Broken Gifts

A MEMOIR

Tyler Auck

PLOTLINE

Bismarck, North Dakota

Plotline Publishing
1108 Hillside Terrace
Bismarck, ND 58501
www.lifeplotline.com

Book Layout ©2015 BookDesignTemplates.com

Ordering Information:
Quantity sales. Special discounts are available on quantity purchases by corporations, associations, and others. For details, contact the "Special Sales Department" at brokengifts1974@gmail.com.

Broken Gifts/ Tyler Auck. —1st ed.
ISBN 978-1-7351489-0-8

Contents

For Dad

"Those who are hardest to love need it the most."

—SOCRATES

Introduction

My name is Tyler Auck and I should be dead!

Many people have told me that I need to write a book. A memoir class was hosted by Humanities North Dakota in 2019. Many people encouraged me to take this writing class, and I was pleasantly surprised by the support and the guidance offered by others. People believed in me when I was full of self doubt. Not being a literary genius, and having only read two books my entire life, Super Fudge and Counting Your Blessings, I wouldn't know a good book if it hit me in the face. But, I am compelled to tell my story of survival and redemption.

January 5, 2011, was a turning point in my life. My eyes were opened after I was no longer masking my pain with drugs and alcohol. Shit was getting real and raw as I started telling my story to others who struggled with the same demons that I struggled with all of my life. There was a shift in the way I looked at my trauma and my failures over my lifetime. There is nothing better than standing in a room of a drug and alcohol treatment center and telling people your deepest darkest secrets and being accepted. It's a beautiful feeling to know you're not alone in the darkness. I proceeded to tell my story whenever I was asked and the healing began to take place. The doors started to open for not only my healing, but others' healing as well. This is where I began to understand my Broken Gifts could be shared with others.

Personally, when I started writing these stories of my life, I began to experience peace and comfort in my lifetime of pain and trauma. I felt more accepting of myself and for a while my nightmares stopped plaguing me.

This spiritual journey is one that I hope continues into the new chapters of my life. I want my kids to someday read this and look back on their life with their dad and see that I not only broke the damaging cycles of addiction, trauma and abuse, but replaced them with beauty. I wish to show them a strength that they never knew existed. I strive every day to use the things that I have learned throughout my life to be my kids' superhero. I feel the things I have gone through in my life give me the ability to be great in the eyes of the people that I love most, as well as in my own eyes.

The last reason for writing this book, and probably the most important reason, is to show people who are still out there struggling with behavioral health issues that there is hope. I want my memoir to help people and give hope to people that may have lost it and may have given up on themselves, like I had many times in my life. I fight every day for the people still out there struggling and the others who are negatively impacted by them.

If you are reading this and you are broken, I want to tell you that I have your back and I send you strength every day. I know a lot of people who are fighting for you. We are not alone. This is a fight that I will continue to fight as long as I live because the stories that are in my memoir are what gives me the strength to share my Broken Gifts with the world. I have laid myself bare for people to see who I really am. And, to be completely honest, I am scared to death to do it. But, if it makes a difference in one person's life then I know it was worth it. I hope that person is you.

I am proud of the person that I am today. Today, I am a dad, husband, brother, uncle, son, and a proud member of the recovery community. I am a fighter for what is right.

CHAPTER 1

Put The Gun Down

There was suicide attempt after suicide attempt. What would be the breaking point? How many times could I keep doing this and getting away with it. I have been knocking on heaven's door most of my life. Failure has always been on my to-do list and I have never been able to stop writing it down and scratching it off again. My confidence had been stripped, hearts had been broken, and my drug addiction and poor decisions were on the top of their game. Everything was spiraling out of control!

"Please help me! Please God, I know that I stopped believing in you a long time ago. "But, please, when I go to sleep, don't let me wake up. I beg you. Please!"

The wind howled through the ravines. There were snow drifts taller than I had ever seen in my lifetime. There was over one hundred inches of snowfall in 2009. It smothered everything and closed the roads. They were covered with mountainous drifts that made it nearly impossible most days to enter the road that led up the hill to our trailer house. This was the kind of winter that we didn't plan for when we moved out of town to our hundred and sixty acres north of Bismarck. Life was very difficult dealing with Mother Nature and perhaps more difficult dealing with myself.

My blue Ford F250 Super Duty diesel truck with a red Heinker V plow attached to the front of the truck that I used to plow snow was sitting in the front yard. This truck went through hell that winter. Mother Nature and the drugs were in control. It was a perfect storm and I kept digging out from the snow and digging my grave, all at the same time. The negative forty-degree temperatures made it difficult to breathe. The feeling of impending doom lurked inside me. My mind was trying to kill me. Racing thoughts of disaster plagued me every second of every day. My gut knew that our life was going to change drastically, soon. Looking into Addison's green eyes I could see that our relationship was broken, and I could feel that her heart was breaking away from mine. Most of my time was spent trying to fix it, but my persistent daily drug abuse just kept breaking everything that we were building together.

One night, my friend stopped by with some meth to help me out. My wife went to town to stay with her grandma to avoid the treacherous travel the next morning to work. Little did I know the tangled web of hurt that was being planned as I sat in my drug-fueled delusion. After my friend left, I stayed up all night smoking meth and cleaning the house, making our home perfect for when my love returned. Everything was in order. Addison had a plan and I had a plan, but they had nothing to do with one another. All my tasks were completed and I was feeling really good. The sun started to shine through the blinds as I opened all of the shades to let the light shine through our perfect looking home and life.

The phone rang the next morning and it was my wife. She told me that we needed to talk and said that she was driving out to the house so I should wait there. I hung up the phone. My paranoia spiked and I had the gut-wrenching feeling that something was going to happen, something horrible. I grabbed my coat and put on all of my winter gear and started walking down the road to get the horrible news faster. My mind was racing!

I walked three-quarters of a mile down the road. The only sounds I could hear were my breathing and the crunching of the crisp snow under my boots. I could hear a vehicle driving a few miles away. I felt my feet moving faster as the noise got closer. Finally, our white Jeep crested the hill right in front of me. Addison pulled up to me and stopped the vehicle. I jumped into the passenger seat, took off my gloves, slid my hand over on top hers, and leaned over and gave her a kiss. She turned her head only giving me her cheek. I kissed her on the cheek, not knowing that this would be our last kiss. She looked at me. I looked into her eyes and something was different.

"What are you doing walking down the road, Tyler?"

"I couldn't wait to talk. It's bad isn't it?"

"Let's go back to the house and talk there."

"Please, just tell me! I can't wait that long. It's bad. I just know it's bad."

She held my hand on the drive back to the trailer. We went in. She sat me down on the couch and sat away from me on the other end of the couch.

"I need to tell you something, Ty."

"Did someone die? Are you okay? It's bad. isn't it?"

"I don't love you anymore, Tyler. I will be grabbing some of my things and I'm leaving you."

Silence.

"Are you leaving and coming back?"

"No, I want a divorce."

I pleaded with her to stay as I watched her grab handfuls of clothes out of our closet. She got into her vehicle and left. I watched the Jeep crest the hill and disappear. I watched in shock until I could no longer hear the Jeep's tires crunching on the snow and the sound of the engine cutting through the crisp, cold air.

I grabbed my meth pipe and slowly put it against my lips, the lighter followed my hand up to the glass bowl. My right thumb was callused with bloody cracks from overuse. The calluses and the wounds made it difficult to get past the childproof slide over the little spinner on my yellow lighter. My eyes locked on the melted meth in the glass bowl. I flicked the lighter over and over until it had a flame. My hand moved the lighter's flame slowly towards the glass bowl, touching it so slightly to heat up the meth until it started to smoke. I puffed little breaths of air in through the glass stem to mix with the heat of the lighter and the already smoke-filled bowl.

I waited until little puffs of smoke shot out of the hole on the outside of the bowl. I inhaled, taking a big hit and held it until my body shuddered before finally exhaling it out into the air. The rush hit my broken heart and blurred my tear-filled eyes. My heart and soul were shattered. I took hit after hit of the meth trying to make the pain go away. I set the pipe and lighter down in the cupboard by the plates and closed the cupboard door.

My hands reached out and grabbed my pistol off the counter and moved the red and white kitchen rug with the cherry prints on it into the middle of the kitchen floor. I knelt down on the rug. My shoulders slouched as my right hand gripped the pistol. Everything was in slow motion. My left hand found its way to the top of the pistol. I grabbed the slide with my left hand and pulled the slide back. The bullet popped out of the clip into the chamber as my hand released the slide. The slam of the slide clanged. The metal slammed against itself. The bullet was now in the chamber waiting to take my pain away once and for all.

My right hand raised the barrel of the gun up to my mouth. Tears ran down my face. I struggled to catch my breath. I stuck the gun into my mouth and tears mixed with the gun oil that I had come to know well from all the years of practicing for this one moment of strength. I could feel the sight on the barrel and the metal bang against my teeth. I positioned the gun at the best angle that I thought would get the job done. Peace and serenity fell over me. The voices inside my head and the hurt in my heart stopped. My finger trembled against the trigger before it came to rest. I pulled the trigger.

Click.

Silence.

The only noise that I could hear was my heart beating in my ears and my breathing.

The firing pin clicked. Misfire. I pulled the gun out of my mouth and set it down on the floor in front of me. I could feel warmth and peace settle into my body. The sweat poured off my face and mixed with the broken tears before falling to my lap. What did I just do? Am I really still alive? I didn't want to die after the trigger was pulled.

I pulled my cell phone out of my pocket and called my mom.

"Mom, will you please come get me and take me to the hospital?"

Her voice sounded frantic on the phone. She kept asking me over and over again, "What's wrong, Tyler? What's wrong? Are you okay, honey!"

"Mom, I just tried to shoot myself, but I am okay."

I reassured her that even though I had wanted to die, I didn't want to now. I just needed help. My mom said that she and Lizzy would be on their way out to my house to help me.

My mom has always been my strength in the moments that hurt the most. She was my angel in the face of pain. She would have taken all my pain away and put it onto herself if she could have. I hung up the phone and looked down at my gun on the floor. I sat back on my feet, still down on my knees. I placed my phone back in my pocket and picked up my pistol. My thoughts raced through my mind as I contemplated putting the gun back into my mouth so I could finish the job that I had started. The more I thought about it the more that I didn't want to die anymore. I just wanted the pain to go away. I released the clip out of the gun onto the floor and watched it bounce off the rug and slide across the linoleum coming to a stop by the stove.

I wiped the spit off the barrel. Anger raged inside me. I was pissed that another suicide attempt didn't go my way. I inspected the gun, looking closely to see why it didn't go off. I jacked the shell out of the chamber. The bullet tumbled through the air, bounced off the linoleum before sliding under the overhang of the countertop. I set the gun down on the rug and crawled over to where the bullet slid and I picked it up and looked at it with disbelief. I could see where the firing pin dented the primer. I dropped the bullet back onto the floor. I stood up, picked up the gun and walked over to where the clip was laying. I picked up the clip and pushed it into the gun, jacked another shell in the chamber and went back to my bedroom and put the gun under my mattress.

All of a sudden, the warm peaceful feeling left my body and I instantly went into survival mode.

I was moving pot and coke at this time. I was scrambling to figure out where I was going to hide everything when I went to the hospital. I gathered up all my white coolers and stuffed them with all of the drugs that I had and hauled them with my 4-wheeler out to a set of trees right over the hill from my house and buried them in the deep snow. I went back to the house and put the large amount of cash that I had in a lock box and hid it in the rafters of my shop.

My mom and her friend Lizzy pulled into the yard and rushed into my trailer house. They asked me if I was okay, then they told me that they loved me and that they would take me to the hospital for help. I told them about Addison leaving and that I was thinking about hurting myself. I was scared and started regretting that I had called them for help. The lies were coming out of my mouth faster that I could make them up. I was trying to hide the fact that I was fucked up on meth. I was so dehydrated that my tongue felt like it was going to choke me to death. I was worried about my dog Keetah and who was going to take care of her. This was the best excuse that I could come up with to get me out of the mess that I was in. It didn't work. Mom loaded Keetah up in her truck and said that Keetah could stay with her. I called my wife who had just left me and let her know that I was going to the hospital and that our dog would be going to my mom's house.

I began to cry uncontrollably as I told my mom that I was getting a divorce and my life was over. Then I agreed to go to the hospital to check myself into the psych ward. Even though I said it out loud, my brain was telling me that I shouldn't do it! A million reasons why I shouldn't go came rushing into my brain and they all made sense. I was still high from the meth. Now it was turning on me. I was overwhelmed with paranoia and crippled with fear. I sat on the couch for a couple minutes in a daze. The voices in my head were telling me that I should be dead now. I should be lying face down in a pool of blood on my kitchen floor with a hole through my head and my brains scattered against the wall and ceiling.

My mom and Lizzy helped me lock up the house. We all got into my mom's truck and drove down the highway towards Bismarck. Mom reached out by phone to a long-time family friend, Scott. He had some years of sobriety, so she put me on the phone with him. He told me that everything was going to be okay and that I was doing the right thing, even if it didn't feel like it. I downplayed everything and blurted out that my wife was leaving me and I was going to be forever broken.

I was not quite ready to verbalize my part in this whole scenario that was playing out. I hung up the phone and started wondering why the hell was I just talking to someone that I hadn't seen in years and what fucking business is it of his anyway? We pulled up to the hospital and my mom escorted me in and got me checked into the ER. I wanted to run from everyone and forget what had just happened! My mom kept telling me that it would all be okay. Every time the ER door opened the fear of impending doom fell over me until they finally called my name. I looked at my mom and gave her a big hug. I could feel her fear as she trembled in my arms. She told me that she was going to take Keetah to her house and Lizzy to her car and that she would be back in a little while.

"I love you, Mom!"

"I love you, Tyler! It's going to be okay."

The nurse took me back and sat me down on a chair. I could hear the giant door shut behind me and the nurse asked, "Are you having any suicidal thoughts?"

"No, just thoughts of harming myself! My wife just left me and I am depressed."

"Have you been drinking?"

"No, I don't drink."

"How about any drugs?"

"No, just a little bit of marijuana to help me sleep at night."

I told her that I used to have a problem with pain pills due to all of my surgeries, but I haven't been on them in some time now. So, just give me a damn trophy even though it had only been days since my last pill use. The nurse called a guard and another nurse over and let me know that they would be taking me to a different floor. I had been through this many times in my life. I knew they were taking me to the psych ward. I calmly walked with them to the elevator and then up to the fourth floor where I was taken to a room. I sat on the bed and looked up at the camera on the wall. My brain was telling me that I wasn't crazy and that I don't have a problem with drugs. My whole life I had always thought that I just had really bad luck. But, what I didn't know at this time was that it had been bad choices that led me to this point. I sat on the bed scared, lonely, and afraid. The doctor came into my room. He was a blunt asshole with no bedside manner whatsoever. He gave me the opportunity to come clean about what drugs I was on. I downplayed everything. I sure the hell wasn't going to tell him that I just stuck a gun in my mouth and pulled the trigger after smoking meth all night or that I am a drug dealer.

What I was willing to tell him was that I smoked a little bit of pot and that I might have a problem with it. He could see right through my shit and he knew I was lying. It must have been my bugged-out eyes, the gallons of sweat that were pouring off my head and face or maybe even the black rings under my eyes or my sunken cheeks from years of hard drug use. One thing that I knew for sure was that I needed to let him know that I was there because my wife left me, and my heart was broken.

My lies only went so far after the son of a bitch dropped a drug screen on me and came back with the results. He had me and there was nothing I could do about it besides tell him that I have a problem and I needed help. He kept questioning me about what I was willing to do and if I was willing to follow through with treatment if they decided that it was appropriate. I wanted to punch him in the face and kick him in the head, but I was willing to cooperate so I could go home and take care of my broken life. He gave me the option of inpatient residential treatment at a facility down the road or treatment at the hospital in an outpatient setting. This was an easy choice for me because I had shit to do, things to take care of, and possibly some really bad people to deal with who I feared would be looking for me if I were locked in an inpatient treatment center for thirty days.

"Outpatient, please!"

They kept me overnight and set up a time for me to start my outpatient treatment the following week.

PART I

Innocence Stripped Away

I was born in Bismarck, North Dakota in 1974, and handed off to young parents who were simply trying to make life work. Everything I experienced as a young kid seemed normal because all my friends were having similar experiences. Even though these things were normal for me and my friends, they sure caused us all a lot of pain. No one ever gets to pick their parents or the situation they are born into. It is just the luck of the draw. So, I just accepted it and learned early on how to survive.

CHAPTER 2

Beat Down Lesson

"Look at this, motherfucker!" Up out of the ditch shot a blue and white truck about one hundred and fifty yards down the road coming right at us.

"Larry's drunk again, Tyler. He can't even keep it on the fucking road." He went down through the ditch and back up on the road again.

"Hang on, Tyler. He's going to kill us!"

I felt my dad step on the gas and the glasspack mufflers on the truck rumbled under my feet. I could see Larry's eyes through the windshield. The closer Larry's truck got to us, the more aggressive my dad's driving became. We were headed for a collision. I started to brace myself. I was full of fear and confusion. Why was my dad trying to hit him? We are going to die! Neither of the trucks were in their own lane. Dad was driving down in the ditch and back up again, following every move Larry was making.

"This son of a bitch is going to hit us, Tyler! He is going to hit us! Hang on!"

Bracing myself for an impact, my eyes wide open, I prayed that we would miss each other. Larry struggled to stay on the road and out of the ditch. It was like a game of chicken; the only difference was that one of the men had no clue what he was doing because he was drunk. My dad was so high on drugs that he thought it would be a good idea, with his kid in the truck, to cause a head-on collision with a drunk man.

The trucks barreled down on one another. The closer the trucks got, the more erratic my dad's driving became. Larry was not even on the road anymore; he was driving in the ditch. Dad cranked the steering wheel, stepped on the gas, and flew down the same ditch where Larry was. We were heading straight for him. The fronts of the vehicles were thirty feet apart. My hands pressed on the dash, bracing for impact. Larry was slumped over, struggling to keep his head up. I could see his eyes looking up at us. The glasspacks on my dad's truck crackled.

"We're going to hit! Hang on! We're going to hit!"

My dad cranked the wheel to the right, narrowly missing the front of Larry's truck. My head jerked viciously to the left as my hands came off the dash. Suddenly, we were back up on the road, then down in the ditch on the right-hand side of the road opposite of Larry's truck. I bounced off the seat from the impact of going over the edge of the ditch. Dad pressed on the gas. We spun a donut and grass and dirt went flying in all directions. Now we were in hot pursuit. No more playing chicken.

"Stop, Dad! Don't crash!"

"Shut the fuck up! This motherfucker just tried to kill us. He's drunk. We need to stop him!"

I was a little boy, but I knew what we were doing was wrong. I couldn't believe that I told my dad to stop. What was I thinking? I was shaking with fear wondering what would come next. Larry finally found his way back up onto the road when we sped up behind him. Dad hit the back driver's side of the truck. The impact spun Larry's truck sideways and back into the ditch. Now we had Larry's full attention. Dad had just smashed the back of Larry's truck all to hell.

Dad shifted the truck into reverse, backing up before driving forward into the front of Larry's truck. His head was jolted from the impact and snapped back. We sat in the vehicles looking at each other to see who was going to make the next move. Dad kept a sawed-off shotgun under the seat of the truck. Out of the corner of my eye I watched my dad, waiting for him to reach for the gun and shoot Larry.

"Get out of the truck, Tyler."

Dad opened the door of his truck and got out. "Get the fuck out, Tyler. Now!"

I Jumped out of the truck as fast as my little legs would go, still not believing we rammed Larry's truck with ours. I stood and waited for the developments. Larry had the door of his truck open with his left foot on the ground. He was slouching down in his seat trying to get his footing. Dad walked over to Larry.

"Get out, motherfucker! You just about killed my kid! Get out! Now!"

"Fuck you, you son of a bitch! You wrecked my fucking truck!"

"Get out, Larry!" Dad reached into his truck and grabbed him by his shirt. His shirt tore almost completely off his body as Dad slammed him to the ground. Larry was struggling to get back up. He was kicking and swinging his arms trying to hit Dad. Dad looked over at me and said, "Watch this! This motherfucker isn't going to get away with this, Tyler. He's going to pay for almost killing you."

I paced back and forth in the ditch. My eyes were glued to Larry's face. I felt bad for him because I knew Dad was going to hurt him. Dad cocked his right hand back and hit him right in the side of the face. The crack was loud. Blood instantly shot out of his mouth and onto the golden-brown ditch grass. He tried to get up off the ground. Dad hit him again, knocking him down face first on the ground.

"Get up, get up, you piece of shit!"

Larry propped himself up to his knees and hands. He was on all fours when my dad walked over and kicked him square in the face. His head jerked back as his body went limp. Dad grabbed him by his head and rolled him over onto his back.

"Look at this piece of shit, Tyler."

He had both of his hands around Larry's head, holding it upright so I could get a good look at Larry's swollen, bloodied face. The images of his face have been unforgettable. It looked like his eyeball was popping out of his head. This nightmare still haunts me as an adult. Lesson learned, Dad.

I stood there in the middle of the ditch with a blank stare on my face. Dad stood over the top of Larry, still holding him by his head. He reached down and grabbed him by what was left of his shirt and pulled his limp body about a foot off the ground and hit him three more times in the face. With each blow, the blood flew in all directions, some even hitting me in my pant leg. My dad's fists were covered in blood and Larry was not responding. He looked like he was dead. His face looked like something out of a slasher movie.

"This is what you do to people like this, Tyler. He tried to kill you, son. I had to do this!"

This was one of dad's ways of teaching me valuable lessons in life.

"Dad, please stop!"

"Come over here, Tyler." He was standing next to Larry's body that was still lying on the ground. I hesitated.

"Get the fuck over here. Now!"

Hesitantly, I walked over and stood next to my dad. Looking down at Larry's busted-up face, I heard gurgling noises coming from his throat. His truck was still idling, the door open, and the stereo was playing old-school country music. The beautiful grasses in the ditch swayed with the wind. Watching the beautiful golden brown grasses soothed the pain and confusion that were tying a new knot inside my guts. I kept looking away to forget what I had just seen.

"Look at him, Tyler. Look at this drunk piece of shit! He can't handle his liquor. He never could. He deserved this. He got what he had coming. We had to stop him before he killed someone."

Trying to convince himself that this was the right thing to do, he justified what he had done. I stood in silence, too afraid to speak. Dad grabbed me by the back of the neck and pushed my head down so that I was looking right at Larry, and his eyes were now open looking at me.

"Do you fucking see this?"

"Yes, Dad."

"This is what had to be done. This is life. Don't you ever let people do this to you." Dad pushed on Larry's face with his foot to make sure he was alive. I could see his eyes moving around under the blood and the swelling. When he was looking up at me, it felt like his eyes were screaming for help, a look of desperation that I will never forget.

I was just a little boy, and I didn't think he deserved this. I felt horrible for him, but I didn't dare say anything. My dad scared me. I had witnessed him do some really bad things to people. Inside, I was having a full-blown panic attack, but the fear kept it hidden. I thought that Dad was going to kill him.

The beautiful grasses swayed back and forth calming the storm that raged inside me. Beauty was happening all around us even when someone was lying on the ground getting beaten almost to death. The flowers still bloomed, and the sunsets still produced beautiful colors. Trauma always slows everything down for me so I can take in the beauty within the storm. I honestly feel that this ability to see beauty around me is what helped me survive all of these situations.

"Get in the truck! Now, Tyler."

He got in the truck, as I stood there looking down at Larry. I felt scared to get in the truck and scared to leave him lying in the ditch all alone.

"Get in the fucking truck, Tyler!"

I turned around and started walking back toward the truck. Glancing back over my shoulder in hopes of seeing him get up, I climbed into the truck and shut the door. I scooted my butt all the way over against my door to distance myself from my dad, my fingers rubbed the little bumps on the seat covers. Every time my fingers crossed over one of the bumps on the fabric, I felt soothed. It felt like everything didn't happen and this was all just another bad dream. The old Ford truck started up. Dad revved the engine over and over. Every time he revved the engine, the truck rocked back and forth, back and forth. He put the truck in reverse and backed up out of the ditch onto the road.

Larry sat up on his butt. He kept wiping the blood off his face. He struggled to get up. We sat there watching him. Larry was able to get his feet positioned under his body and he used his arms to push himself off the ground. He kept looking up at us. I often wondered what he was thinking and feeling. Dad reached under the seat and pulled the sawed-off shotgun out from underneath his seat.

"If he has a gun Tyler, I will have to shoot him."

Larry got into his truck and shut the door. I prayed that he didn't pull a gun on my dad. Larry sat there in his truck with his hands drooped up over the steering wheel. Dad continued to rev the engine. The power of the truck rumbled beneath my feet. The sawed-off sat next to us on the seat. The gun scared me and I started to cry. The tears slowly started to run down my cheeks. I tried to wipe the tears away as fast as they came out so my dad wouldn't see me crying.

"Stop crying, you little pussy! He deserved that!"

Larry just sat there in the ditch. We drove away and back to our trailer house.

"Do not tell your fucking Mom! Do you know what a 'rat' is?"

"Yes."

"Not that kind of rat. A fucking rat is a little pussy that tells on people. Don't you ever be a rat, Tyler! You don't ever tell on anyone for anything."

"Okay, Dad. I won't be a rat."

I would have promised anything at that point.

"I hope you paid attention, so this never happens to you."

I paid attention. I watched everything and felt everything. I was sick and afraid, but too scared to show any emotion. My dad turned this into a life lesson. Honestly, I think that he thought that he was doing "good dad" shit.

Over the next few days, I struggled to get the images out of my head. They constantly plagued me when I was awake and in my dreams. When I closed my eyes at night I would hear the crack of the knuckles on the bare skin, seeing the blood splatter on the golden-brown grasses in the ditch. I fought against the negative images. Instead, I tried to see the beautiful grasses blowing in the wind. I tried to remember the swishing noise they made brushing against each other.

CHAPTER 3

Head Shot

The car drove up the bleak desolate road towards Main Street in Sterling, North Dakota. As it approached, the noise from the engine and the gravel off the tires pierced the evening quiet. Who was it? What did they want? The car slowly drove up the hill right below Sterling Elementary School. The car took a hard left and parked on the front side of the yellow and white trailer house. The car doors opened and then slammed shut. Two men approached the trailer house and stepped into the semi-lit yard. The trailer house's interior lights were off, but the yard light by the front door was on. Someone peeked out from behind the curtain inside of the trailer and then quickly disappeared out of sight before the two men saw that someone knew they were there.

The men were talking when another man appeared out of the darkness and stepped into the light. This man walked up to the two men and the argument started immediately. The man who was being yelled at by the other two men was now just out of reach of the yard light. The only thing that could be seen were their silhouettes with their hands moving around. The voices grew louder. The two men were now yelling at the guy who showed up late. There was some shoving and a couple of punches thrown. Now, all of the men were standing in the middle of the yard in the light. A pair of eyes again gazed out through the partially open curtain and observed the men in the yard.

Their voices would get loud and then quiet. One of the men who got out of the car had a stick resembling a baseball bat in his hand and the other man wore a white tee shirt with a motorcycle on the back. The man that showed up late wore a black leather vest and jeans. He had long black hair that was pulled into a ponytail. The two men stood in front of the man with the leather vest. The arguing increased and then stopped. The man in the white shirt pulled a gun out of the back of his pants and aimed it at the guy with the black vest on. The man with the gun yelled at the other man as he stuck the gun closer to the man's face.

Bang!

A bright flash erupted from the end of the gun.

His head jerked backwards as he dropped to the ground. He laid on the ground in the yard as the two men stood over him looking down at his lifeless body on the dirt. The man who shot the guy kicked him a few times and after each kick his body jerked. The two men disappeared out of the yard light, came back, and grabbed the guy's arms and legs and loaded him into the trunk. Then they returned to where the man had been laying. The gunman had a shovel and the other man had a pail. The man with the shovel bent over and scooped up whatever was laying in the yard where the man's lifeless body had been laying and then dumped a shovel full into the pail. They walked about the yard scooping up different items and placed them in the bucket. The men walked back over to the car, put the shovel and pail in the trunk, and slammed it shut. They got into the vehicle and drove off. The curtain inside the trailer slowly shut as the tail lights disappeared down the street into the darkness.

The eyes that peeked out from behind those curtains were mine. I ran back to my room that night, crawled into my bed, and cried myself to sleep. Any noise outside of the trailer house jolted me awake with paralyzing fear. My mom was sleeping in her bedroom and I wondered if the gunshot scared her. I wondered if my aunt and cousins next door or the kids across the road heard and saw what I had seen.

The next morning when I woke up and got dressed, I went outside to look at the spot where the man had been lying on the ground. Looking down observing the ground, I could see the shovel marks. I followed the trail where I watched the men drag the victim and saw a few different spots of what looked like dried up blood. I used my shoe to kick the dirt and rub the spots away so I wouldn't have to look at them and no one else would have to know what I had seen. The knot that was tied in my guts that night continues to hurt. Nightmares still plague me.

CHAPTER 4

Stuck In The Outhouse

There was a weathered, storm-damaged, beat-up outhouse right along Main Street in Sterling, North Dakota — a town with a population of what felt like fifty people. The door was beat up with a drop lock on the outside to keep animals out and the door from slamming around in the wind. The once white paint was peeling and the boards were riddled with holes from knots that had fallen out. Many years without a fresh coat of paint had allowed the rot to set in. The roof was missing most of its shingles and parts of the rusted-out metal patches allowed some sunlight into the dingy interior. Once inside, you could see the rays of the sun that filtered through the swaying canopy of trees that covered the surrounding area. Cobwebs lined the roof, glimmering in the sun's rays. Mice spent a lot of time running around the inside of this structure. You could also find an occasional sparrow's nest that would only last for a little bit of time before some kid from the town would bash it with a stick. The inside floor was falling apart, and the smell of aged feces and urine seeped from the splintered-up platform from where many a butt sat to take care of business.

As kids, we would hide inside and have shootouts with fake outlaws and hide out from the town bullies. We would lean our bikes up against the building and use them as a stepping pad to climb up to the roof and stand up there as if we were on top of the world.

One summer, a couple of younger Sterling boys and I thought it would be a good idea to start a gang and call ourselves the Red Devils. We heard a lot of talk from the older kids that they were starting a biker gang and that they would not let us join because we were too little. So, we all found white shirts (well, mostly white anyway), a red marker, and then my mom helped us write out "Red Devils" on the front with a red pitchfork sticking up through the lettering as our logo.

Little did we know the hell that we were going to pay for doing such a ballsy thing. We thought they would respect us and think it was cool. Not! They were a bunch of teenaged pricks. They clearly didn't want anyone else being cool. We all took off on our bikes, pedaling with a vengeance with our chests puffed-up high above our handlebars to show off the logo of the gang that we had just established. We peddled around town for some time with freedom blowing through our souls, no helmets - just like Hell's Angels. The older kids in the neighborhood were out and once they caught wind of our little gang, they chased us down to make us pay for this offense to their dignity.

When I saw the older kids peddling their asses off trying to catch me, my little legs went as fast as they could peddle that bicycle while images of what they could possibly do to me raced through my mind. But, I was not fast enough. Jon rode up next to me and kicked me in my side, knocking the wind right out of me. My legs slipped off the pedals as my balls bashed off the middle bar of the bike and my hands lost their grip on the handlebars. My body slammed into the ground, scraping the skin away. I panicked, gasping for air. I knew this was just the beginning as I watched them all drop their bikes.

I watched their silhouettes coming at me through the sun as they called me, "little pussy," and taunted me, "Who the fuck do you think you are? A Red Devil? You little pussy."

Jon's foot hit my shoulder, rolling me over on to my back as he leaned down and screamed into my face, "You little fucking pussy. Stop crying and get up."

I rolled over to my knees and proceeded to get up just like he asked. But, before I could do anything, I was met with a hard shove and slammed back down to the ground. Darrin spit a large loogie into my face. I felt it hit my hair and run down into my eyes. It mixed with sweat and tears. Now, they surrounded me.

"Who the hell do you little pussies think you are trying to make a gang?"

"This is our town. You need to take that shirt off."

The two other boys grabbed my shirt. They ripped the shirt right off my body. I heard the fabric tear as they jerked me off the ground and then threw me back down.

"Get up, boy!" Jon's hand latched on to the back of my neck like a claw.

"Let me go!"

I squirmed around trying to get away. The harder I tried to get away, the tighter his grip became. He marched my ass to the outhouse.

If I would have known what was about to happen next, I would've fought for my life and just let them beat the shit out of me instead of enduring the next few hours of hell.

Jon randomly threw a knee at me, slamming it into my side while his claw clenched deeper into my neck as his anger flared. They grabbed my arms as I screamed for help.

"Please, let me go. Please! You're hurting me bad, please stop!"

Now, Darrin and Jon had me by the arms and were twisting them with brutal force behind my back. It felt like they were trying to dislocate my shoulders from their sockets. We all stood there looking at the door of the outhouse as Damon took the metal clasp off the door. The door swung open. I felt a huge shove as my body slammed into the back wall of the outhouse and down onto the gross, urine-soaked floor. The door slammed shut behind me faster than I could even think about pulling myself up. The clang of the metal clasp fell into place, locking the door with me inside.

I couldn't even begin to imagine all the possible things they were going to do to me.

I felt relieved that they were outside away from me, but that relief didn't last long. Moments later they proceeded to take sticks and jam them towards me like swords through the rotted holes of the outhouse. A number of their jabs drew blood. The name calling stopped and they grew tired of poking me. Their voices got farther away until I finally felt brave enough to snap off the longer sticks inside of the outhouse so I could get to the door. I slammed my body against the door with all my might trying to open it. No such luck. The clasp held.

I yelled for help, but soon stopped in fear that they would quickly return. I proceeded to bust pieces off the sticks, trying to find a perfect piece to jam through the door to knock the clasp off the hook. Again, no luck.

They were coming back.

I heard one of the guys lean his bike up against the outside wall as Jon's shadow blocked the sun's rays from shining through the cracks and holes. His feet kicked against the wall as he tried to push himself up on top of the roof.

"Now what?"

I anticipated sticks sliding through the holes in the roof. I could see Jon's face at times and his eyes were looking at me as he plotted his next evil move. My heart raced when our eyes met.

There was lots of laughing and name calling.

"You're dead, you little fucker. You little silly girl. Keep crying, pussy."

I heard the sound of urine splashing against the top of the outhouse. Soon it found its way through the rotted holes in the shingles, dripping and running over my head, face, and body. It was warm and the odor was overwhelming. The taste was salty and bitter. He kept pissing all over me. I screamed and cried for him to stop.

"Please stop, it's in my mouth. Stop!"

I spit out as much as I could while trying to block it with my hands. I scrambled to the other corner trying to get away. It was too late. Now I was covered in piss. The sweltering heat from the day along with the urine in my mouth made me thirsty. Jon jumped down from the roof. I could see them standing out on the road talking. Just then, Darrin came sprinting towards the outhouse and climbed up on top. I could hear him unhooking his belt and taking down his pants. He started pissing on the roof and, as the urine made its way through, I was able to only get hit by some of it. He jumped down when he was done. He was laughing and taunting me the whole time. I was covered in sweat, urine, blood, and dirt.

I tried my best to not make any noise, but in brief moments of panic and fear, I would lose my shit, attacking the door, kicking and punching it. It was not budging! I was humiliated, hurt and crying so hard that I struggled to catch my breath. I could hear the chatter once again as the sticks came alive, poking and jabbing at me. Then an ominous silence fell. I could hear whispering. What now? I could hear footsteps getting closer. My body trembled with fear. Were they going to kill me?

Pop!

A hot sting hit me in my pants right below my waistline. The pain was excruciating. I looked down, saw a hole in my pants, and a spot of blood that started to seep through my jeans. One of the guys had shot me with a pellet gun. Pellets are shaped like an hourglass and when you use a pellet gun instead of a BB gun, you wanted to make it hurt. Pellets were made to penetrate skin.

My heart pounded with each pump of the pellet gun. It was pumped up to ten pumps and sometimes more. I kicked at the door and screamed for help. I wasn't quite sure which hole they would stick the tip of the pellet gun in to shoot me from next time, but I knew it was coming.

The only thing worse than listening to the giggling, was the pellet gun being pumped and then the moment when the pumping stopped, I knew what was next.

Pop!

This time the pellet found its way into the side of my stomach, ripping the skin open. I screamed at the top of my lungs for help. I could hear their voices outside talking about shooting me again. Each time they pumped the gun, I could feel fear choking me. The tip of the gun peeked through the different holes. They continued to taunt and laugh at me. I'm not quite sure what was worse, getting shot or when they would stick it through the walls and not shoot me. The anticipation made my knees wobble from fear.

The tip of the gun came through the hole on the door.

Pop!

This time they missed, but I still screamed. I pleaded to Jon, "Let me go! Please let me out, I won't tell on you. I promise!"

They had enough for now. Or did they? The sounds of their voices diminished. I pictured them picking up their bikes and peddling down the street. I continued to scream for help, hoping the lady in the yellow house would hear me.

But, no one was around to help me.

Now, I began breaking pieces off the sticks trying to stick them through the door to jimmy it open so I could get away. The heat was stifling. The drying blood mixed with the piss that was seeping through my pants made the piss all sticky. I used a small piece of a stick to perform emergency surgery to dig out the pellet that was stuck in my side like I had seen on many episodes of MacGyver. Where were my friends? I hope they got away. I was also hoping that they would come back and let me out.

I wanted to get out so badly and run home to find my mom, but I was already thinking of how I could hide this and explain what happened to my pants and my shirt. I came up with a story. "I wiped out on my bike!" Yeah, that's it! That's what I will tell them!"

It felt like I sat in the stench of the outhouse for hours. Occasionally, I let out a random scream for help or viciously assaulted the door in order to pass the time. The tips of my fingers were bleeding from trying to claw my way out and my legs were sore from kicking at the door. Usually, I could hear their bikes coming. But, this time they were sneaky and I didn't even hear them coming,

Pop!

The pellet hit me in my left forearm, ripping the skin open. But, this time the pellet didn't get lodged in my skin.

I screamed and cried, "Let me out and leave me alone!"

Threatening them with violence, I promised, "My dad and my cousins are going to kill you! My dad will kill you; he will fucking kill you!"

It felt like the sun was right outside the door pounding on my skin. Fear and claustrophobia attacked me as I anticipated their next assault. Where did they go now? Are they going to shoot me again? Every time I heard the branches sway in the trees, I thought they were back. I felt really sick to my stomach. I began puking up yellow stomach bile.

"I am going to die!"

The next thing I knew, a bike rode up. I could see the shadow blocking the sun from the door. I braced for the worst. But, this time it was different. This time I heard the door latch come undone. The shadow left the doorway, allowing the door to slowly swing open. The sun flooded into the outhouse. I waited until I could hear that the bike was gone. My body trembled in fear and I wondered if this was a trap.

Were they waiting to shoot me when I left? Were they going to beat me up? Shit! I waited a little bit longer until there were no sounds except the occasional truck over at the grain elevator. Finally, I built up enough courage and pushed the door open all the way, peeked my head out slowly, and braced myself for the worst. Nobody was around. I took off running from the outhouse. On the south side of the yellow house, behind some bushes, I waited, looked, and listened. I heard some kids playing off in the distance making noises, dogs were barking on the other side of town, and I could hear a radio playing country music over at the grain elevator.

I began to sob uncontrollably. I suddenly feared that my parents would find out what I just endured.

I ran over to the neighbor's house and turned on the garden hose. Warm water sprayed into my mouth and I gulped so much that I threw it up. I sprayed the dirt and piss off my skin. The water started to get cold as I gulped frantically until I threw up again. I ran to the bushes outside our trailer house and listened to see where my mom was. My dad's truck was gone–good thing because there would have been hell to pay for everyone, especially me.

See, everyone was scared of my dad. And they should have been, because he was a scary man with a temper that impacted everyone when it went off. If you messed with someone that he loved, you were screwed. He would come after you. I was scared of my dad, but I was even more scared of what he would do to the kids who had just hurt me.

I cut through the alley between my aunt and uncle's house and I could see my mom sitting in the lawn chair talking to my aunt. The pain was so bad that I felt sick. Once at our trailer I rushed inside, took off my pants, and buried them in the bottom of the laundry hamper. I cleaned myself up, hiding what had just happened. I hid the pain deep inside, along with the hurt caused by my dad. The more I stuffed the hurt deep down, the more it helped me keep living life as normally as I knew how.

CHAPTER 5

Burn The Cat And Sit In The Front Row

When I was a kid, I spent some time out on a farm with a very devout Catholic family. And I watched this family display a hard work ethic that surpassed much of what I had witnessed during my time on this earth.

During this time in my life, I enjoyed the thought of God. I looked at God as something that was beautiful and exciting. But, during my short stays on this farm I witnessed a lot of bad things that made me think a little differently about God. I watched the man of the house kill baby kitties so that cats wouldn't over run the farm. As a kid, this was very disturbing to me, even though I had been through a lot of shit up to this point in my life.

I was told by the man that, "This is the way of life, and it is cheaper than a bullet."

After watching this man kill the kittens, I stood next to the tractor that was parked in the middle of the farm yard. I was in shock and not quite sure if I would be able to catch my breath. The smoke from the burn barrel slowly danced out of the metal fifty-five gallon drum. I looked at the dead kitties laying on the ground, kitties that I had just played with over the last two days, and I was shaken to the bone. My hands fidgeted in and out of my pockets. I wasn't sure what to do with them. I wanted to run, but where would I go? I wanted to cry, but I was scared. I wanted to lash out, but I knew that I wasn't big enough. So, I just stood there with a broken heart. I closed my eyes and wished that this was just a bad dream and that when I opened them the kitties would be running and playing on the neatly stacked hay bales next to the trees along the road. But, when I opened my eyes, the kitties were still laying on the ground. I finally found enough strength to start walking over to the barn away from the pain. But, the pain still followed me. Farm life didn't slow down for moments like this. In fact, it seemed like I was the only one who this tragedy affected. It seemed like everyone else was able to continue on with their daily chores.

But, not me. The look on the kitties' faces hurt my heart. I wouldn't wish what was done to them to be done to anyone. I never wanted to experience this kind of pain again.

Then when Sunday morning would come around, everyone acted differently. I was asked to sit in the living room that morning and clean the dirt out of my fingernails and trim back the cuticles on my fingers. I was being prepped to attend the little Catholic church down the road. Once at church, I sat looking around at all the different people who were sitting on the long wooden church pews, six people to a pew. A cross hung over the doorway of the church. Candle stands were lined up next to the pulpit which had a Bible laying open on. The pulpit was dimly lit by the flickering candles. Sheer looking gold banners swayed in the draft when the door opened and closed. No one talked except for an occasional "excuse me." I could have heard a pin drop onto the wood floors because it was so quiet. The smell of incense filled the room with a glorious calming scent. But, I couldn't seem to make sense of how the people who I had watched murder the little kitties could just sit there all nice and calm like nothing had happened. This disturbed me so much. Then they prayed to a God who sounded like he might brutally destroy me like an unwanted cat. I couldn't think of God as beautiful and exciting any more. I now saw God as hateful, and it scared me.

CHAPTER 6

Walking On The Roof

I remember driving around in my dad's Ford truck when I was a kid. This truck was badass. It was green and had loud pipes. Sometimes, my dad would reach over and pin me against the passenger side of the truck door by my neck and choke me. This happened a lot. Sometimes he did it just because I was breathing too loudly or I would burp and he would hear it. There was no good reason really, but let's just say I watched how I would breathe when I was with him.

Whenever my dad would do something like this, he would look at me and say, "I'm doing this for your own good! You're going to need to learn how to deal with this, Tyler!"

Sometimes when he was really upset at someone else, he would choke me instead of them. As I gasped for air I seriously thought he was going to kill me.

When I was a kid, I went to a lot of doctor's appointments with my dad and sometimes I would wait outside in the truck. On this particular day, it was beautiful and sunny. We had the windows rolled down in the truck as Dad and I drove to the pharmacy to get some pills. The roof in his truck had carpeting on it and as a kid I would always look up at the carpeting and think about walking on it. I wanted to lay on my back and walk with my feet on this carpeting. This carpeting was an orange, seventies shag carpet that looked really inviting to my feet. I obsessed about being able to put my feet on this carpeting and walk on it. I fantasized about how good it would feel under my feet.

"Dad, can I walk on the carpet on the roof?"

"Don't you dare, Tyler!"

No arguments from me. Dad went into the pharmacy and left me to wait in the truck. He was in a lot longer than expected so I kept looking at that carpeting on the roof and fantasizing about putting my feet on it. Against my better judgment, I eventually found enough willpower to take my shoes off, lay on my back on the seat, put my feet up on the roof and walk on the carpeting. It felt soft and freeing to finally get to do something that I had wanted to do for so long. I tried to be as fast as I could, but I was not fast enough. All of a sudden, the driver side door opened up. It was my dad. I was still lying on my back with my feet on the roof of the truck. I was caught red-footed.

"What the fuck are you doing, you fat fuck?"

He grabbed me by the hair and pulled me across the seat towards him. My feet slammed down into the passenger door. I looked up at him and he looked down at me. He still had me by my hair when he open-handed slapped me on the left side of my face three times, maybe more. I lost count as stars flashed in my head with each blow.

"I fucking told you not to do this and you never ever listen, you fat piece of shit! What the fuck did I tell you?"

He finally let go of my hair. Sitting myself up, I scurried back across the seat to the passenger side. He climbed into the truck still cussing at me and glaring at me. He reached across the truck and grabbed me by my hair again and bashed my head into the door over and over again. I screamed for him to stop. I was crying, I just wanted him to stop. He started his truck and we drove away.

"Put your fucking shoes on! Now!"

Once we got back to the house, I jumped out of the truck, ran to my room, and shut the door. My head hurt bad. I just wanted him to stay away from me. I laid in bed and pulled the covers up over the top of me. I cried. Twenty minutes later Dad came into my room and sat down on my bed next to me and pulled the covers from my face. I anticipated another beating, but this time he was different.

"Tyler, I'm sorry! I'm sorry that I got mad at you for doing that. I just don't want the carpeting in my truck wrecked! This is all that me and your mother have, and we want our things to be taken care of. Please just listen, Tyler. Please, just listen to your dad."

Whatever he got from the pharmacy must have started to work because he was definitely feeling a lot better than he did just a short time earlier. I always wondered how he could do something so horrible to me and then turn around so quickly and act like nothing had happened. He would use his words to try to smooth it over. But honestly, I don't think that some of the things that he did to me could ever be fixed by words. I was very happy that he had a change of attitude because when he was high, he was a happy-go-lucky man who would've given the shirt off his back to people. My dad was easy to love when he was on a happy high. I craved his attention and it felt good to see him calm.

CHAPTER 7

Junkyard

The junkyard was a place we went to daily to mess around. There was shit up there that you couldn't imagine. It was heaven on earth for a kid who had an amazing imagination! It was a place to escape to. A place where a kid could disappear from all the troubles of the world. My favorite part was breaking glass that didn't have a mark on it. After all, it is just a junkyard so they didn't need any of this crap anyway. All of it was just junk. But, it seemed like some people had a connection to the junk, because they would occasionally chase us away. We would run and hide. We thought if they caught us, they would hurt us. One time, a white work truck came flying through the junkyard and a man jumped out and tried to hit me with a shovel. He missed. He was fat and slow, and it might have helped him if he would have pulled the cigarette out of his mouth before trying to catch a kid. Dumb ass! Later, I found his truck on Sunday and let the air out of all the tires. Take that, asshole!

We dodged the workers on a daily basis. It was always fun to sneak up on workers when they were working on a piece of equipment. Shit, we would get ten feet away and listen to them talk. Sometimes they would talk about getting drunk and one of them even said that his ol' lady was a whore. If I remember correctly, she was banging his best friend. Not the kind of friend that I wanted in my life, even if I didn't have a girl. I hated when men would call their girls their "ol' ladies." My dad called my mom an ol' lady even though she was a young lady.

Weekdays at the junkyard after five p.m. and Sundays were the best, not a worker in sight. I could bust every window without worrying about the noise that it made. During these times, we owned this junkyard. We were Kings of the junkyard.

Our junkyard was located at the end of the glide path for planes landing at the Bismarck Airport. One day we loaded our pockets with throwing rocks, waiting for the next plane to come in low to land at the airport on the other side of the road. Ranger, Maddox, and I stood on top of cement culverts that were stacked thirty feet tall. We each had a rock in our hands. Ready. Waiting. We made a bet that whoever could hit the airplane with a rock first would get a pop bought by the other two. We all had pretty good arms and we could throw a rock a long way, but trying to hit an airplane was much more difficult than it looked. You needed to think about timing, how far to lead the airplane, and which way to run if you connected. We didn't know shit about airplanes. We thought that the rock could possibly put a hole in the bottom of the plane and make it crash. We never even took into consideration all the people on board who could get hurt. It was all about pride and free pop.

We planned our getaway down to a spot on the fence we would crawl through. We hoped that the rock would just bounce off the plane like it had done before and everyone would go about their day. Plus, we wanted to stay in the junkyard and play all day if we could. We threw rocks at nearby targets, honing our skills while we waited. We scanned the skyline, looking and listening for a plane. No plane, yet. We climbed down off the cement culverts and scoured the ground looking for the perfect rocks to restock our pockets. Once our pockets were full, we climbed back on top of the culverts and waited.

While we waited, we talked about kid stuff: what we were going to do for the rest of the day, our BMX bikes, and girls' tits and asses. The usual stuff that we didn't know much about.

Ranger yelled out, "Here comes a plane. I can see it. Get up, shit dicks."

I replied, "There it is! It's mine, fuckers!"

Maddox said, "Eat shit, you are both going to owe me a pop."

We all stood up and got rocks ready. We knew from past experience that you only had enough time to throw one rock. We stood there with our backs to the runway looking at the big jetliner lowering through the sky.

Ranger yelled out, "Get ready, fucker."

"Fuck you, dick! I am going to win," I replied.

Maddox said, "You pussies are going to miss. It is mine today."

I made sure that my footing was stable so I could throw the rock without falling thirty feet to the ground. The plane always looked like it was barely moving until it was right over the top of you. The engines whistled as it got closer. I could see the front cockpit windows and the landing gear was down. The glare of the rising morning sun was reflecting off the bottom of the airplane.

I was ready. I had saved the best rock for this moment. I needed to win. The plane was just about in perfect distance when all three of us wound up and threw our rocks as hard as we could straight up into the air towards the plane. My rock veered out to the left and did not even get close. I had the height, I just pulled it at the last minute from trying to throw too hard. Maddox's rock was short by twenty feet. The plane was directly over us. Ranger's rock was perfect. We all watched it contact the bottom of the plane before finding its way back to the ground.

"Fuck you both in your ass! You suck and you both owe me a pop!"

We climbed down off the culverts as fast as we could and ran through the junkyard to the opening in the fence. Ranger was in first place, with Maddox not far behind him, and then me bringing up the far rear. I was not a runner. I turned my head back to see if the plane crashed. It landed without any problems, so I started to walk. We all met at the opening of the fence.

"Do you want to buy my sodas now or later?"

We both replied, "Later!"

We felt that we were in the clear and that we could stay at the junkyard and play for the day. The junkyard was a beautiful place. It was actually a stocking yard for a local construction company. There was old equipment, vehicles, and every kind of building material that you could think of. Rock piles and dirt piles were scattered through the yard.

There was even a pond. No, it wasn't a pond, it was just some big ass hole that was the size of two small trailer houses, five feet deep and filled with water from the rains. Fifty-five-gallon barrels of God-knows-what were stacked around one side of the pond. Some of the barrels were leaking brown, nasty, chemical smelling substances into the earth and down into the pond. The pond had an oil slick that covered the water's surface on the end by the barrels. Frogs still frequented this pond, even with all of the contaminants. We were up in that junkyard every chance we got. This was a beautiful place to get away from our homes. We had limited supervision, so we were free to do whatever we wanted to do.

CHAPTER 8

New White Shoes

Mom took me back-to-school shopping to get new shoes, shirts, and jeans. I was always a pain in the ass when she took me shopping. I always wanted the most expensive items, even when I knew that my parents had limited funds. I also knew how to get my mom to cater to my way of thinking. For example, instead of getting four pairs of jeans for a hundred bucks, I would want two pairs of nice jeans for a hundred bucks. Shirts I wasn't too picky about, just as long as I was able to get them a size up to hide my fat.

"Mom, I want these shoes."

"No, Tyler, they are too white."

"Mom, I will take care of them. I promise."

"It's a no, Tyler. Pick a different pair."

"No, Mom, I need these so bad and I promise I will keep them clean."

"No!"

This arguing went on for some time, but then my persistence started to pay off. I could see that she was breaking and that meant that I would get my way.

"Please, Mom? I promise I will take care of them."

"You little shit, you better not wreck them. This is all the money that I have for shoes for the whole year."

"Thank you, Mom. I will take good care of them. I promise."

I walked out of JC Penny with a pair of my new jeans on and my shiny brand new white tennis shoes. I felt like a million bucks and my mom even had a big smile on her face. She loved making me happy, even if it was out of mom guilt. It was a special occasion for me when I got new clothes and I really enjoyed it. We went home and Ranger was sitting on my steps waiting for my return.

"Nice shoes, Tyler!"

"Thanks, man."

"Thank Mom, Ranger. It was my idea."

"Tyler, your mom picked out your shoes?"

"Yes, it was all her idea." I looked over at my mom and smiled.

"Tyler, you take care of those shoes."

"Mom, stop it! I will!"

"Have fun boys. Tyler, be back by dark, please."

We jumped on our bikes and peddled up the road.

"Let's go to the pond," Ranger said.

"Let's go, shithead."

Ranger and I met Maddox at the end of the street. We sat on our bikes talking about who got which raft once we got up to the pond. We had made rafts out of board insulation and wood pallets. The pallets were stuffed with sheets of board insulation. We would nail them back together so the sheeting inside of the pallets had another piece of the board insulation nailed to the top of the pallet. Some of the other rafts were pieced together with any kind of material that you could imagine, such as milk jugs that acted as extra flotation devices. These things would float. Well, sort of. Okay, not very well, but it didn't really matter what they looked like or how good they floated. We felt cool when we set sail off the bank of the pond using longer sticks or a 2x4 to push the rafts from one end of the pond to the other. We struggled to balance on top of our vessels and it was pure luck if we stayed dry.

Today was going to be a great afternoon with my new pants and my new white shoes on. I even took a 2x6 and laid it on the ground out to my raft so I wouldn't get my new shoes dirty. My thinking was on point with the confidence that this day was going to be different. I thought that I would be able to float on my raft without falling in, because if I wrecked my new shoes, Mom would kill me.

I pushed myself around the pond using a long stick, gazing down at my new shoes feeling proud and on top of the world. Life was great until I lost my balance and fell into the dirty pond. I struggled to swim to the shore. The negative consequences were already flashing through my mind of how pissed off my mom would be when she found out.

"I'm screwed! How am I going to tell my mom and dad what happened to my new shoes and my pants?"

My brain was already crafting up the perfect lie. If I crawl out of the pond I will just stay outside until I dried off. Perfect! Climbing out of the pond was a bitch because the banks were covered in slippery mud. Maddox docked his raft and stuck his push stick down into the water so I could grab it and pull myself out of the murky pond. I looked down at my once brand new white shoes that were now covered in so much mud that I couldn't see a speck of white on them. And my new pair of stone washed jeans were now mud washed jeans. The tears instantly came fast, because I knew how hard my mom and dad had to work to get me these nice things. I had messed up again. When I got home there definitely would be screaming. And, if my dad was home, there would be name calling and some hits to the top of my head and possibly a choke.

As I sat on the bank of the pond crying. Ranger and Maddox stood around me, feeling my pain. They all knew what was going to happen to me for being so stupid.

Maddox said, "Why did you wear your new shoes?"

Ranger replied, "Shut up, Maddy. This isn't the time."

"Guys, I am so dead!"

Ranger said, "Take your shoes off. I will wash the mud off from my raft."

I took my shoes off and watched Ranger climb on his raft and clean all the mud off my shoes.

"Tyler, take off your pants. Maddy, throw them to me."

I stood up and took my pants off. I stood there in my underwear, afraid to take my shirt off because my dad was always calling me a fat piece of shit and I believed him. Maddox walked down the bank and threw my pants down the slope to Ranger and then Ranger tossed my shoes up the bank to Maddox. Ranger scrubbed the mud off my jeans, Maddox brought me my shoes and handed them to me. They were no longer covered in mud, but they were no longer white, they were more of a grey color. I thought that if they had time to dry the white would come back. Yeah, right. I was screwed. Ranger finished cleaning my pants and came up the bank and hung my pants over the fence.

Ranger said, "Give me your shoes, Tyler."

He took my shoes and wrung out as much water as he could and then hung them up on the fence to dry. Maddox had to be home earlier than we did, so Ranger sat with me in the junkyard until it was almost dark. Ranger always had my back. I went home with wet pants and wet shoes and everything that I expected happened. My mom screamed at me and told me how stupid I was for wrecking my new clothes and my dad was home and he slapped me in the face twice and hit me on the top of my head with his knuckles. He was about to choke me, but my mom came down the hallway so he stopped. He tried to hide the mean shit that he would do to me so Mom wouldn't see, because she would give him hell if she saw him hitting me. I had to wear my now grey shoes for the rest of the year. I should have known that I am not a white clothing kind of kid even if I felt cool for a few hours. Mom was right, "No Tyler, they are too white."

CHAPTER 9

Nice, Butt At What Cost?

Palmer was the most beautiful girl that I had ever laid eyes on. She was a year or two older than me. Never mind, that is not important. She was hot, and that's all that mattered. Palmer was a goddess. We always thought about "palming" Palmer. She had beautiful brown hair with the most beautiful blue eyes. She was older, so she had boobs. Boobs were always a plus.

One beautiful summer day, I was chasing her through this little park trying to catch her. We were playing tag. I was hot on her tail, just about to tag her bare skin. She wasn't naked, she was wearing a swimming suit. It was a hot day, or maybe she already knew what she could get accomplished with her attributes. Anyway, I was hot on her tail when, as I reached out to touch her shoulder, I tripped on the grass. On my way down, my first instinct was to catch myself. But, the only thing around to grab hold of to catch myself was Palmer. On the way to the ground, my fingers slid down her tanned soft back then got hooked in her swimsuit bottoms. My momentum from the fall pulled her bottoms down to her ankles. As I smashed off the ground, my eyes became glued to the first bare ass that they had ever laid witness to. It was perfect. This is something that a little boy never forgets. I was stunned and I felt horrible because I didn't try to pull her suit down. It was an accident

She looked back at me and yelled, "You little pervert."

"I'm sorry."

"Get away from me."

She gave me no time to explain before she ran off, pulling her bottoms up on the way. I felt embarrassed and knew that there wasn't any chance that I would ever share a lifetime of love with Palmer. Even though I had no clue what I would do with such a beautiful girl, I thought for sure that I would marry her and spend the rest of my life with her. You know, fairy tale stuff. I would have loved her with my whole heart and soul. I would have kept her safe and never called her a name or hurt her. She did not think of me the same way, because in her eyes I was just a little piss ant and a pervert. What I had seen that day was unbelievable, but it was never the same with her after that. From then on, I only saw Palmer from a distance. But, that was nice, too. Maybe she was right when she called me a little pervert. She shouldn't have been so damn pretty. It was impossible for little boys not to look. I was only human and no one in my life ever talked to me about how a boy should approach a girl or all of the feelings that I was feeling inside. With limited parental guidance on the birds and bees, I was confused. So, when she called me a pervert it hurt.

CHAPTER 10

This Is How You Get A Girl

One day after the school bell rang, I was walking home on the south side of the Bismarck Expressway headed for our trailer park. Palmer was on the north side of Expressway. My eyes quickly scanned the yards on the edge of the trailer court looking for a flower that I could pick and go across the street and win her heart over. There were no flowers in sight. So, the dumb little boy in me thought that it would be a good idea to throw a rock in her direction so she would look over at me and smile. Yeah, right. Great idea to get a hot girl's attention. Throw a rock at her. Yeah, that will work. My intention was to not hit her, I was just hoping to hit the ground next to her so she would look over at me.

I searched the ground for a nice rock that I knew that I could get the distance that I needed to cross the street. I cocked my arm way back, and as I let my arm go the rock shot out of my hand like a rocket. I had more heft than I wanted, but I knew that I had the distance down perfectly. This was going to be perfect. She is going to love it. My eyes were glued to the rock as I watched it sail through the air. It was close. Oh, shit it's too close. Whack! The rock struck her right in the head, knocking her to the ground. Instantly, I heard her crying and yelling. My God, what did I just do? I just hit the school's most beautiful girl in the head with a rock. Fear and embarrassment rushed over me. I ran away. Boy, that didn't go as planned.

I scurried behind one of the trailer houses and hid. She got up off the ground and ran up the hill towards her house, holding her hands over her head. I ran home, my heart was hurting because I knew that I had hurt her badly. The next thing I knew her parents called my parents and let them know what I had done. My dad came into my room screaming at me, telling me that she had to go to the emergency room to be checked out.

"You hit her in the head with a rock! You stupid little fucker! Do you want to see how it feels to get hit in the head?"

I watched his fists clenched as he took a swing at me. His knuckles smashed off the top of my head. Whack! I got what I had coming to me. An eye for an eye, my dad thought.

"You need to go to their house today and apologize! Do this tonight! Don't fuck this up, you stupid little shit!"

I didn't really care what my dad was doing to me because I was more nervous that I had to go face the girl who I was in love with. The girl that I just whacked in the head with a rock. I would have never been able to find the courage to go knock on her door on my own, but now I had some motivating circumstances that forced me to take that step. I walked up the hill to her house and stood there in the driveway looking at the door. My brain was telling me to run so bad, but I knew if I ran, I would have to go back home and see my dad and that was not an option. I walked up to the door and stood there trying to find the courage to press the doorbell.

Ding dong.

I could hear it ring through the door. Hearing some movement in the house made my heart pound, my mouth was dry and I was sweating profusely. Her dad came to the door.

"So, you must be Tyler?"

"Yes, I am Tyler. Is Palmer okay?"

"You hit her in the head with a rock, Tyler."

"I am sorry, I did not mean to."

"You didn't mean to? You threw the rock, right?"

"Yes, I did, and I am sorry! Can I tell Palmer that I am sorry?

"Palmer! It's the boy that hit you with the rock. He wants to talk to you!"

Palmer came to the door as her dad walked away. I stood on the cement step looking through the glass screen door, but then my attention was captured by the flower bed along her house. There were beautiful lilies, bright orange lilies. My mind raced, trying to stop my body from walking over and picking one. I was thinking that there is no better way to say sorry than with a flower. I tore my eyes away from the flowers and back up to the screen door where Palmer was standing. She looked pissed and had a white bandage that covered her beautiful brown hair on the right side of her face. She opened the screen door two inches.

"What do you want?"

Long awkward silence, I froze up.

"What?"

"I'm sorry, Palmer."

The screen door shut and then she slammed the house door. I had fully expected an ass chewing, but nothing coming out of her mouth was worse than an ass chewing. I ran over to her mom's flower bed and picked a dark red lily to make myself feel better after getting the door slammed in my face. Then I wandered down the street towards home to let my dad know that I did what he wanted me to do. I pulled the lily up to my nose and took a big whiff. It smelled so good. This lily was beautiful. It had my heart from the moment that I laid eyes on it. Hopefully, her mom didn't see me pick it, because then I would have to say sorry for that, too. But, it didn't matter; this lily would be worth a few whacks on the head from my dad. I laid the lily down on the cement by the mailboxes, just in case someone else needed to feel better.

Once back at the house, I took another really good ass chewing and a few hard hits to my head. My dad was even more pissed than Palmer was, and she was the one I hit with the rock.

Shit, there goes any chance that I had with her.

Another one bites the dust. Literally!

CHAPTER 11

Pop Machine

Ranger and I started working out together down the street from our trailer house. They recently built a new gym called Third Street Gym. Ranger was in a lot better shape than I was and financially he was able to get a gym membership. But, Ranger came up with a brilliant idea. Because it was a twenty-four hour gym, it had card access after hours.

"Tyler, we can go late at night and you can come with me and use the gym for free."

"Awesome! Thank you, Ranger. This is going to be epic!"

We went down to the gym at midnight using Ranger's card access and the doors opened. It had every piece of gym equipment that you could imagine. Ranger showed me how to use the equipment. This kid always had my back. He was like a big brother to me. One night, as we finished up our workout, both of us were tired and sweaty. A pop sounded great. We talked about going down to the pop machine by the mailboxes in the trailer park and scoring some free pop. Did you know that you can stick your arm up inside of a pop machine through the opening where pop comes out and grab a free pop? This would only work on some machines because the pop machine companies started figuring out that kids were stealing pop, so they put some safety measures in so you were unable to get your arm all the way up into the machine. But, the pop machine companies didn't know that if you tilted the machine towards the front, pop would fall out of the return slot. When we would do this, we would usually get about five to eight cans. Ranger and I walked down to the entrance of the trailer park and scoped out the area, looking for anyone who might catch us getting our free soda. Ranger went around to the back side of the pop machine and I stood on the front side waiting for Ranger to push the pop machine my way. I would slowly lower it down until the pop started coming out and then I would push it back up again.

Ranger wiggled in behind the pop machine and the wall and started pushing the pop machine towards me. It began to tilt my way. I reached up and grabbed the top of the machine to slowly lower it down. But, this time he ended up pushing it a little harder than I expected. I tried my best to stop it with my arms, but the momentum was too much. The pop machine caught me off guard, and I struggled to hold the pop machine up. It was tilted way too far. I could hear the pop falling out the bottom and I felt it hitting me in the legs and feet. My arms were giving out. I could no longer hold the heavy machine.

Crash! Smash!

The pop machine came crashing down on top of me, pinning me underneath it from the chest down. I could feel the light bulbs inside of the machine breaking and the heat was burning my legs, chest, and stomach. I tried with all of my might to push it off me. But, no such luck! Not even a wiggle. Ranger came running over to me. He bent over and grabbed the pop machine and attempted to pick it up. He was able to pick it up just enough so I could wiggle out about four inches. Then his hands slipped off the machine and sent it crashing down on my battered body again. I felt the air get sucked out of my lungs from the impact. I was afraid I was going to be electrocuted. The noises the machine was making had me concerned and so did the heat and the broken glass that was stuck in my legs from the bulbs that once lit the Coke emblem.

"Ranger, get it off me! I'm hurt. Please."

"I'll lift and you wiggle out!"

"Okay!"

Ranger lifted and I wiggled. Then he would lose his grip and the machine's full weight would crush me again. We did this over and over again until I was finally free.

"Let's get out here. The cops are going to come."

I laid on the cement trying to catch my breath, knowing that my leg was hurt bad. I struggled to get up. Ranger grabbed my arm and helped me to my feet. The machine was making noises like a sign in a horror film that was broken after a zombie apocalypse scene. The electrical current was making that eerie buzzing sound. Glass from the light bulbs stuck in my legs, my elbows and the back of my head was bleeding. The pop that we were supposed to be enjoying was now soaked into my clothing. Ranger hoisted me up and draped my arm over his shoulder. He helped me limp across the street. Out of the corner of my eye, I saw two people walking towards us. Shit! It was my grandma and grandpa's good friends out for a late evening stroll. They lived in a trailer house right across from where the pop machine was now laying, smashed on the ground.

"Go Ranger! Go! They can't see us!"

"Here they come! They are following us."

We crossed the street and cut through some backyards. The pain was too much. I needed to stop. Ranger lowered me down next to a shed. Two shadows were coming through the trailers. "Are you okay, Tyler?"

"I'm okay. Please do not tell Grandma and Grandpa. Please!"

"Tyler, we just need to know that you are okay. We will not say anything."

"I'm okay. Thank you. Thank you for not telling."

They walked away leaving us next to the shed.

"Tyler, what should I do? Should I go get your mom?"

"No! Just help me home to my door."

"Holy crap, dude! You could have died! Do you think your insides are bleeding?

"I hope not! I'm okay. Just help me home."

Good thing we were only three trailers away from mine. Ranger helped me to my front door before running down the street towards his house. I crawled on my hands and knees into the house and down the hallway to my room. I slumped on my bedroom floor and managed to get my clothes off before crawling into bed. I listened for the cops. Nothing. No noises besides the random car driving through the trailer park. Finally, I was able to fall asleep. The next morning, I woke up before everyone in our house and went into the bathroom barely being able to walk. I had a bad limp and I was in a lot of pain.

I took a shower and tried to wash off the mess. That day my mom had planned my birthday party at one of the local hotels. It was a swimming party, just like I had wanted. My mom was always concerned for my well being.

"Mom, I wiped out of my bike last night after we were done working out. But, I'm okay."

Then I called Ranger and let him know that we were ready to go to the swimming pool. Ranger, and a couple other kids from the trailer park met us at our trailer house. We all got into the car with my mom. I sat in the backseat. We were driving out of the trailer park when Ranger looked at me with "Oh, shit!" written all over his face. We both knew that we were going to go by the pop machine and the last time we saw it was smashed on the ground.

Shit! The cops were there. They were standing around the pop machine surveying the damage. Mom looked over at the cops and the pop machine laying on its front side.

"Oh, no! Look what someone did to the pop machine." Her eyes instantly looked at me through the rearview mirror.

"You little shit. You didn't! Tell me you didn't do this, Tyler! Ranger! You little shits!"

"No, Mom. I didn't do that. I have no clue what happened to that pop machine. Right, Ranger?"

"No, Cindy. We were at the gym last night."

We went to the pool and had a fun time at my pool party. Mom knew that we were the ones who had screwed up the pop machine. Later that evening when we were home, Mom came into my room and said. "I know you did that, you little shit! Don't you dare tell your dad!"

I told her all about how we tilted the pop machine to get free pop and how things got out of hand and Ranger pushed it a little too hard and it landed on top of me and crushed me.

"Tyler, have you ever seeing those little stickers on that pop machine that tell you not to tilt the pop machine?"

"No, Mom. That is why we didn't know not to do it."

Sure, a sticker that tells you not to do something would have stopped us! My leg was fucked up for a couple of weeks. I was worried that the police were going to get our fingerprints and then I would have to deal with my dad and what he was going to do to me. Years after this incident I would have family members tell me, "Tyler people get killed every year from tilting pop machines in California." Apparently, California was the Mecca of pop machine tilting. That was the last time I tilted a pop machine. You could say that I learned my lesson the hard way. I guess I am lucky to be alive because pop machines kill lots of people every year in California. There is a sticker on every machine. Who would have thunk?

CHAPTER 12

Boobies For Everyone

Wild seventeen-year-old girls lived at the end of our block. We would often hang out by their trailer house because they were always up to no good and it was exciting for a fourth grader to watch them drinking beer and doing other stupid shit. One day, these girls told a bunch of us kids who were outside of their trailer that they were going to show us their tits today. The only other time that I had seen tits was when I caught my mom's friend laying in our backyard sun tanning.

We were full of excitement at the possibility of seeing some real tits, not the ones in the dirty magazines that our parents hid under their mattresses. We stood outside the trailer with great joy. The girls came to the window and stuck their chests out with their clothes still on giving us a peak at their bra straps to get us excited. It worked and we were excited and nervous. All of a sudden, I realized I had to shit! I rode my bicycle down the street to my house and ran inside as fast as my legs would go. I needed to make this quick so I could get back to the action. I plopped down on the toilet and took the biggest, nastiest crap. I tried my hardest to get my business taken care of, but shit turned south. I started itching all over and then broke out in hives while sitting on the toilet. Big red welts covered my body. When I would break out in hives, Mom always told me that it was from garlic. I was not quite sure about this, but one thing I knew for sure was that this sure put a hamper on my tittie gazing for the day.

Maybe it wasn't the garlic—maybe it was girls. If I break out in hives every time a girl is going to show me her tits, no girl is ever going to want me. I spent the rest of that evening shitting myself in the bathroom and taking a soda bath that my mom made for me to stop the itching. I was so disappointed that I couldn't make it back to watch those girls hang their tits out of that trailer house window. The next day, when the hives finally cleared up, I jumped on my bike and went down and talked to my friends. They told me all about how nice the tits were.

"Hey, Tyler, they showed us everything, even their underwear."

"You guys are full of it."

"Nipples and panties. You could even see some bush sticking out the sides."

"Did they have nice tits?"

"The nicest we have ever seen."

"Screw you, guys!"

I couldn't believe I missed it.

"What happened to you, Tyler?"

"Once I got home my dad made me stay there, he wouldn't let me come back out."

I had to lie. I could not tell them that I got the shits and then the hives because I was so excited to see some tits. Later that afternoon we all went back down to the trailer house hoping that the girls would be back. I prayed that day that they would come back, but we were disappointed. No tits.

CHAPTER 13

Crack Therapy

Most people look at cracks in a sidewalk as an eyesore or irreversible damage to a sidewalk. But, beautiful things happen in the cracks in sidewalks. Little flowers grow. Daisies are usually tough enough to pop up through a crack. Daisies are tough to kill. If you have never seen a flower growing out of a sidewalk crack, you are definitely missing out on a beautiful expression of life that only exists to the ones with grit. These are the badasses that grow where no others can grow.

These beautiful little green patches of weeds would cover a crack in the concrete, sometimes from one end to the other. Some of the cracks even had small, beautiful yellow flowers with tiny brown stigma. The outer petals had black dots. The only way that you could see these black dots is if you laid down on the sidewalk and looked really closely. The purple flowers and white flowers usually shriveled up and disappeared into little knobby balls when the summer heat was too hot. If you pay close attention when you are walking on a sidewalk in the summer, you will see a whole new world that is happening under your feet.

As a kid, I sometimes wished that I was tiny so I could disappear in a sidewalk crack and explore all the jagged edges. I would lay down in the green crack meadows and smell the tiny little yellow flowers while looking up at the whites daisies against the blue sky. It had always looked so comfortable in a crack of a sidewalk. Cracks in sidewalks consumed me as a child. It was like a maze that I struggled to escape, but kept going back to. The busted up jagged cracks in a sidewalk soothed some of my pain and caused me great sorrow all at the same time.

It all started as a child. I had no clue what it was that was brewing inside of my soul. What it was doing in my life was keeping me alive so I would not go completely crazy. In my earliest memories, I remember that the counting in my brain consumed me. I would trace everything with my mind, and if I was not able to complete the task at hand, I felt like I was going to die. Anxiety rushed through my body as the car I was in passed a sign on the side of the road. My brain would trace the sign from top to bottom and everything in between. At fifty-five miles per hour, signs were a killer because we were usually traveling a little faster than that and it was hard to trace everything at those speeds. I would usually get the shape of the sign and one of the fives traced. We would pass the sign before I completed my task. It felt like a little piece of me died, but I had no time to mourn my loss, it was on to the next sign. The anticipation was horrific and the letdown from my failure was catastrophic.

I improvised for fast moving targets such as signs that moved with TV commercials, license plates, and even lettering on people's shirts at stores. I always hated it when someone had a wrinkle in their shirt so I couldn't see the complete letter or number. Women were difficult because their boobs always hid parts of the word. Depending on the size of the boobs or the angle, it could make it difficult to get the job done. Trying not to get caught looking like a little creep for staring at a woman's chest for too long was tough, too. Don't mind me, I am just trying to trace the words that run across your chest using my brain. I swear that the disappointment in my face is from not being able to trace the T in lettering across your boobies that read, Best Mom. The damn T is always in the cleavage. I bet you didn't know that. Damn it, lady, can you please adjust your boobs so I can finish tracing the T?

Once the trauma from my daily life built up to a point that it was no longer treatable with tracing in my mind, I struggled to find what worked. It was all starting to backfire on me. The anticipation became too much and I felt overwhelming failure when I was not able to complete my tasks of tracing. Something needed to change. The task that once soothed me was now breaking me. The fear that people would find out what I was doing became a reality. I was no longer able to keep it under control. I couldn't stop it and it was embarrassing.

It was pure insanity that I participated in daily as a young boy. This imaginary knot that was tied in my guts that only I could feel and see, felt like a rotting hollow corpse. The sickness in my stomach was from a million different traumatic moments that cut me deeply. I was not able to cope with the trauma and the feelings. This was all normal in my daily life. Inside of my soul, where no one was able to see, was anything but normal.

"What the hell is wrong with me? I am a deranged piece of shit. Just do it! This is too much, just kill yourself, Tyler. Life would be easier if I was gone. My dad would be nicer if I was dead. I hate life. I am a fat, fucking pig. I am the reason he hurts me. Please hit me again because words hurt too much."

I started to fantasize about my death at the age of seven. Standing at the crosswalk with all of the other kids after school, I would think about stepping out in front of a car that was driving by on the street. My legs would twitch and take a partial step towards my death. I just wanted my pain to go away. I wanted all of the bad shit that happened in our home to stop. I thought the only way this would stop is if I was dead.

When I was riding down the highway with my family, my teeth would frantically start tapping off each other: left tap, right tap, left tap, right tap! My fingers and toes would follow suit. Left toe, left finger, left tooth tap. Right toe, right finger, right tooth tap. I would perform this task at frantic speeds, always fearing failure. I would count the divider lines on the road for hours at a time. It felt like the taps were so loud that everyone in the car could hear what I was doing. But, no one ever looked at me. I was good to go. The white center lines would whiz by so fast that I would have to prop myself up so I could get a clear eye shot over my dad's left shoulder. If we would pass another car, I would lean to the right and look over his right shoulder.

I dreaded changing sides because I knew that I would have to sacrifice counting a line if I wanted to get the next hundred lines. I hated the solid yellow, no passing lines. This interrupted my pattern, throwing me into a panic. I would clench my jaw, hands, and toes until I could see the white lines approaching. Instantly, I would pick up the beat with the next white line. My teeth bouncing off one another with each white line that went by. My guts would sicken when I could see a hill coming up, knowing that the solid yellow no passing line was going to throw off my task. The yellow solid lines felt like death to me. Some days I would switch to power lines or even people walking. My brain raced; it felt like a million red ants that went crazy after their mound was stirred up, the panic setting in as they raced for survival. I was surviving just like the ants.

My legs were wiggling, and I was chewing on my fingers. Blood covered my lips and the fingernail on my left pointer finger. I quickly licked the blood off my finger with my tongue trying to hide the damage that I had done. The anxiety was taking over. The last bell for the day sounded and startled me up from my desk. My legs felt spiritless. I walked out of my fourth-grade classroom and down the hallway. I procrastinated leaving the school. I was sad that the day was over. All of the other kids were running and laughing, leaving the school as fast as they could to get home. I would have spent the night on the floor at the school if they would have let me.

I didn't want to go home due to the turmoil that filled our trailer during this time. Some days I would walk in the door of our trailer house after school and I would get a dad that was smiling and joking around and then the next day he was pissed off about something. This is what drugs did to my dad. They made him very unpredictable. I could tell when he was high because he was fun for a moment. It was hard to enjoy when he was in a good mood because he could blow at any moment and then, look out! I would walk through our front door and I could smell the pot that he was smoking in his back bedroom. I tried to avoid contact with him if at all possible. I was always scared that he would be going crazy and call me names. I can still hear them.

"You, fat fucker! I suppose you need to eat, piggy!"

Squealing noises came out of his mouth. "Don't cry little pussy! Your mom will be home to fucking take care of your fat ass! I suppose she needs to hold you and feed you!"

I hated days like this. The words cut deep and made me sad. The words made me want to kill myself. I was verbally abused for so long that I believed what he said to me. I preferred the days when the verbal abuse was put on the back burner. I liked the days when he would choke me or hit me on top of my head with his knuckles. This hurt bad, but when it was done, he walked away. The knots on my head from his knuckles and the red marks from the open hand slaps were a constant reminder that I needed to stay on guard. After the onslaught, he would go into his room, do drugs, and later come find me and apologize in a way that made himself feel better and made me think that I deserved it.

We walked home from school, which was about four blocks from the front door of our trailer house. Once I left the safety of the school, I took the longest way home. But, I made sure to not take too much time, otherwise my dad would come looking for me. I didn't want that. Out in front of the school there were Petunia plants. I would stop and look at the beautiful red, blue, and white flowers. I would sit down on the ground and smell them and admire their beauty. The flowers would give me the strength that I needed to make the trek home. Flowers were always an escape for me. They made me forget about everything for a moment. I stood up and prepared myself for the grueling walk home.

The sidewalk was the place that my task would start. My first step was always the toughest one, but once I planted my feet on the sidewalk without stepping on a crack, I could feel the confidence run through my blood. At these moments nothing else mattered. The only thing that I needed to do was make it all the way to my house without leaving the sidewalk, trace all of the cracks with my mind without missing one, and to avoid stepping on any of the cracks. Sounds simple? It wasn't. My mind started tracing the cracks on the sidewalk leaving school.

This was tough because all the kids were running around. The sidewalks were full of kids. There were lines of cars on the street with parents waiting for their kids so they could go on with their day. It felt like everyone was watching me, but in reality, no one was paying any attention.

My mind raced with anticipation of the next crack. Some cracks had multiple branches that ran off the bigger cracks. I traced them all, trying not to get confused and miss any. If I found myself confused about a section, I would do it all over again so I wouldn't have to go back to the school and start over. I couldn't start over because my dad would definitely come looking for me if I took too long. My eyes scanned each section of the sidewalk, sectioning off the sections into smaller sections. My footwork had to be precise and my mind had to be fast. No time for playing or laughing with my friends. Business as usual.

As I approached the intersection of 12th Street and Bismarck Expressway, I started to panic. How would I manage all the cracks on the busy road? My eyes gazed out into the intersection tracing the lines in the road in between the white crosswalk markings. Section complete. I needed another red light so I could finish the second half of the intersection. Second half complete. Now I felt confident to start walking without stepping on the cracks that I just traced. Green light, go! I took off walking making sure to step over every crack. All the cracks on this section were completed. Anxiety dissipated once I was across Bismarck Expressway. I was able to move on. Task complete!

I went from relief to a full-blown panic attack. I was getting closer to home. I followed each line, being extra careful not to step on a crack. I couldn't make a mistake and turn back now. I had put in way too much work up to this point. The tracing made everything feel like I was going to be okay and the walking made me feel like I was going to die because with each step I was closer to home.

I would stop in different sections of the sidewalk that had weeds, grasses, and dandelions growing out of the cracks. I got lost in the foliage, admiring the beauty and the strength of a plant that was tough enough to grow out of a crack in the sidewalk. I would do my best to guess what the crack looked like under the foliage making sure nothing was missed. I couldn't miss anything.

This was life and death. Cars zoomed by on the Expressway, but I paid no attention. My task consumed me. With each line that passed under my feet and through my mind a sickness in my stomach started to churn with thoughts of what might be happening when I walked through the door of our trailer house.

Everything shifted into slow motion. I felt my bowels start to turn on me as my butt cheeks clenched. I could see the little park up ahead. I knew that I was getting close. I wanted to run, but if I ran I would get home faster - and my task would not be complete. I needed to finish my task. I needed to continue to feel the relief. The reality of shitting my pants took priority. I made a mental note of where I stopped tracing and frantically left the cracks in the sidewalk and ran behind a trailer house. I struggled to get the button on my pants undone and the zipper down. I looked around as I leaned against a shed in the backyard of a trailer. Will I get caught again? My pants were down around my ankles. I relieved myself. I hurried and pulled my pants back up as fast as I could before someone saw me. I always hated pulling my pants back up without using toilet paper, but I had no choice. I was just relieved that I didn't shit my pants.

The fear of what went on at our home made me physically sick and I would get the shits and sometimes my body would get covered in hives from the anxiety. My mom always told me that the hives were from garlic.

"You are allergic to garlic, Tyler."

I wasn't allergic to garlic; I was allergic to trauma.

Once I finished relieving myself, the only thing that I could think about was getting back to the same spot in the sidewalk where I had to tragically alter my path due to the sickening feeling that overtook me. I was embarrassed that I had to put myself in such a vulnerable situation while all the other kids were walking by me out on the sidewalk and through the park. I could hear them laughing happily as they ran towards their happy destinations.

The fear and anxiety set in as I left my pile of sickness on the ground in fear of being caught. I looked around to see if anyone saw me. Nope! I ran across the section of grass back to the area where I had left off. There it was, the spot where I stopped tracing. I found it. I felt relief for a moment before getting back on the sidewalk over the same crack that I had left. I wanted to run all the way back to the school to start all over again so I could finish my task without interruption, but the fear of being late and having to deal with my dad overrode my insanity and my task.

I backtracked a few cracks to make sure that I didn't miss any. I struggled to get back to my task; it was difficult. The anxiety was too much to handle. Once I started tracing, I could feel the anxiety leave me, until I took the steps necessary to complete my task. As I got closer to the entrance of the trailer park, my guts started to rumble again. This time I ignored the thought of shitting my pants. The cracks were way more important in this phase of my task.

Now I added to the task by tracing cracks with my fingers. My fingers were frantically trying to catch up with my mind. Tapping with my teeth came next. I would tap my teeth at the end of every expansion joint. Two taps on my left teeth and two taps on my right teeth. My mind honed in. All my worries about going home went away. I was in my zone. It was like fast forwarding a commercial, just the one shot was moving at high speeds, never getting to the end of the commercial. This is what it looked like in my mind.

The tapping, counting, tracing and then carefully stepping continued down the sidewalk on the south side of the Bismarck Expressway. Everyone was participating in their own lives. I was doing my life the way I needed to so I could survive.

There was a little part of me that wanted to step on a crack so I could start all over again, but my racing mind would not allow that to happen. When I would pause to catch my breath, I could hear all of the kids playing on the playground at the little park that was situated at the entrance of the trailer park. I played there a lot as a kid. There was a tornado slide on the north side of the Expressway and my favorite sledding hill straight ahead but the only thing that mattered right now were the cracks in the sidewalk.

Everything slipped back into slow motion and fast forward all at the same time. The noises disappeared and all of the places that

I found joy in no longer existed. The feeling of anxiety rushed through my body. The stress of knowing that the sidewalk would end soon shook me to my core.

"How will I stop? Is there another way to complete my task?"

I was already picturing the curb where the sidewalk ended. The little line above the curb that was always hard for me to step over and then down on to the street. I knew that I needed to leave the sidewalk that was my safety from everything. The cracks that soothed all of my pain would be no more.

Back to the task at hand. No thinking about the end just quite yet! Once the sidewalk turned south into the trailer park, it narrowed by at least two feet. This section I was able to make short work of and it was one of the newer sidewalks so only a couple of cracks. The end was just two sections of sidewalk away. I could see the curb where my task would end. I was sad that I was almost complete with my task, but happy because I was exhausted. I prepared myself to face the worst possible situation once I walked into our home. I always expected the worst because it's better to have relief that it was not as bad as I thought than to think that it wouldn't be bad and find out it's worse.

I stood at the end of the sidewalk. I took a deep breath and stepped over the last line that I traced and counted. My feet hit the street and everything became real again. Sweat ran down my face as I realized that if I didn't move quickly I would shit my pants.

No going back now, it was over, my mind was no longer okay. The pull to go back and start over at the school was strong. The fear of what might be in front of me became much bigger and scarier. The anxiety and depression overran my body. I was sick. My body was trembling.

I paused in the middle of the street and started tracing all of the numbers on the trailer houses that surrounded me. My fingers were sore, and my brain was tired. I stuck my hands in my pockets to make them stop. My fingers twirled a million miles per hour, rubbing against my soft cotton pocket, surrounded by denim and flesh. My mind traced every hard line there was from license plates down to the vents on the roofs of the surrounding trailer houses. All of these movements stimulated my brain and made the anxiety and depression lessen.

I could see our trailer house through the back sides of the other trailers that surrounded ours. I was starting to feel the sickness that was behind the windows. My eyes scanned the bathroom and bedroom windows to see if my dad was looking out. I waited for him to yell at me.

"What the fuck is taking you so long? Get your ass in the house!"

What would it be like today? My stomach needed help again. I was so close. My feet shuffled under me. My feet continued to move in the direction of our door. I wanted to turn around and run away. I walked up to the trailer house, my legs trembling as I lifted them up each step. The fear was overwhelming. I could hear my heart beating inside of my chest. My breathing became frantic. My hand reached up to push in the handle on the screen door. I pulled it open, stepped inside of the entryway and hung up my coat. My fingers felt raw, my teeth throbbed, and my eyes were exhausted. One door left. I turned the knob and opened it. I was as ready as I could be. The house was clean, quiet, and safe this time. I ran down the hallway to the bathroom and shut and locked the door. I could hear my dad snoring in his room. Everything was okay for now!

CHAPTER 14

Catching My Breath

Growing up and getting to spend lots of time at my grandparent's house was a beautiful time in my life. My grandma and grandpa were hard working, loving people that always gave me a place to catch my breath. We would go fishing and camping in the summers and this was a very special time in my life. My grandpa Alvin was a hard-working concrete man. He had the softest heart and soul. Grandma always took great care of me and loved me with all of her heart.

I remember one particular summer night on West Sweet Ave. The air was filled with the noise from the loud speaker that broadcasted the play by play action from the baseball diamonds down the street. Grandpa and I listened while getting the boat ready to go fishing the next morning. I loved fishing with Grandpa. This particular time, he invited the neighbor guy Ben to go fishing with us and, I tell you what, Ben was a real character. I learned lots of life lessons about how to treat people whose lives were usually spiraling out of control. Grandpa always treated Ben with respect and dignity even if he would scratch his head at some of the off-the-wall comments Ben would make. The next morning all three of us climbed into my grandpa's truck and headed down to the bait shop. I loved going to the bait shop. There was a picture hanging on the wall of the bait shop of me and grandpa holding our fish that we caught. We bought minnows and worms and then headed out to the river and put the boat in the water. Grandpa ran the boat from the back and Ben sat on the bow and I sat in the middle. Ben cussed like a sailor because we were on a boat and that's what sailors do. Grandpa told him many times, "Ben, there is a kid in the boat, so use your kid words." The fish were biting that day and we all were busy reeling fish in. In between catching fish, I would relax into the seat and look at the beautiful scenery as we floated down the river. At that moment, there wasn't a worry in the world. I always watched my grandpa's every move, learning what I could from him about fishing. Once our limit was caught we called it a day. We would always come home with lots of fish and a renewed outlook on life. Once back at my grandparents' trailer, Grandma always had a home-cooked meal waiting for us and a bed where I could lay my head down at night to catch my breath. I spent a lot of time at their house over the years being loved like I was their own.

One day, some buddies of mine and I were playing football in my backyard. Through the trailer houses we could hear the loud mufflers on my dad's Ford truck coming from half a mile away and once he hit the turn to the trailer park he would squeal the tires around every corner. My buddies and I would stop playing and run to the driveway so we could watch Dad come around the last corner. This was awesome for me and my friends to see. There is no better smell than rubber being burned off of tires on a hot summer afternoon. Dad greeted all my friends with high fives and laughter. He had a deep laugh that made everyone smile. My buddies and I went in the backyard and continued our game of football. Dad came back with us and tossed the ball around and challenged us to running races which he won. He was really fast for a big guy. I was happy during these moments that I was able to play with my dad and catch my breath. I loved that he was always shifting gears and when you were with him you better hang on because it would be balls to the walls. Everything that he did he did for his family. He tried his best to be the best dad that he could be. He would give the shirt off of his back to help people out and often made sacrifices for his family.

Spending time with my mom was always a little scary. When she drove she had a lead foot and would have to stick her arm out to catch me when she braked so I wouldn't go through the windshield. As scary as her driving was, I felt like I could catch my breath with her at times. My mom protected me with all her heart and pushed me to look at life outside of the box. When I was with my mom we dreamt about fields of wildflowers and took turns picking shapes out of the clouds. She could talk people's ears off. I swear I actually watched people walk away from her missing an ear. She always said, "I am a sales person and I talk to make a living." I always enjoyed my mom's creativity and big heart. I remember the mornings in our house with my mom. The candles were all lit and the stereo was turned up loud playing Janis Joplin's "Piece of My Heart." She would have a hot dish cooking on the stove while driving the vacuum cleaner so fast that the wheels squealed. As she rounded the corner with the vacuum, she would dance and sing at the top of her lungs while blowing me kisses. All of this sounds like it would be hard to catch my breath, but it was times like these that she helped me by filling my heart and soul with love and laughter.

PART II

Anger

I was now entering a time when I was able to finally fight back. But, my anger came out in all the wrong ways and caused damage throughout my community. My heart hurts today over the pain that I caused others, but at the time I wasn't able to stop it or control it. I didn't know how to self regulate my emotions and I did my best to make everyone around me feel my pain when I felt they deserved it. In many ways, I am the same person today that I was back then, it's just that I am able to make better choices about how I act in certain situations today. Damage to others runs through some of the following chapters, and it breaks my heart today. Today, I take great pride in being a kind and accepting man that cares for others the way I wish to be cared for.

CHAPTER 15

Quit Crying, You Little Pussy!

It was June, 1986. Helena, Montana. The excitement inside of me was almost too much to handle. Finally, we were able to go on a vacation as a family. Mom, Dad, little brother, and I traveled out to Helena, Montana, to visit Grandma Irma. I loved my grandma with all my heart. My dad was a saint when she was around, so that was always a plus. She had some kind of power over him that no one else did. She brought out the best in my dad and kept him in line. Losing my grandma was a big fear of mine. Every time that I would see her, I would think that this would be the last time that I would get to see her. I always made it extra special even with the looming fear that lurked in my brain that induced large amounts of anxiety. I experienced my grandma's death hundreds of times over in my life before she passed on from this earth. She always made me feel safe to cry in front of her. In fact, she was the only one that I felt safe to cry in front of as a kid.

Grandma was an amazing, beautiful person who always provided support for me in my life. The only problem with this support was that it was far away. The distance from Bismarck to Helena, Montana, is 613.2 miles. This particular visit was my first to her house. Her backyard was so beautiful with all of her flower beds and a giant mountain as a backdrop. One of the days I spent some time with her in her backyard. It had just rained. The smell of the rain and the aromas of the foliage that surrounded her yard was a sensation overload for me. She brought a towel from inside the carport and wiped the water off the patio chairs. The birds were eating out of the feeders. Butterflies started to shake the rain drops from their wings. Black, orange, and blue hummingbirds floated through the garden with grace and beauty.

Grandma sat down on one of the lawn chairs and watched me walk through her yard, admiring the beautiful rocks in her flower garden and smelling all of her beautiful flowers. She told me the names of each flower and gave me a little education on how to love them. She would always tell me, "Tyler, the only thing that you need to do is love your flowers and water them when it doesn't rain."

"Grandma, I can do that! I have lots of love in my heart."

"I know you do! You are such a sweet little boy!"

That moment that I had with her that day in her yard was one of the best memories that I had as a kid with my grandma.

I was the "sweet little boy" until I said the word fucker in front of her. When I said it, she grabbed me by my ear, yanked me up, and pulled me into the bathroom. She jammed a bar of soap into my mouth. The bar was too big but that didn't stop her. My teeth shaved off the edges of the bar of soap until she jammed it in far enough to cover my tongue. It hurt badly and the soap tasted horrible. I look back on this today and I think it's funny because she was washing my mouth out with soap for saying the word fucker. But, she must have said the word fuck fifteen times while she was jamming the bar into my mouth. It didn't make much sense to me. But, I knew that she loved me and what she did to me, I deserved. When I got older, using the word fuck or fucker was okay. It's just off limits when you're a kid.

My step-grandpa George was a fun guy. He went on hikes with us and took us exploring. He had a very playful side to him that brought joy into the room. He was the only grandpa that I knew on that side of the family. My dad's dad died before I was born. I heard a lot of bad shit about him and the vicious things that he used to do to his kids, in particular, my dad. I am kind of glad that I didn't get to meet him because the stories scared me to death. Family members always said that he did the best that he could with what he had. Then I would hear a story that during dinner my dad reached for a piece of bread without asking for it first and his dad wound up and punched him right in the face, knocking him off his chair to the floor. This made a lot of sense when I heard these stories. No wonder my dad was such an asshole. Even as a kid I knew that I was going to be nice to my kids someday and that I would never call my wife names like my dad did. Grandma always told me that "Your dad is doing better than his dad did for him."

There were all these wonderful things to do in Helena. Dad said that someone would always give him the middle finger when he was in Montana and, sure as shit, someone did and everyone in the car laughed except for me. I had never seen my dad give anyone a pass that gave him the finger.

We climbed the mountain that was behind my grandma's house. This was the first mountain that I had ever climbed. My grandpa George climbed it with my mom, my little brother and me. The smell of the evergreens and the different colors of all the jagged rocks were awesome. The heat felt like it was only inches away from us once we made it to the top. The thrill of making it to the top was inspiring. I was able to use each of these experiences to slow down my mind for a moment. My mind constantly raced a million miles per hour, constantly tracing every shape there was from stop signs to doors on the houses. Sometimes, I even tried to count people's teeth when they smiled. This anxiety that I was participating in every minute of every day was overwhelming, but climbing the mountain, smelling the scents on the mountain and in my grandma's flower beds did something for me that was unbelievable. My mind slowed; I could breathe. The insanity in my brain was able to rest for a few minutes at time.

My dad gave me so much anxiety. He was constantly criticizing everything that I did from the way that I opened the door to the way that I shut the door. Shit, he even used to tell me to stop breathing so loudly and that I was blinking my eyes too many times. Grandma knew everything that was going on in our lives and she had some control over my dad. She was the only person who I had ever seen have control over him. She used to always tell him, "Come back here, Ricky, into the backyard and look at these beautiful flowers and butterflies."

"No! I'm not going to waste my time looking at some stupid flowers. Mom, you're going to turn my boy into a little pussy having him look at flowers and shit."

"Ricky, you're a pussy for not looking at flowers."

I got a kick out of the way she talked to him. He always had to act tough and grumbly. I had witnessed different times in our lives where he would find the beauty in the things around him. I watched him smell flowers and look at wildlife. He would let his guard down every once in a while. But, when he refused, he was the one missing out on the beauties in life. Grandma pulled me over onto her lap and said, "Don't listen to him, Tyler. He is the one that is missing out on the flowers. He is just a big baby."

I spent a lot of time with my grandma on this trip. I kept thinking that this would be the last time that I would ever see her. The anxiety that I had inside me was unbearable most minutes. Constantly thinking about her death was overwhelming and it played through my mind every minute of every day that we were there. Dad was constantly trying to irritate his brothers and start fights. There were a couple blowout fights and then everyone would leave grandma's house because of what my dad would say. Mom kept trying to cover his tracks. She would always justify his actions. Everything felt like it was falling apart towards the end of our trip. That last night at grandma's I cried myself to sleep knowing that we were leaving early the next morning. The next morning, we packed all of our belongings in the vehicle and said our goodbyes. I felt sick to my stomach when I looked at Grandma. I held her so tight. She kissed me on my cheeks and I kissed her back.

"I love you, my sweet Tyler."

"I love you, Grandma! I will miss you so much."

I had all of these feelings inside of me, but I was scared to show them in front of my dad for fear of being judged and the things that he would say. The tears welled up in my eyes and my heart felt like it was pounding out of my chest. Grandma looked at me. She knew the pain that I was feeling inside and the struggle that I was having trying to hold back my tears.

"Hang on, Tyler. I will be right back."

She walked into the back yard and came back out holding a Tiger Lily. She handed me the beautiful flower.

"Tyler, when your tears start to flow, think about this beautiful flower that was watered by the tears of God that gave it life. If you are feeling scared on the drive home, smell this flower and think about happy thoughts."

"Thank you, Grandma. I love you!"

I hid the flower behind my back so my dad wouldn't see it. We all climbed into the vehicle. I looked out the window at my grandma and blew her a kiss, mouthing the words I love you. She said I love you back. The feelings were overwhelming. The tears poured out of my eyes. With my hand, I tried to wipe the tears away as fast they were coming out. The thoughts were running through my brain that Grandma is going to die soon. I struggled to catch my breath. I was seated in the backseat right behind my dad's seat. I tried to hide my head against the door so I was out of sight of the review mirror. I was doing my best to minimize the noises that my body was making while crying. Mom heard me. She looked back at me and said. "I know you love your grandma honey and she loves you. It's going to be okay, Tyler."

No! What the hell? She was blowing my cover. No, Mom! We pulled away from Grandma's house and as we rounded the block, I heard my dad's voice.

"What's wrong with you?"

I looked up and I could see my dad looking at me through the rearview mirror. His eyes locked on to my tear-filled eyes.

"What the fuck are you crying for?"

"I love Grandma and I'm going to miss her."

Mom said, "Stop it, Rick. Leave him alone."

"Shut your mouth, Cindy! He doesn't need to be a little pussy! Get over it, Tyler."

He turned the radio up so he didn't have to listen to my mom or me crying. I tried as hard as I could to stop the tears from flowing, but they wouldn't stop. I clenched my fists together trying to make all of the rage that was inside me now go away. My eyes glanced up at the mirror. I could see his eyes staring at me. He shook his head in disappointment.

"Stop crying, you little pussy! Only pussies cry! Little baby Tyler."

These words sent me into a full outrage that rumbled through my soul. My tears dried up and my thoughts turned to thoughts of killing my dad. I was looking up at the seatbelt thinking I should wrap it around his fucking neck and put my feet on the back of his seat and choke him to death.

I will show you who the little fucking pussy is now.

I sat directly behind my dad over the next hour fantasizing about killing him. His words cut me deep and I wanted them to stop. Honestly, I thought that I could kill him with the seat belt. In reality, I would have never been able to overpower him.

I would have been screwed. It felt like I had my heart ripped out when we left my grandma. My dad condemned me for the feelings that I had about someone who I love so much.

I held onto that flower that grandma gave me for the whole trip. For thirteen hours that flower made everything okay. I smelled that Tiger Lily and lost myself in its beauty. When my tears fell on its orange petals, it made me think about the rains that helped this flower grow.

Whenever I felt overwhelmed by the counting and tracing, I would go back to that moment in Grandma's backyard when we talked about the flowers. I loved my grandma and that is something that I will never hide as long as I live. Tears are beautiful, even if you are a boy. We all cry, even my dad. He was just scared to let anyone see him.

CHAPTER 16

Couch And The Shotgun

On the weekends, my dad would go drinking with his friends at the Corral Bar. This particular weekend my mom was playing bingo with my grandma. I heard the garage door open at three in the afternoon. I had been downstairs in my room playing video games and time had slipped away from me. I had missed both breakfast and lunch. The garage door opening interrupted my zoned-out video game session and I realized that I was hungry. I went upstairs thinking that it was Mom coming home after bingo, but my dad was standing in the kitchen. He was in a really good mood. He was slurring his words and stumbling when he walked. He was drunk.

"Where's Mom?"

"She's playing bingo with Grandma."

That pissed him off.

"She is fucking wasting money. What the fuck is wrong with her? Where did they go to play bingo?"

"I don't know, Dad. I'm not sure."

"What are you doing up here?"

"I need to get something to eat. I haven't eaten yet today."

He mumbled some shit under his breath and walked back to his bedroom. I propped the fridge open and looked inside. I was looking for something that I could grab really quickly and take downstairs to my room to avoid the whole situation with him. He came walking back down the hallway, out into the kitchen, over to the sink, filled up a glass full of water, and set it on the counter. My guts churned because I could see in his face that he was looking for a fight.

"You're still standing in front of the fridge, you fat fuck."

I shut the fridge because I knew that I needed to get the hell out of there. I turned around to walk away and he was standing there right in front of me. He stuck his arms out and shoved me against the fridge. He reached up with his right hand, grabbed me around my throat, and started to choke me. He pulled his head right up against mine and smashed them against one another. He was looking me in the eyes. I could smell the alcohol on his breath.

"You fat, fucking pig! That is all you do is fucking eat all of our food, you fat fuck! You're a fat fucker! What the fuck do you have to eat all the fucking time for?"

I couldn't talk because he was choking me. I couldn't breathe! I was trying to get away from him, but I couldn't shake his grasp. He was way stronger than me. He must have seen my face turning blue or the fear in my eyes, so he let go of my neck.

"Get the fuck out here, you fat son of a bitch! I don't want to see your pig ass for the rest of the day!"

"I didn't eat breakfast or lunch, Dad. I'm sorry!"

I took off from the kitchen and ran downstairs as fast as I could. I went into my room and shut the door. I looked into the mirror at my neck. It was swollen and red. I could see his hand marks. I was so pissed and hurt. I didn't really care about getting choked. It was the words that cut me deep. I hated myself and when I looked in the mirror all I saw was a fat, fucking pig and I wanted to die.

I could hear him walking around upstairs for the next thirty minutes and then it became quiet. I thought maybe he passed out in his bedroom and now it would be okay for a little while. I snuck up the spiral staircase, peeking upstairs to check out the situation. I could hear my dad snoring and I could see his feet sticking up over the edge of the couch in the living room. I walked up to the top of the stairs so I could see him. He was completely passed out.

I stood there for a moment thinking about killing him and wishing that he would die. I looked over at the knife set on the counter in the kitchen, fantasizing about sticking a knife into his chest and killing him. This thought really scared me, because I didn't think sticking a knife into his chest would kill him right away and he would get his hands on me and probably kill me before he died.

I opened the gate and walked into the kitchen. The images kept going through my brain over and over again of different ways that I could kill him. I looked at the fridge and remembered what he had just done to me a little while ago and the words that he had said. I went back to his bedroom and thought about stealing some of his drugs out of his safe, but it was locked. In the corner of his closet was a 12-gauge shotgun with a box of shells on the top shelf of the closet. I grabbed the shotgun. I loaded two shells, pumped a shell into the chamber and then put in another shell. I was fantasizing about killing him. I wanted to kill him so bad! I was so sick and tired of what he was doing to us. I walked out into the living room being as quiet as I could.

He was still lying in the same spot on the couch snoring away. His snoring and his breathing were so bad that it sounded like he was dying. I stood next to the couch, about three feet away, with the shotgun pushed against my shoulder. I was aiming it at his chest. I had my finger on the trigger. I sat there for some time aiming the shotgun at him. I was shaking with fear.

The voice inside my brain was saying, "I'm going to kill you, you fat motherfucker! You piece of shit! I'm going to shoot you right in the chest and when your eyes open, I will shoot you in the fucking face!"

I ran the scenario over and over again, trying to find the nerve to pull the trigger. He would stop snoring and move around a little bit. I was hoping that he would wake up and see me pointing the gun at him, because then I would have to kill him before he would kill me. I prayed for him to wake up. The tears flowed down my face. All the years of pain and abuse came bubbling back up to the surface. I wanted him to die so bad, but I couldn't do it. I thought about the blood that would be all over the couch and how sad my Mom and brother would be.

I thought about the good times when my dad was nice and funny. I finally pulled the shotgun down from my shoulder and walked back to his bedroom. I emptied the shotgun and put it and the shells back in the closet. I went back downstairs. I sat on my bed crying uncontrollably. I was very upset with myself because I couldn't do it. I had him right there and I couldn't kill him. I felt like a failure and now he was going to continue to hurt us. I loved my dad; I just wanted the pain to go away and I knew that once he was dead the pain would go away forever.

CHAPTER 17

Broken Heart, Just Hanging There

I found myself finding girls that I liked and then going all in before I even knew their last names. I would buy them flowers and cards before we would even go on a date. I was bass-ackwards for sure. I was planning our future together before I even knew they liked me. If this didn't scare them away, I don't know what would have. My heart was in the right place, but there was too much other shit that was attached that clouded my judgment. I wanted a girlfriend so badly, but I did everything in my power to fuck it up.

There was this particular girl that caught my eye. Her name was Imani. She was beautiful. She had beautiful dark black curly hair. She was half black and half white. I thought she was the most beautiful girl I had ever laid eyes on. I lusted over her at school and took any opportunity to walk by her and say hi. I told all my friends that I liked her, but I was afraid to say anything to her besides a random hello. I had zero girl-getting skills.

My dad always told me that he didn't care what I did in my life, but if I would ever bring home a black girl, he would kick me out and disown me. I struggled with this inner turmoil of wanting to listen to my dad and the way that I really felt deep down inside about the whole race issue. I didn't care that she was half black. This would have never been an issue if my dad wasn't here. I spent a few months lusting over Imani. She would smile at me and show me a little bit of attention. This was just enough to make me think that I had a chance. I was getting excited and actually started thinking that I would get to go on a date with her. I was fucking delusional.

One Friday at school I decided to have a dozen red roses delivered to her house, even though I never really had a conversation with her. My twisted mind kept running through all of the scenarios thousands and thousands of times until I convinced myself that it would be a good idea. So, I went for it. I went to the flower shop on my lunch break and picked out each red rose, making sure to get the nicest ones in the shop. I was in heaven that day in the flower shop. My mind stopped trying to kill me for a moment and the flowers were magical. I felt a serenity that I have struggled my whole life to find. I set up the delivery for 3:30 p.m. I picked out a card and wrote, "Hello, Imani, I hope you find these flowers as beautiful as I have and that they make you smile. Have a beautiful day." I saw a miniature teddy bear that reminded me of a teddy bear that I had as a kid that my dad threw away, so I got that, too.

That afternoon at school was stressful. I was unsure if it was the right choice to send her the flowers. Was it too much? Will she like them? Later that day, I found out through a mutual friend that she received the flowers and that she thought they were beautiful. I also found out that she would be going to a house party on Saturday night. Imani told our mutual friend that she would like to talk to me there if I was going to go. Hell, yeah, I can come. The thoughts in my brain wouldn't stop. I thought that this was going to be the time of my life. Maybe she liked me. Maybe I would actually have someone fall in love with me like I had always dreamed.

Saturday night came around and I prepared. I put on the best clothes that I had. I even went and got a haircut a couple hours before the party. I showed up to the party early. I stole a 1.75-liter bottle of Canadian Windsor out of the cupboard at my house. Once I was at the party, I started to drink. I filled a glass up with the Canadian Windsor and guzzled them, one after another. I was nervous to meet Imani in person and actually have a real conversation. I thought if I got drunk it would be a lot easier to talk to her. I continued to get so fucking drunk that I could hardly stand. I was falling down the stairs and causing all kinds of problems at this house party.

They finally got me settled down when Imani showed up. I walked over to her and told her that I was glad she was there and had a small conversation with her. She thanked me for the flowers, and I let her know that I was happy that she liked them. I told her that I liked her a lot and that I would like to get to know her better. She really didn't say anything back to me. She just kind of looked at me. There I was with my heart hanging out of my chest trying to hand it to her and she had nothing to say back to me.

We separated and started talking to other people. I couldn't stop admiring her beauty. I started getting down on myself thinking about how stupid I felt. I was embarrassed and all of the negative thoughts that I had about myself came rushing back and flashed through my mind. She shot me down completely and now she was standing over in the corner talking to another guy. She was actually talking to him. She was smiling and touching his shoulder. This instantly made me sad and I started to cry. I ran into the bathroom and hid out for some time crying, drinking, and feeling sorry for myself.

I wiped the tears away, then went back out to the party and started to cause a shit load of problems, just like I always did. I was done holding myself together for this girl who slapped my heart right back into its dark lonely dungeon. I was pissed off at the guy that she was talking to so I thought it would be a good thing to confront him. I walked over to this individual, called him a pussy and punched him in the side of the face. The blow from my punch sent him falling over the side of the couch onto the floor. Everyone started screaming for me to leave him alone. I looked around and Imani was nowhere to be found. Now I felt in control. I showed this little pussy that he shouldn't be talking with a girl that I was in love with. I was told to leave the party and to not come back.

I grabbed my bottle of whiskey and went outside. I walked around the outside of the house talking to people that were coming and going from the party. Then reality set in. I had really messed things up with Imani. Self-pity reared its ugly head. I started to cry and feel sorry for myself that nobody will ever love me. Nobody will ever want to go on a date with me. I walked down the street taking straight shots out of the bottle of whiskey. I knocked over a bird bath and kicked the side of a couple different vehicles leaving dents. I walked down the street for about twelve houses.

Desperation set in and I started thinking about ways to hurt myself. I thought about getting into my car and driving it into a wall as fast as it would go so it would kill me instantly. I started to look around one of the yards and I saw an extension cord rolled up next to the garage. I grabbed the extension cord and looked at the tree in the front yard. I unraveled the extension cord and tied it around my neck. I struggled to climb up the tree, but I was able to get about eight feet off the ground. I laid on the branch hugging it with my legs and arms. I tied the extension cord in a knot around the tree branch. I rolled off the branch and let go.

I felt the extension cord tighten around my neck, cutting off my circulation. I felt my feet and then my ass slam against the ground. I couldn't breathe. My hands instinctively reached up, trying to pull this extension cord that was strangling my neck. I wanted to die so fucking bad, but when it was choking me to death I was trying to get it untied from my neck. I was able to pull myself up off the ground and get it untied from my neck. Once the pressure was off and I could breathe again, I was instantly pissed. I was pissed that the extension cord stretched. I was upset that I was still alive.

I climbed back up the tree and untied the cord from the branch. This time, I doubled up the extension cord, tied it around the tree, and my neck once again. I clawed my way back up the tree to the same branch. I was exhausted from all this work. I struggled to get the doubled-up cord tied around the tree. Finally, I got it! I rolled off the branch feeling the cord tighten up instantly choking me. I felt the panic set in. I hit the ground. This time the cord was tight. I struggled to stand up. I was flailing around on the ground trying to get the cord loosened around my neck. This time the cord stretched and my knot around the branch didn't hold and let loose. I was able to get my fingers in between the cord and my neck enough to catch a breath. I was gasping for air. I was able to get the cord untied from my neck. It's crazy that I wanted to die so bad, but once I was dying, I fought as hard as I could to stay alive.

I laid on the ground feeling the cold damp grass under my body. I lay there for some time crying. I sat up and leaned against the tree. I looked at the cord laying on the ground, but I was done. No more attempts on my life tonight. My neck was hurt bad and so were my hands and my side. This completely took all of the fight out of me. I pulled myself up off the ground and rolled the extension cord up and laid it next to the house in the same spot that I took it from and grabbed my bottle of whiskey.

I walked back down the street and found my car. I got into my car and drove home. Tears streamed down my face the whole drive home. I was so broken that I couldn't drink any more whiskey. I was upset with myself about the problems that I caused at the party. I felt stupid for sending the flowers to Imani without getting to know her and I felt like a complete failure that I couldn't even kill myself. I laid in my bed that night cursing God for not taking my life. I begged God to not let me wake up, so I didn't have to face the pain any longer.

CHAPTER 18

Not The Way I Dreamt
It To Be

I went to Bismarck High School in Bismarck, North Dakota. I struggled immensely with girls. I had a giant heart and I wanted and needed it to be handled with care. I wanted to find a girl who I could spend the rest of my life with, but I had serious issues. Unresolved issues. I had been raped by an older lady my first year of high school while I was drunk. I was partying with some older people and they decided to go skinny dipping in the Missouri River. It was dark outside, and I was too embarrassed to take my clothes off to go swimming, so I sat on the shore just watching these naked adults jumping in the water. I was drinking whiskey to the point that I could no longer sit up. Two of the people decided to have sex on the dock and the other lady came over to where I was laying and started fondling my penis. I told her to stop, but she kept going. I tried to push her away, but she pinned me down and started sucking on my penis. I kicked and tried to get up, but the alcohol had me good.

I begged her to stop. She pulled down her pants and then mine. She climbed on top of me and started rubbing her vagina on my penis. I couldn't feel anything. I told her to stop. She grinded herself on my penis until she finished and got off me and left. This really hurt me inside. This scarred me forever. This event in my life really hurt me because it messed with feelings of my heart. I wanted a girl who I could spend the rest of my life with to share my virginity with, not some drunk slob on a dirty shore along the river in the dark. I thought that I was confused before, now it was confusion on steroids.

CHAPTER 19

I Have Arrived

Experiencing a narcotic pain medication high is life changing. I felt like I had arrived at a new and beautiful life. Everything felt perfect. Love flowed out of my heart to the people who had harmed me over my lifetime. Forgiveness was given out daily without processing the past negative feelings. Nothing hurt physically. All my self-doubt left my body instantly. I looked in the mirror and loved the person who looked back at me for the first time in my life. The tracing and counting ceased in my mind. I didn't want to die anymore. I wanted to live.

The safe in my dad's closet always had bottles of pain medication that my aunt would give him to help him with his pain. I would grab two sandwich size baggies out of the kitchen drawer and sneak into my mom and dad's bedroom when they weren't home.

I would open the closet door, kneel on the floor in front of the safe and pray that it wasn't locked. The safe was grey with a little spin dial number code that required a special combination to enter and a silver handle. My hand reached for the handle and pushed it down. It wasn't locked. Now, all his drugs were my drugs. Well, not all the drugs, just enough that he wouldn't be able to tell that I took any. There was a one-ounce bag of pot, a gallon Ziploc baggie that was half full of white pills and a pill bottle that contained a cream-colored powder with a McDonald's straw cut in half next to a pipe made out of deer antler.

I opened the Ziploc baggie and grabbed two large buds and five or six smaller buds and put them in one of the sandwich baggies that I had in my hand. I fluffed up my dad's bag of pot before I sealed the bag back up and put it back in the exact same spot where it was before. The smell of the safe was a strong smell of pot. I took the baggie of pills out of the safe and sat down on the floor between my knees and opened it. I opened the other baggie that I had in my hand and reached into the large baggie of pills and took two handfuls of the pills and put them in my baggie. My sandwich baggie was half full of pills. Scored once again. I reached back into the baggie and grabbed about 20 pills and placed them in my mouth and started chewing them up.

I got up and went to the bathroom, turned on the water in the sink and cupped my hands under the water and scooped two scoops of water in my mouth to chase the pills down into my stomach. I dried my hands on the bathroom towel. I looked out the bathroom window to make sure that I was still in the clear. Good to go. I kneeled in front of the safe and put my dad's bag of pills back into the safe. I grabbed the straw and the pill bottle. I opened the pill bottle, stuck the straw up to my nose, plugged my left nostril and stuck the straw down into the bottle and took a big snort. It burned so bad. My eyes watered. I could feel the powder that I snorted start to run down the back of my throat. I put the top on the pill bottle and placed the straw and bottle back into the safe. I could feel the drugs starting to kick in right away.

I noticed on the inside of the door of the safe, two Philips headed screws holding a metal plate over the combination dial. This intrigued me. I ran to the garage and got a Phillips screwdriver. I opened the walk-in door to the garage and looked down the road and listened for any vehicles that might be coming. All clear. I shut the door and locked it. I ran to my dad's bedroom and kneeled in front of the safe. I used the screwdriver and took both screws out, one at a time and laid them and the metal plate on the carpet next to my baggies of drugs that I just stole. My ears were constantly listening just in case someone came home early. I looked in the hole in the safe that the metal plate once covered. I could see the inner workings of the combination dial. I could see the cogs on the wheels inside with some springs and switches. I wondered what would happen if I turned the dial. Would it make it so I wouldn't be able to close the safe back up again and I would for sure be caught by my dad. What if I can figure out the combination. I thought about it long and hard for a whole fifteen seconds. Screw it. It would be great if I had the combination for the safe for the days that he didn't forget to lock it.

I started to turn the combination wheel while looking at the cogs inside. I noticed that there were different spacings in each cog. I knew that I needed to get each cog lined up with the locking mechanism. I spun the combination to the left twice until I watched one of the springs move. I slowly spun the combination knob to the right until the cog with the biggest spacing was lined up. I looked at the number on the combination knob and it was ten. I spun it back to the left until it lined up and looked at the number and it was twenty-six. I spun it to the right until it lined up and it was fifty-two. I pressed down on the handle and it unlocked. I put the metal plate back on the safe with the two screws and made sure everything was in order. I closed the safe back up and spun the wheel to the left two times, then to the right until it was on ten, then back to the left until it was on twenty-six and then back to the right until it was on fifty-two. I pressed on the latch handle and it opened. Yah, 10/26/52 was the combination to my happiness. Or, so I thought. I picked up my baggies full of drugs and stuck them into my pockets. I grabbed the screwdriver and put it between my teeth. I took my hands and rubbed them across the carpeting to raise it back up from where I pressed it down with all my activity. I slowly crawled backwards out of the bedroom grooming the carpet to hide my tracks.

CHAPTER 20

The Start Of The Gang War

The war started when I was a junior at Bismarck High School. I was a fighter, drug addict, thief, and a very respectable kid when I wanted to be. Most of my friends' parents loved me until the cops showed up to get their kid for questioning on a bunch of crazy shit, most likely a felony that I committed.

I had a long history of street fighting and the reputation that I was down to fight anyone. I never backed down from a fight and I did it on a regular basis. There were times that I was in multiple fights per day. Shit, there were times that I would fight three times per week. No matter where I was, I would fight anyone. My dad always told me, "Hit the motherfucker first." I listened. It worked. I was not scared to hit anybody first and I really didn't give a shit if there were more than one of them. Most of the time it didn't work out when I was outnumbered, but sometimes it did. I was six feet tall and weighed in at three hundred and twenty-five pounds. I was fast for a big guy and I could hit hard, most of the time knocking out the person on the other end of my punch.

None of this made me happy. This made my life miserable, but it became the survival of my pride and my life.

One day in the commons area at Bismarck High School three gang members had a girl tell me that they wanted to meet with me. I told her I didn't want to meet with any of them. The leader was Joe. He was a bigger guy whose hands were as fast as lightning when he would fight, and his mouth would run all the time. The next in line was Hud. He was huge. No one knew if he could fight, but we all knew that he looked like he would hurt you if he got his hands on you. They were trying to recruit new members into their gang. They were a side gang of the DEG gang out of Minot, North Dakota. The DEG gang was much larger and well organized. They meant business and nobody really wanted to mess with them. One week at school I had a couple of guys walk up to me from the local gang. They were getting up in my face trying to intimidate me. I wasn't scared and I sure didn't want to be in a gang. Joe told me that I needed to join their gang. They let me know that when I joined, I would be part of something great. I guess I didn't respond correctly to what they wanted to hear.

"Fuck off, I am not going to be part of your piss-ant gang." Not the words that they were looking for.

Things became heated and a lot of really bad shit was said. I was not backing down. I was ready to fight right then and there. I looked at Hud and figured if it went down, I would hit him first and see what happened after that. I thought it was going to be just a fight, but boy was I wrong.

This one encounter turned into more encounters and finally into years of all-out war. The reaction towards me was instant and the news spread like wildfire. Everything got blown out of proportion from the very moment that it started. There are no rules in war and, even if there had been rules, none of them would have been followed. After the altercation in the commons area I told my group of friends what had happened and this didn't help the situation. This actually fueled the fire. My friends loved this shit until it became directed at them. Over the course of that month there were some fist fights that happened between my group and their gang. My group basically consisted of a few friends, mostly jocks and a bunch of innocent people that got caught in the crossfire. We definitely were not a gang, but most of us wouldn't back down from a fight.

Walking through the hallways of that high school was tense. Venomous words were spewed from both sides. Words hurt and everyone knew it. I figured if I was willing to punch you in the face, I should be able to call you every name in the book. Today, if I could take my words back, I would.

One night out at my friend's party north of Bismarck, the alcohol and the drugs were flowing heavily. Some of the local gang members showed up at the party. I am not sure what they were thinking. There were two individuals in the car, one of the guys was Scott and the other guy was Everett. Everett and I had fought a couple times over the years. It was always a good fight; he was a tough son of a bitch, but I was much meaner and I always seemed to get the upper hand and this bugged the shit out of him.

They walked into the house just like they owned it. Things started getting said by both sides. Threats of violence started to flare up from both sides. They basically were saying that I should have never screwed with them and that I would pay the ultimate consequence. They threatened to hurt my little brother. Wrong thing to say to me. Threaten me and my family and I will hurt you bad. The consequences did not scare me. I was pissed and now I wanted to fight. They were threatening me with physical violence from their families. They let me know that they had people who were going to kill me.

"Fuck you. Bring your families and let's do this." I followed them out of the house into the driveway. They got in their car. The windows were rolled down. I threw three punches through the passenger side window at Everett, knocking him over in the seat. He was bleeding. They threatened me repeatedly, letting me know that I would pay for this. I blurted out some very horrible words. Tensions were high and the hate came right back at me. The threats were still being yelled out the car window as they were backing out of the driveway.

The words that night were dark and evil. The car sped out of the driveway before disappearing down the road. We all wondered what was going to happen next. Lots of shit was being talked about after they left. My buddies justified my actions. If you're going to threaten me and my family, I am going to threaten you back.

The next Monday, when I walked into the school, the atmosphere was different. I could feel the tension in the air. By now, the rest of the gang and a bunch of other kids that had nothing to do with this war were involved because of the things that I had been saying. The day was being filled with verbal attacks. Horrible words. The war was started and the lines were drawn.

A week had gone by with no violence, only vicious words. A couple of my buddies and I went up to the north Taco John's on our lunch period. We loved Taco John's and we went there almost daily. We were sitting at a table inside the restaurant talking and eating our tacos. I noticed a black car pull into the parking lot. This car was loaded with four different people. The driver was Joe and he had Hud riding shotgun with two other kids in the backseat. They proceeded to hang their head out the windows as they drove around the building. Joe had his arm out the window banging on the side of his car with his hand. Around and around the building they went. I think they circled the building about six times.

"Fuck it, I am going out there and get this over with." I walked outside; my friends followed. My friends wanted to watch a fight, not be in one. I made eye contact with Joe. The car stopped. I walked over to the passenger door of the car where Hud was sitting. I crouched down.

"What the fuck is your problem?!!"

"Fuck you, piece of shit!!"

"Fuck you!"

"Get out of the car, Hud!! Let's do this, you pussy!! Get out now!!"

I stood up from my crouched position expecting the car doors to open. None of them moved! I thought that Hud would've gotten out of the car because he was a big boy. He was the one who I was worried about the most, but he didn't move. I noticed that his eyes got really big. I could sense fear. I took advantage of the fear that I saw in his eyes.

"It's just me and you today, Hud! Get out, let's go now!!"

"Fuck you, Tyler! Fuck you! You want to fight right here?"

"This works for me!"

Joe was telling Hud to get out and fight. I could tell everyone in the car was scared.

I backed up from the car and took my sweatshirt off and threw my hat and sweatshirt to my friend Kimmo Slurpy.

"Come on, get out before the cops come."

Joe stepped on the gas. The tires squealed. The car sped out of the parking lot flying down the street away from us. I looked over at Kimmo Slurpy.

"Shit, Ty, they are going to get more people. We better get the hell out of here!"

We walked back into the restaurant and sat down and finished eating our tacos. I was on high alert, waiting for a bunch of cars full of people to come back for revenge. Kimmo Slurpy was scared.

I didn't want my friends to get hurt so I said, "Let's go. I will fight another day."

We went back to school that afternoon and it was eerily quiet. There was nothing crazy that was happening. I knew that something was going to be happening from this altercation. I called them out and none of them were willing to get out of that car. I wanted to get this fight over with the hope that this would all stop.

The battle of words went on for some time as the tensions heightened. Death threats were being made towards my friends and my family. The phone in our house would ring at 3:00 a.m. on a regular basis. I would hear my dad answer the phone. Then the yelling would start. My mom and dad's bedroom was right above mine so I could hear everything well. My dad would yell, "Fuck you! Come out to my house and try to kill us! I will kill you all! Come out! Now!"

These threats on our lives were happening on a regular basis. Dad instructed me to have all the guns in the house loaded. I felt horrible that my parents were being dragged into this mess. I was worried what my dad would do. They shouldn't have threatened him. He was not right in the head when he or his family were threatened. I knew that my dad would kill them all if it came down to it. I guess, so would I if I needed to. Our house was on high alert 24/7.

CHAPTER 21

Hit! The Wrong Person

Kimmo Slurpy talked me into going to Minot, North Dakota, for a big party that was happening over the weekend. He knew some kids who he was in wrestling with that we could stay with. We road tripped, literally. We had coke, whiskey, and a bag of some killer pot. Once up in Minot, the party started. We were drinking and smoking pot. We hid the coke from the kids we were staying with. Coke is something that you never wanted to share with anyone. The kid whose house we were staying at had a Dodge van. This van was a badass. It had a cool paint job and a souped-up engine. I'm not sure what kind of engine was in it, but when he started it, I could feel its rumble deep in my chest.

"Let's go. I'll give you a ride in the van."

I was so high from the coke and the pot. He took off down the street squealing the tires. When he stepped on the gas pedal, I was instantly sucked back into the seat that was located behind the driver's seat. He stopped in the middle of the road and using the gas pedal and the brake, he could get the front end of this van to bounce a foot off the ground. We bounced for a whole block before he stopped. We were having a great time smoking pot and drinking whiskey. We ended up going back to the house to drink and smoke some more.

"Time to go to the party boys!"

I had some concerns about this party due to being in the DEG's back yard. I was on their turf now and I might have said some stupid crap letting them know that I would be at this particular party. Kimmo Slurpy and I followed the van full of kids out to the party. I drove my own vehicle because I wanted to be in control of the situation. I didn't know these kids whose house we were staying at, and I sure didn't trust them. There must have been four hundred kids standing around in this field where the party was. Cars were everywhere. Everyone was getting blitzed. After we walked around for some time, I started to hear my name being talked about, but none of them knew that it was me standing in the field next to them. I could hear random people talking.

"There is going to be a fight."

"DEGs are on the hunt."

'They are going to fuck this Tyler kid up now."

Different groups were huddled up all over the field. My eyes constantly scanned for kids in black DEG clothing. Kimmo Slurpy begged me not to start any shit with them because we were outnumbered. I agreed I was not going to go looking for any trouble, but if it found me I was going to fight. The feeling was tense and uneasy. I knew something was happening and it wasn't good. I knew they were looking for me. I could see large groups moving through the field. Next thing I knew, there were a bunch of screams as the field full of kids instantly scattered. I could hear some faint pops. It sounded like a small caliber gun was being fired. Everyone was running and getting into their cars and leaving. I could hear people yelling.

"They fucking shot him! They shot him!"

"Run! Let's go, run!"

"He's dead! They killed him! Go, Go, Go! Now!!"

Kids were running in all different directions. Kimmo Slurpy and I jumped in my car and took off. We pulled over in a parking lot and talked about what we were going to do next. He was really shaken up and wanted to go home and I thought it was best to leave now. Little did I know that I was the one that was supposed to get shot. The word on the street was that there was a hit out on me and the DEGs were supposed to carry out the hit at the party. They knew that I was coming to Minot because my dumb ass told them that I would be at the party. They ended up shooting a guy in the leg with a .22 caliber pistol. They thought this individual was me. Holy shit, this little game just changed, they were trying to kill me. Thank God that there was no social media back then because they would have known exactly who to shoot. I feel bad for the guy who was mistaken for me. Poor bastard! Well, at least they missed and only got him in the leg.

Now, it was my turn to dish out some of the pain. It was my turn to cause damage to these motherfuckers who tried to kill me. Enough was enough. Paybacks are a bitch.

CHAPTER 22

That Escalated Quickly

I was sitting in English class when the principal stuck his head into the classroom and said, "I need to see Tyler, please." I got up and walked out of the classroom. I was met by a police officer and an FBI agent. They took me into a room and started questioning me about a note that I supposedly had written. The note threatened to kill a student and said I would set off bombs. I was completely blown away. I didn't write a note, and if I had, I sure wouldn't have signed my name to the goddamn thing. The FBI conducted a handwriting analysis on me. The word instantly got out and there was an uproar within the school and the community. I did not write the note. Somebody else did, trying to stir the pot to watch more action. Honestly, I think it was one of my friends who wrote the note. Not only was I being watched by my peers, but by the FBI for terrorist threats that I didn't make.

I remember that parents marched into the school looking for me. They were met by teachers, security guards, and police. Tensions were high that day. News crews were positioned off the school grounds waiting to get a piece of the action as it unfolded. There was a line of concerned parents at the school to take a stand against me due to the death threats I had supposedly made. The kid who received the note and the threats was a good kid who I had no problems with. He had nothing to do with the DEGs or the fighting. Maybe that was the intention to take the spotlight off what was really going on. The assistant principal grabbed me and rushed me up to the third floor of Bismarck High and hid me in a classroom for my safety. I was scared and broken that it had come to this. We talked up in that classroom and I told him how this all got started.

There was a picture being painted that was not completely accurate. This was about a war with a gang that had turned into something else.

CHAPTER 23

Aggravated Assault

It was 2:00 a.m. on a Saturday night and we had just left the last house party on North Washington Street. We had just passed Interstate Avenue and went under the Interstate bridge. We were driving by Turnpike Avenue when I yelled for Kip to flash his lights at a grey Monte Carlo that was heading north.

I said, "Hey it's Ron. Let's pull over, talk to him and see what's going on."

I knew Ron had hard drugs, so I was hoping that I could just jump in with him and go party some more. Kip pulled over on the west side of Washington Street and stopped in front of the dark brown apartments. I was watching the headlights coming up next to us. The vehicle pulled up in front of us on the side of the road. I told Kip, shit it's not Ron. It was just another car that looked like his. I jumped out of the car to tell them that we thought they were someone else. Kip also was out of the car. The driver's side door and the passenger door opened on their car. A woman got out of the driver's side and shut her door and a man got out of the passenger door and slammed it shut.

I hear, "What the hell do you want?"

"Hey, we're sorry. We thought you were our friend, Ron." The woman stayed on the driver's side of her car standing in the street.

She was yelling for us to, "get back in your car."

She was out of control at this point. The guy she was with kept telling her to calm down. She finally shut her mouth. I just wanted her to get back in her car and shut up. The guy came up to me on the boulevard and confronted me. I could see his face and his brown hair in the glow of the streetlights. He walked up closer to me so I shoved him and told him to stay away from me. He became upset and came at me again, but this time he slipped on the wet grass of the boulevard almost falling to the ground. I told him that I didn't want any trouble and that we should go before the cops show up.

He kept asking again. "What's your problem, man?"

"Nothing, I just want to go."

I was getting ready to punch him if he got any closer. Kip was standing in between the cars talking to me.

"The cops are going to get called. Let's go now. I don't want to get a DUI, Tyler."

I had my eye on the guy. I was waiting for him to punch me. I told him, "Let's just get into our cars and leave before the cops get called."

He said, "I don't want any trouble, but I want to know why you pushed me?"

I stuck out my right hand and said, "We have no problem. Shake my hand and we'll call it good and go."

He walked over and shook my hand. I was ready to smack him in the mouth if he tried anything. He continued to be aggressive and by now I was done with his crap.

I told him, "Get in your car now before I kick your ass."

The woman started screaming at me.

I looked across the top of the car at her. "Shut up, you dumb bitch."

This was the first time in my life that I had ever called a woman a bitch. I could see the guy out of the corner of my eye lunge at me. He grabbed me by my shirt and pushed me up against the back of their car. His hands were wrapped up in my shirt. He kept shoving me against the car jamming his fists into my chest. I grabbed him by the shirt, spun him to my right side and I blasted him with my right hand. I could feel his grip loosen on my shirt. His legs buckled under him as he smashed onto the asphalt. I stepped back with my fists up getting ready to blast him again, but he was knocked out. The woman ran around to the back side of the car and kneeled down on the ground next to him trying to wake him up.

She yelled, "You killed him, you killed him!"

Kip grabbed me by my shoulders and said, "What the hell did you do that for, Tyler? Let's go now!"

Kip jumped into his car and turned his headlights on. I stood there looking at this man knocked out on the ground wondering, if in fact, he was dead.

Kip yelled out the driver's side window, "Let's go now or I'm leaving you!"

I turned around and ran back to Kip's car and jumped into the passenger seat. The guy was sitting up. He then attempted to stand up, but before he got all the way up to his feet, his legs buckled again, and he crashed back down to the asphalt. I could see his face bounce off the asphalt viciously. Kip pulled out into the road and stepped on the gas. As we went by the man, he was still lying on the ground and the woman was still screaming. Kip was upset that I had hurt the guy. I told Kip that he grabbed me first.

Kip drove me back to the party the night started at, dropped me off at my car, and then drove off.

No one was around so I got into my car and went home.

The next morning, I woke up around 11:00 a.m. My head was foggy from all the pot, beer, and Southern Comfort from the night before. It took me sometime to pull myself together to even get out of bed. Having to throw up motivated me to run to the bathroom. I squatted down on the floor in front of the toilet and the burger and fries finally had enough. They were coming up whether I liked it or not. I threw up all my stomach contents. I was sweating and shaking uncontrollably. I hated this part of the party. I was physically and mentally sick.

The night before started to come through the fog in my mind. I started to remember everything that I had done. My mind wouldn't stop. It was too much. I tried to block it out, but this only made it worse. My body was failing me and my mind was trying to kill me. I got up from laying down by the toilet and went back into my bed. I pulled out my one hitter and took a couple hits of pot thinking this will make it all better, but it made it worse. I was finally able to get up for the day. Over the course of the day, all the images of what I had done raced through my mind hundreds of times. I struggled to have conversations with anyone because I couldn't think of anything but this mess happening in my head. Every time the phone rang, I thought it was the cops. Every vehicle that I heard go by, I prepared to face the consequences of my doings.

Reality always sucked after I messed up. I was worried that the guy that I hit did in fact die just like that woman who he was with was screaming. I tried to process what would happen to me if I had killed him. The images of my fist hitting him, his eyes rolling back into his head, his knees buckling under him and his head bouncing off the asphalt plastered my thoughts. I could see it all the time. This increased my anxiety and my fears. Please stop brain, please stop trying to kill me. I was exhausted to the point of tears.

I ran through every scenario of how I could get caught. Did the woman get Kip's license plate number? Was someone looking out the window of the apartment watching it all unfold?

I knew that if the cops talked to Kip I was screwed. I knew he didn't have it in him to lie to the police. I felt bad for dragging him in this. He was a good kid who had a lot going for him. I wasn't planning on following through with my threats to hurt him, I just thought that he could use the motivation to do what I needed him to do for me.

Over the following week, I was plagued with anxiety and fear that controlled every moment of my day. I looked in the newspaper daily to see if it was on the front page. I thought the caption would read: "Man Was Assaulted on North Washington Street and Died. The Police Are Looking for Any Leads."

The days passed and nothing. I was starting to think that I was in the clear, but little did I know what was brewing. My mind continued to be consumed with the images and thoughts of getting caught. As the time went by, I started to justify everything that I had done and spun it so it was everyone else's fault. I think that I did this to manage my brain from assaulting me daily. My brain always was trying to kill me.

The phone rang and I answered it, "Hello."

"Tyler, it's Kip."

I instantly became sick to my stomach. Anxiety and fear came rushing back in and hit me like a semi full of frozen ostrich meat.

"What's up, Kip?

"I heard the cops were looking for the person that hit that guy."

"Did the cops talk to you?"

"No."

I reminded Kip of the story that I had come up with and prepared him for when he talked to the cops. Kip was scared, I could hear it in his voice that something was up. I knew in my gut that he already had contact with the cops. My plan was crumbling all around me and I knew it would be a matter of time before I was arrested.

Kip said, "I have to go. I'll talk to you later."

He hung up the phone.

I started to prepare the story that I would tell the cops. I believed that I had the right to protect myself after the guy grabbed me and pushed me up against the car. I did in fact shove him first to stop him from coming at me. He started it. I even shook his hand to try and stop the fight from happening. This all sounded great in my mind. The guy shouldn't have put his hands on me.

The word was out on the street that he was looking to press charges. Kip let me know that the cops had contacted him. He told me that they were looking for the guy that did this and there was some serious physical damage done to him. I heard through some friends that they arrested one of Kip's good friends. I heard that Kip's buddy who they arrested was out of the state the night that it happened and that he was getting his plane ticket stubs to prove to the cops that it wasn't him. I knew that it was a matter of time before Kip started running his mouth to the police. I guess I couldn't really blame him. I had put him in a bad spot and his best friend was being questioned. I knew that he would have to give me up soon. I was proud of him that he was holding out this long, even if it was out of fear. Yes, I did threaten him but that was strictly out of fear. I wasn't going to hurt him. I actually felt bad that I had caused this mess and he was trying to cover it up for me.

My mom was an office supplies salesperson in downtown Bismarck. One day while she was at work, she had an individual come in asking for her by name. My mom called me right away and said,

"Tyler, there was a guy that came into my work asking me for money for you hitting him."

"What are you talking about? I didn't hit anyone."

"He could barely talk to me Tyler, and he looked hurt. Did you do this? You need to tell me now."

"Did you pay him? Tell me you didn't give him anything."

"No, I am not paying him, Tyler. He said that he is going to the police and he will be pressing charges."

"If he comes back Mom, call me and don't give him anything."

"He left on a motorcycle. I watched him ride away."

"Mom, I'm in trouble. I punched him a week ago. I thought that this was all going to go away."

"Well, we'll have to wait for the cops to arrest your stupid ass. I can't believe you did this shit again."

That night when Mom got home, she confronted me and asked me who this person was. I told her all about what happened. I convinced her that this was self-defense. The next day at 8:00 a.m. I got a call from the Bismarck PD. I answered the phone.

"Hello."

A man's voice said, "May I talk with Tyler Auck?"

"This is Tyler. Who is this?"

"This is Detective Brown from the Bismarck Police Department."

I started to panic. This is it, shit.

"I need you to come to the PD for questioning on an assault that happened on North Washington Street."

"Okay, I will come in now if that's okay."

"You need to come in now or we will come out and pick you up."

"I will be there in twenty minutes. Am I under arrest?"

"Not at this time. We need to talk to you."

"Okay."

Click. The phone was hung up.

I called my mom and let her know that I was going to the police department for questioning. I went to the police department and was met by three officers who placed me in handcuffs immediately. I was read my rights and the questioning began. This time I told them everything, because I thought that I was just protecting myself since I was the one that was smashed against the car first. Officer Brown let me know that I am being placed under arrest for aggravated assault and they will be taking me to the detention center until I have a chance to see a judge. They let me call my mom.

My mom came to the jail with cash in hand for my bond money. I waited a couple of hours before I could see the judge. I was told by the judge that I had a $2,500 cash bond. Mom bailed my ass out before they had a chance to make me bend over and cough. I love my mom. She was always there for me through thick and thin. She stood up for me when I fucked up throughout my whole life. In reality she should have left me in jail. She should have let my dumb ass feel the pain instead of bailing me out and giving me a soft place to land. Moms love their kids even when everyone else runs from us.

The next day I had a visit from two different Sheriff's deputies who served me with more papers. Kip and his friend Jason filed restraining orders on me because they were afraid of me. I did threaten Kip. The restraining orders and the aggravated assault charge just fueled my fire. New badges of honor.

I ended up getting a slap on the wrist because my mom and dad hired a damn good attorney. I had an aggravated assault charge with a deadly weapon. I thought this was also pretty bad ass, that they considered my fists deadly weapons. My mom and dad paid the fines like they always had and I got to go on my merry way. I still thought that the right thing to do was to punch people no matter where we were, no matter who they were, and no matter what the situation was, just as long as I could justify it in my little mind. This was the first charge on my record as an adult. Little did I know the trouble that it would cause me over my lifetime and the good jobs that it would cost me.

At this time in my life, I really didn't care. I was going to do what I was going to do no matter what. I thought about the man I attacked over the years. I would tell people about what I had done to him with great pride. This was not the first or the last person who I would look at while they laid knocked out on the pavement as I left wondering with a sick, twisted feeling in my stomach thinking they were dead.

PART III

Fucked Up

My drug addiction was out of control and it controlled everything I did. I shifted gears and turned my anger inwards. I was an adult now, my innocence was gone, and I was heading no place, and fast. When I thought my life couldn't get any stranger I just shifted into another gear. During this time in my life, I still thought that I could control my drug and alcohol addiction, but I was slowly losing any control that I thought that I had. I stooped to lows that I didn't know were possible. I thought I hit rock bottom, but I still was carrying around a shovel and digging my hole deeper and wider.

CHAPTER 24

Really A Fart

I started preplanning how the night would unfold. Hopefully, better than my day had gone so far. I had already endured one drug-induced vehicle accident that ended me up in the ER with bleeding on my brain. But, this little hitch in my giddy-up wasn't going to slow my roll. I had to make sure everything was cleaned up from the accident, just like nothing had happened. Once everything on the exterior of my truck looked okay, I detailed the inside of the truck and wiped everything down with Armor All until it shined. I went into the house and called Josh and let him know that I would pick him up early so we could get a good buzz on before we went to the Mandan Community Center for the boxing matches. I showered, shaved and put on my best-looking clothes. My coke stash was dwindling fast, so I focused my attention on meth over the next couple hours. I showered again to wash the sweat off my body and changed shirts because the one I was wearing was all pit-stained. I threw a hat on to cover the large lump and shade my eyes from the sun.

I headed into town to pick up Josh. The whole way into town I had the air conditioning on high with my arms elevated, my back separated from the seat to allow the cool air to slow the sweat. It was inevitable that I would have to settle into the sweat sooner or later. I pulled over on a residential street and took a couple snorts out of the bag of coke, making sure to look closely into the mirror to see that there was no white residue on my nose, feeling the paranoia that everyone would know what I was doing. I was getting very frustrated that my stash was shrinking, and the anxiety of running out was almost unbearable. I was not going to have enough to last me the rest of the night.

I picked Josh up in a parking lot where he planned to leave his vehicle for the evening. He jumped in with a case of beer in a cooler covered with ice. He handed me a beer as we made our way north out of town to get primed up before we attended the boxing match. I made sure to go a different direction with the paranoia still present from the fence incident earlier that morning. We drove out into a field, parked behind some trees and sat there drinking and smoking pot until it was time for the fight. I kept thinking that he was going to know that I was on more than beer and pot. My mind raced back and forth as I tried not to make eye contact. I got out of the truck to take a piss and stuck my tooter in my coke bag and took a snort without being caught. Once we were about nine beers into the night we felt ready to go to town!

We ended up stopping at the supermarket to take a piss. I grabbed my stash from under the seat where I stuffed it, went into the bathroom into a stall and sat down on the toilet and hit my meth pipe until I rushed so hard that I almost threw up. I had to be sure to muffle the flicking of the lighter with an occasional cough so no one would hear what I was doing. I got up off the toilet and stood up, but before I even pulled my pants up, I dumped some coke on the toilet seat and snorted it off that nasty ass seat without blinking an eye. I pulled up my pants and checked my nose in the mirror and then was out the door and back to the truck.

We drove over to Mandan and went into the facility where the fight was scheduled to take place. I went into the bathroom and snorted more coke while I was pissing. I was too paranoid at this point to flick the lighter due to all the people in the bathroom waiting in line for the stalls, so I took a chunk of meth out of the bag and wrapped it in toilet paper and gut-bombed it.

During the fight I was drinking beer and thinking about how badly I wanted to take a hit of the meth that was in my pocket. My brain was just screaming for the coke to the point I thought I could just pull it out and snort it in front of everyone with no negative consequences.

The fights were finally over. By now, I was so high that I was stumbling. We ran into our friend Billy and decided to go out and party for the rest of the night and celebrate the weekend. Billy was sober at the time only to witness his two friends already completely blasted. He grabbed my keys out of my hand.

"Give me my keys back."

"You can't drive."

"I drove here."

"You're too drunk. Just let me drive. "

"Okay, just for a little bit."

I knew that it was for the best if he drove, I was blasted.

We left the facility and climbed into my truck. Billy was driving, Josh was in the middle, and I was positioned by the door. Once in the vehicle, I struggled to hide my shit under the seat, so I just left it in my pocket. I was tired of covering my tracks.

We headed to Josh's house so we could drink some more before hitting up some parties.

We were about three blocks from his house when Billy farted and it stunk so bad that I started to gag. I puked in my mouth a little then, with a beer in my left hand, I reached for the door of the truck to open it to puke. As I opened it my hand slipped off the door handle that was covered in Armor All. I tumbled out of the vehicle headfirst bouncing on to the pavement. I felt the flesh on my body tear open. The black flash of going in and out of consciousness was followed by bright flashes of stars. My head thudded as it bounced off the pavement traveling thirty miles per hour. When I finally came to a rest, I rolled up to my knees before I was stable enough to stand up. Josh and Billy came running up to me shocked at what they had just witnessed.

"Holy shit! Are you okay?"

The blood began to trickle out of my head and the open wounds from the road rash started to sting. My left hand was still gripping tight to the now crushed beer can. Beer was running down my arm, and I mumbled that I could still fight. They picked my hat up off the ground and loaded me into the truck to leave the scene as fast as we could before someone called the cops. We ended up bypassing Josh's house to get out of the neighborhood as fast as we could. They were concerned for my head injuries, but at the same time giggling uncontrollably at my dumb ass. This is what we did, we laughed at the things that should have killed us. We kept talking about what just happened repeatedly until I convinced them and myself that I was okay to still go out and party.

"Do you have to go to the ER?"

"No."

"Do you want us to take you home?"

"No, just get me a beer and I will be good."

It was insane that it had become a normal feeling to turn something horrible into a comical badge of honor.

We went to a couple house parties and told everyone about what happened as if it were the greatest event on earth. As the night went on, the story became funnier and the pain and the fear became more intense. At this point I had no interest in getting any more messed up. I took great pride in screwing up my life. I was okay with physical pain because that was something that I knew well. Emotional pain was a whole other issue because it felt like the physical pain triggered the emotional pain. I was lonely and very depressed. I tried to self-medicate, but let's be honest, I sucked at that, too. I pulled my hat down over the bloody mess of missing hair. I wiped the tears off my cheeks so that no one would see them and think that I was weak.

After the party was over and we all parted ways, I spent some time laying down on my bed hoping that it would all go away so I could forget about the damage caused. What a day. My only thought at that moment when the pain and fear became too much was to get high.

The sun started to come up and my hat was still stuck to the blood on my head and the fear set in that I might have to take a good look at what happened. It always felt worse in the daylight. Shit was getting real when everyone else woke up in the house. By now, I was starting to think that I might have to go to the ER again, but I quickly shut that thought out with deep denial.

"Is my arm broken? It sure feels like it." I was only doing a little bit of coke at this time knowing that I needed to control it or else I would be screwed. I scrambled to compose myself enough to go upstairs and look at my mom and dad, who I could hear walking around for some time now.

I finally got up enough nerve to go upstairs to get it over with. I walked over to the spiral staircase and looked up for a moment listening to what was going on. It sounded like my dad was in his recliner watching TV and my mom was in the kitchen probably cleaning.

"Screw it, just do it now."

I went up the steps and opened the wrought iron gate.

"Good morning, Mom."

"Good morning, honey".

I made my way to the living room where my dad was sitting. I was trying to feel things out and to not lead on to everything that was happening in my mind. I sat down on the couch, but instantly I felt the room spinning. I tried to stand up to go back downstairs. Halfway back up to my feet, I felt my knees buckle under me as I crashed back down into the couch, jostling my hat off my head enough to show the bloody wounds.

My dad yelled out, "What the hell happened to you?"

My mom began to go into a panic as she ran to the living room. "Oh, honey! Oh, no! What happened?!"

I was hesitant to tell them as my body froze up in fear of the truth and my dad's reaction. I was filled with fear as we sat there in the living room contemplating what to do next and by now my mom was in a full-blown panic attack as she stood right in front of me staring into my eyes. I was trying to keep my head down due to the black rings around my eyes as they darted all over the room trying to avoid eye contact.

"Is it bad enough to go in?"

"I don't know. Call the ER and ask them."

Mom and I went out to the kitchen and sat at the kitchen table looking the number up in the phone book. My dad was disgusted as he voiced his embarrassment.

"I was drunk (yah drunk, another half-truth to throw everyone off the trail) and fell out of my truck."

I had to make sure that I called the other hospital so my mom would not know that I was there the day before. This whole time my mind was racing trying to cover up all the tracks that I laid over the last forty-eight hours. The lies kept coming, one after another until I was once again convinced.

I talked with the nurse from the ER by phone while listening to my dad cursing under his breath in the other room and my mom right next to me supporting me through my struggles making everything okay like she had done all of my life. The ER nurse highly suggested that I come in to get checked out, so I did.

My mom took me to the hospital. On our way there she told me of a time my dad fell out of the box of a truck all drunk and explained why he is so embarrassed and upset.

We finally arrived at the ER.

"Name please. What is your emergency?"

"Tyler Auck. I called a little while ago and talked to a nurse about falling out of my truck."

"Okay, we have you down. Have you been drinking?"

"Yes, a lot."

"When did you have your last drink?"

"This morning at around 2:00 a.m."

They took us back right away and did a brain scan, x-rays and cleaned up the bloody wounds on my body making sure to pick all the rocks clean that were embedded in my road rash. The doctor came in and told us, "You had bleeding in your brain, but it has stopped."

He showed us the scanned images, we could see a little spot on my brain that looked like dried blood.

"Your arm is not broken, but it will be tender for a few weeks. It is safe for you to go home now. If you have any issues, come back in right away."

The car ride home was quiet, and the anxiety was gone, but The Jones started to creep back in. I had just dodged another bullet. I went downstairs to avoid my parents and straight to the bathroom to start the insanity all over again. This time it will be different. Or will it?

CHAPTER 25

Wrong Trip

Fuck Bismarck! The cops were on to me and I was sick and tired of the harassment. There was one particular cop that kept harassing me. His name was Dan Donlin, a real special kind of pig! This guy tried to get me put in prison for thirty-five years for some burglaries that I had to commit to keep the high going! A geographical move will fix everything, because that's what's wrong me. If I move, all of my legal issues will be behind me, and so will the gangs and Dan. I am over this shit! It can't be me and, if it is, I sure as hell am not ready to look at that or say it out loud. I am out! New beginnings, a clean slate! This time will be different.

So, I bought a 1972 VW deluxe high roof camper out of a barn in Mercury County and moved myself to Boulder, Colorado, to live in my van down by the creek. Let's be real, I moved for the accessibility to all the drugs. Seemed like the right decision, since I was full of right decisions. But, that prick Dan probably called out to Colorado and warned all the other pigs about me, so I needed to be extra careful. My luck had to be better somewhere else. Peace out, Bismarck!

I did my best to fit the part of a Coloradan by wearing tie-dyed shirts with the Grateful Dead on them and a hemp necklace with a real peyote button the size of a tennis ball. I was really putting my best foot forward in becoming a hippie. Peace, love, and tripping out. In reality, I was in Colorado because I was running from my past. I knew that I couldn't live in North Dakota after everything that I had done. I felt like a failure and completely lost in every aspect of my life. So a geographical fleeing felt appropriate. When I finally arrived in Boulder, I parked my van on a side street and laid down on the bed and cried uncontrollably. I was now in a new place where my life was supposed to be magically different, but it wasn't. I don't know if I was thinking that once I crossed the state line a rainbow of beautiful feelings were going to shine down upon me. I honestly wanted to leave the instant that I got there, but I couldn't be the pussy that tucks his tail and runs. I needed to stick this out. Little did I know all the shit that was about to happen. Once my little giving-up cry session was over I did what I knew best: I went to the liquor store and got fucked up to numb all my confusion. I sat in my van all alone with my curtains closed and drank until I passed out in hopes of a different feeling when I awoke. The next morning when my eyes opened I stepped out of my van and saw the beautiful Flatiron Mountains peeking up over the evergreens. I stuffed all of my feelings and started my new life with hopes of it being different while being the same person that I was when I left Bismarck.

CHAPTER 26

Guns, Coke & The Jones

The night was black and the trees were flying by as we sped down the two-lane road headed away from the mountains towards the flats. There were three of us packed into a rusty-red colored '80s model Chevy truck with a five speed. It had more rust around the wheel wells than good metal on the whole truck. The alcohol had been flowing before the telephone rang letting us know to meet out at an abandoned gas station between Lafayette and Denver. I was stuffed in the middle of this little-ass truck trying to avoid the smoke that was rolling out each window, the cherries of the cigarettes, and all the arms moving up and down as the cigarettes crackled and smoked.

My friend's beautiful girlfriend, Summer, sat next to me with her hand almost in my lap. The sexual fantasies of what I wanted to do to her swerved along with the driving, back and forth across the center line, cutting morality and the law to pieces. I had heard them many times having sex in the other room which just fueled my desire for her. But, my loyalty as a friend stood far stronger than any deception and deep desire that I had for her. So, no sex.

Out of the darkness came flashing lights as they bore down on us with speed and purpose. We pulled over to the side of the road. The chatter in the truck was, "Keep it cool. Smoke that cigarette so he can't smell it."

The windows were all rolled down as the jumbled mess of paperwork was spilling out of the glove box in anticipation of covering our ass. The beam of the flashlight hit us in the back of the head as the officer walked up illuminating our every move. My first thought was, "Son of a bitch. There goes our chance at scoring some coke." I really did not give two shits if my friend was going to go to jail for a DUI. Summer and I would have to tuck our tails and go back home empty-handed.

The officer's voice out of the darkness said," Do you know that you have a taillight out?"

There was a pause as my friend's cigarette flared up and smoke filled the cab. "No officer, I didn't, but I can fix it now."

"Stay in the truck. I don't want you trying to fix it in the dark on this road."

My face was calm as I looked ahead in fear and disappointment. My voices were screaming, "Shut the fuck up," and "Let's go get our shit." It sucks how fast your buzz gets sucked out of you when scary shit happens.

"License and registration, please."

"I don't have my license with me, officer. I lost it."

My voices became louder, screaming, "You seriously didn't know your tail light was out and you're driving with no license on you?"

"Name and address, please. All three of you."

We gave him our names and addresses as he turned around and walked back to his cruiser. I was scrambling sitting in the middle trying to find a seatbelt. There wasn't one. The chatter in the cab was of despair. We knew we were done for if he could smell the alcohol. I was struggling inside because I already let my mind go to the place where I was thinking I was going to score some shit. And the anticipation for coke is a life and death feeling. It felt like saliva was running down my chin. I was afraid to wipe it off because I didn't want to give away what I was thinking.

Summer could not help herself. She kept looking back even when we told her to keep looking forward. But, she would not listen.

"He is coming! He is coming!"

The officer had a ticket, a warning ticket, for the taillight and not having a driver's license. He also told Tommy that he needed to get that tail light fixed.

"Have a good night," he said.

"Thank you, thank you, thank you." Tommy poured out his relief.

Relief. We dodged one bullet. But, now I had to deal with The Jones which was still at work.

I was scared that the officer was going to see us swerve as we pulled away from him. I couldn't bear the thought of our plan being ruined again. But, my fears started to dissipate as The Jones for the coke took over, churning my insides.

I told Tommy to pull over on the side of the road and call the Mexicans to see if the meetup was still on, or if the cops had taken up too much of our time. I could hear the phone ringing over and over again, even though it was muffled against his ear. My stomach felt sicker with every ring. Finally, I heard a muffled voice that confirmed it was still on.

We drove about ten miles down the road and pulled into this sketchy, run-down abandoned gas station. We sat there in the pitch dark with the windows rolled down and the engine turned off. Crickets chirped in the background and the wind rustled the leaves on the trees. I heard a car approaching from what sounded like a lifetime away. I kept scanning the road wondering if the cop had let us go because he was onto us. A beat-up sports car skidded to a halt and all four doors flew open. Four men jumped out of the car in a practiced, tactical maneuver. As we climbed out of the pickup we wondered what was going to happen. At first, I just saw their silhouettes. But, when the interior light of their vehicle hit them, I saw guns.

At this point, everything went into slow motion as I gazed at the silhouettes outlined by the glow of the moon. I could feel the tension in the air, not knowing what they were saying because they were speaking in Spanish. Summer walked over to these men as if she had tits of steel. You could see the men focus their attention on her because no matter how hard these men were, seeing a hot little piece of ass like that at an abandoned gas station in the middle of nowhere did it for them, too.

I had the cash in my pocket, so I pulled it out with anticipation and excitement that this was actually going to happen now. Tommy was still running his mouth being dramatic as he always was, out of touch with reality. I walked with the man who had the shotgun over to the interior light of the truck and showed him the money. I counted it out in front of him and he handed me a sandwich bag that was almost half full of rocks and some loose powder. I opened it up and smelled it. Yes, this was some good shit. The smell was so strong that my nose went numb. I sealed it back up and pushed it down into my pocket. Now, how were we going to make it all the way back to my apartment with this dumb bastard swerving all over the road with no taillight?

But, I was willing to take the chance once Summer slid in next to me. I could feel her body trembling from the fear and excitement. I wanted the seat by the door in case jumping out and running became necessary. Tommy jumped in the truck and slammed his door. I wanted to choke him, punch him in the head and hug him all at the same time. I was watching the men climb into the car with their weapons. My heart was pounding out of my chest still wondering if they would shoot us just for fun and take Summer.

Once back at the apartment we all got blasted on coke. I was so messed up my eyes stopped working. I could see shapes, but visual acuity was gone. I was able to calm The Jones for a short period of time until it once again took control.

CHAPTER 27

Closer To Death Than I Thought

What the hell! Why do I continue to lead with my heart? The feeling that I got by helping people was amazing and I was good at it - for a short period of time anyway. It felt like I was supposed to help people, but at what cost to me personally? Drugs were clouding my judgment and my heart was leading me down a path of pain and suffering. I couldn't wait until I figured out how to use my gift of helping people correctly without a shit storm coming down onto my life. I would just let people into my apartment because I had a bad habit of making other people's problems mine. I could feel their pain in my heart. But, this time would be different because he had kids and their mother was a crack whore. The kids were what got me this time.

Tommy knew this guy named Skip who was living in the back of a vehicle repair shop in North Boulder, Colorado. Skip was a motorcycle mechanic and, get this shit, I had a Yamaha street bike that needed some work. Tommy introduced me to Skip one day up at the shop and I bought an air cleaner for my bike. Skip told us that he needed to find a place to live temporarily because he had to move out of the back of the shop today. I knew that Tommy was hoping that I would let him stay with me for a bit until he found a place. I was thinking that there was no way I wanted this guy to move in. I just met him. Skip took us to the back of the shop and over in the corner sitting on the floor there were two little boys. They both looked really sad.

"These two little guys are my boys; Luke is six and Pat is four. They are scared because we have no place to go and their mom is really screwing up our lives."

I walked over to the two little boys sitting on the cement floor and I tried to make them laugh or smile. They looked sad.

"Hey Skip, can they have a candy out of the machine out in the front, and a soda?"

"I don't have any money, Tyler."

"You don't need money. I have some quarters that I was going to use for laundry in my pocket. It's on me."

"They would love that. Right, boys? And don't forget to say thank you to Tyler."

Both of the kids stood up and walked over to me. Now I got their attention. I would get these little dudes to smile yet. We walked out to the front of the shop to the candy and pop machine.

"What kind of candy do you want? You can pick anything in the machine besides the jaw breaker because I don't want you guys to choke."

Luke pointed to a Snickers bar and then he whispered something in Pat's ear. Pat nodded his head. Luke pointed to the barbeque chips. I put fifty cents in the machine and had Luke press the numbers. The machine dropped the chips first. Luke grabbed the bag of chips and opened them up and handed them to Pat. Still no smiles. Luke got his Snickers bar out of the machine and tore the wrapper open and took a big bite. It felt like they hadn't had a treat in a while.

"What kind of pop do you want, Luke?"

"Coke, please."

"How about you, Pat?"

He walked over to the Pepsi machine and pointed to the Mountain Dew. I panicked because I thought that he was too little for a Mountain Dew. So, I lied to him.

"That one is sold out, little guy, how about this one?"

I pointed to the Orange Crush. He nodded his head and smiled. I handed Luke fifty cents and Pat fifty cents. Each put the quarters in the machine and pressed the buttons. I kneeled down to grab Pat's pop out of the machine and acted like my hand was stuck. I struggled for a couple seconds before I asked for help.

"Boys, I am stuck, and I need your help."

They both looked at me like I was crazy, but they set their treats down on the floor and walked over to me. I was down on my knees with my arm in the hole of the Pepsi machine.

"Okay, I need you to both pull on my shirt to help me get unstuck."

They both grabbed on to my shirt and started to pull.

"Pull hard! Harder! It feels like it's coming loose. Almost!"

They yanked and yanked until finally I pulled my hand out of the machine and fell backwards onto my back holding the Orange Crush can straight up into the air like I just had retrieved something really cool. I was looking up at these two little boys and they were giggling. I did it! I knew that I could make them smile. These two boys had my heart from that moment because I understood that look of fear and uncertainty in their eyes. They both grabbed their treats off the floor and I handed Pat his soda. They both said thank you. We all walked back to the back of the shop. Tommy and Skip were smoking a joint. I could smell it.

"What are you guys doing? Put it away, now!"

Tommy just laughed and said "Chill out, dude! Come take a hit."

"The kids! No! Put it out now or else, Tommy!"

I took the kids back to the front of the shop and played thumb war with them until Tommy and Skip came out from the back.

Skip said, "It's just pot, Tyler. The boys smell it all the time."

"I know that they are your kids, but that's messed up, man! Don't you ever do it in front of me when your kids are around! No drugs or I will hurt both of you when the kids leave!"

Skip and Tommy just stood there looking at me in disbelief. I got my point across and Tommy knew that I would punch him right in the face if he didn't listen to me.

"Skip, why don't you and the boys come stay at my apartment until you find a place. I have food and a bathtub so you can clean your kids up."

Tommy said to Skip, "I told you he was cool, man."

"Tyler, are you sure?"

"Yes, Skip. No drugs in my house when the kids are there."

"I won't, Tyler. Thank you! Thank you so much."

"I have blankets and I will go buy you each a pillow now."

"You don't have to do that, Tyler."

"Your boys need a pillow at least."

"Thank you, Tyler."

I wrote my address down on a piece of paper and handed it to Skip.

"Come over at five tonight and I'll order a pizza."

I got to know Skip really well and I found out that he was trying really hard to be a good dad. He only had one really big problem and that was his crack whore wife, Linda. Linda was all strung out on crack and meth. Skip tried his best to keep his kids away from their mom when she was strung out, but he kept getting pulled back into it by manipulation. He was trying his best to save her while sacrificing up his own life and his kids'. The boys and I got along great. They now thought that I was funny.

The whole no drugs in the house when the kids were there was tougher than I had thought. I hid my pot over at my uncle's shop a few blocks away. I was a daily drug user, so I needed to be very creative to hold the feelings that I had in my heart about kids and drugs. Let's just say that I went for a lot of walks. The weekends that the kids were gone it was back to getting high every minute of every day. Linda started coming over every once in a while to see Skip. She was always up to party. I went against my gut feelings and I let her in.

Usually, she would have a random boyfriend drop her off out in front of the apartment. I could see the pain in Skip's eyes. He loved this woman and he continued to enable her in hopes of her getting her shit together so they could be a family again. She, however, would come in and then she would leave. Tommy used to talk about how Skip would sit and watch his wife screw other men for drugs to make sure no one would hurt her. Skip told me that this really bothered him, but he didn't know how to live without her.

I was dumbfounded, wondering why this dumb bastard kept this crazy woman in his life. His kids didn't need to see any of this. Skip ended up sending the boys to live with their grandparents after three weeks at my place. Saying goodbye to the kids was hard. I cried when they left. I met Grandma and Grandpa and they were good people, so I was happy for the kids to go someplace safe away from their mom.

Skip continued to sleep on the floor in my living room and Linda started to visit more frequently. I didn't mind because she was always selling meth or heroin so she could get her fix. One Friday night after work, when Linda stopped by, we picked up two cases of Corona and started drinking and smoking pot. Linda spent most of the night trying to score meth. I didn't even have time to shower. I was still in my work clothes with some of my work tools still in the pockets of my brown Carhart overalls.

We were all really drunk when Linda's beeper went off. She made a phone call and when she got off the phone, she told me she could get me an eight-ball of crystal for a hundred dollars, but we would have to drive out east of town to pick it up. I told her that I wanted to get the meth and I would share with them, but I wasn't going to give her the hundred dollars without me going with her. She told me that the guys that she gets the meth from are some bad guys. I didn't care, not the first time I had dealt with bad people. I just knew that if she left with my money, I would never see it or the drugs again. She hesitantly agreed that I could come with her. Skip stayed back at the house.

We got into her car and drove east of Boulder towards Longmont. It was spitting snow and sleet. The roads were getting icy. She talked about the guys that we were going to meet. I guess this one guy had a used car dealership out of town that he used as a cover for his drug business. We started to get closer and she said that she needed to drop me off in the ditch and then when she was done with the drug deal she would come back and pick me up. I looked around and had no clue where I was at. It was dark and snowing and there was no way in hell I was going to let her drop me off in the ditch. Finally, she said I could stay in the car, but she warned me that I had to tilt my seat all the way back and be quiet. I reassured her that they will never even know that I was with her. I wanted her to just go inside, get the stuff, and come back out so we could get the hell out of there. We pulled into this farmyard and up to a trailer house that was surrounded by trees and used cars for sale. I peeked my head up over the dashboard to see what we would be dealing with. Then I handed her my money.

"I will be right back. Stay quiet!"

"Hurry up." She was in the trailer for forty minutes. I had to piss really bad, but I knew that I better not get out, so I held it.

I passed out in the seat only to be woken up by a bunch of yelling. The yelling started getting closer! I sat up in the seat to look at what was going on. I could see six to eight men and Linda walking towards the car. I could see that one of the men had a crowbar, another man had a baseball bat and the big fat dude had a tire iron that he set down on the hood of the car. He was walking over to the passenger door.

He opened it and started screaming at me, "You're a fucking narc, cop bitch! What the fuck were you screaming for?"

"I wasn't screaming! I was sleeping!"

"You were fucking screaming you motherfucker! Get out of the car!"

Linda was screaming for them to leave me alone. One of the guys had her by the hair with her face pushed down on the hood!

"Are you a cop?"

"No, I'm not and I didn't say anything when I was out here!"

"You're a fucking cop! Pig bitch motherfucker! Let's kill this fucking pig!"

I was getting ready to fight, but I was outnumbered and they had weapons. A fist came flying through the car door hitting me on the right side of my face, knocking me over into the center console. I could feel the blood running down the side of my face as I used my hand to wipe it out of my eyes. He grabbed me by my shirt and my hair trying to drag me out of the car. I knew if he got me out of the car, I would be done for so I did my best to fight him off and keep my ass on the seat. He walked to the front of the car, grabbed his tire iron, and came back to my door. I shut the door. He was screaming at Linda calling her a dumb bitch and telling her to give him back the meth.

She screamed back, "Fuck you! I paid for the meth! You're not getting it back!"

I screamed at Linda, "Give him the meth! Linda, listen Linda, give the meth back and let's get out of here!"

She wasn't giving it back even with her face pinned to the hood and her hair being pulled. The other guys now surrounded the vehicle yelling. The fat guy ran around the front of the car and grabbed Linda by the hair. He slapped her in the head and threw her down to the ground. The other guys who were with him were standing over her yelling at her to give the drugs back.

Then he came running back around to the passenger side of the car. I was scared so I pulled my screwdriver out of my overalls. I was ready to jab it in this fat asshole's face.

I could hear the tire iron get set on top of the car. The car door swung open and I was blasted with three more punches. I couldn't hold my piss any longer. I pissed my pants. He grabbed the tire iron off the top of the car. I slammed the door and locked it. I screamed at Linda to get in the car! Linda was pulled up to a standing position by her hair. She was kicking and screaming. Linda finally pulled the meth out of her pocket and threw it at one of the guys. Linda was able to fight her way free. She climbed into the car and started it.

The guy with a baseball bat came running around the driver side of the car and grabbed Linda by her hair. She put the car in reverse and stepped on the gas. She screamed for him to let go of her hair. He was trying to jab her in the head with the bat. Finally, the momentum of the car caused him to lose his grip on her hair, but he took a handful with him. We took off in reverse as these guys chased us across the farmyard. Linda shifted the car into drive and we sped out of the farmyard down the road.

She was crying and screaming uncontrollably.

"I told you to wait in the ditch! I told you it was not a good idea for you to come with me! This is your fault, Ty!"

My eyes were swelling shut as the blood dripped on my chest and piss covered my lap.

"What is wrong with you? You should have just given the meth back to him so he stopped beating on me!"

She wanted the drugs so badly that she was willing to sacrifice my life for it. On the drive back to my apartment, I questioned her over and over again about who these people were. I wanted revenge. She gave me the phone number of the fat guy. Once back at my apartment I cleaned myself up. I called him and I threatened him. I told him that I was going to kill him. He threatened me back and told me that I didn't know who I was messing with. I threatened him over and over again until I finally had enough. I hung up the phone and I had Linda give me directions back out to the farm where we just left.

The only mode of transportation I had was a motorcycle my cousin had given me. I put on a bunch of warm clothes and grabbed my bow and arrows. I stuffed the arrows down into my coat and I put the bow strings over the top of my head around my neck. It was still sleeting and starting to snow again. The roads had a thin cover of snow covering the asphalt, but I didn't care. I went outside and got on my motorcycle. I sat out there for a good ten minutes trying to start it until the battery finally went dead. I went back to my apartment and begged Skip to help me start my bike. He refused to help me and tried his best to get me to stay in the apartment. I put my bow and arrows back in my closet. I called back out to the farm.

When the guy answered, I said, "I am going to kill you!"

I hung up the phone. I called back, "You don't know who I am, but I know who you are. One day I am going to come out and act like I am looking at some of your used vehicles and I am going to shoot you in the back of the head!"

He screamed, "You're dead!" and hung up the phone.

I could hardly sleep that night. My mind was planning every single detail of my revenge.

The next day when we all woke up in my apartment, Linda was apologizing over and over again for what had happened to me. She told me that the group of people were being investigated for two murders in Denver. They also had stabbed a prostitute twenty-six times and threw her body off a train bridge and she lived. Linda let me know that these guys were big time meth dealers. Shit, I can't believe that I just threatened these guys over and over again and they were killers. Once I sobered up, I was happy that the motorcycle didn't start that night. I think God was looking over me. I told Linda that I didn't need her to repay the hundred dollars that she lost. She sure the hell did not have any money to pay me back. I asked Skip to move out and he did.

CHAPTER 28

Dumpster Kind Of Friends

Thud.

My body slammed down onto the dirty apartment floor. I felt like I was choking to death. My hands reached for my throat, trying to pull away the heavy weight that I thought was smothering me. BK and the two other guys who we just scored some white H and coke from stood over me. I felt myself going in and out of consciousness. I could hear voices talking.

"Call 911"

"Fuck that! This motherfucker will come out of it."

"Call 911! He's dying! He's OD!"

"What about the drugs?"

The voices turned to whispers as I felt myself going in and out of consciousness. I felt hands on me rolling me over. I felt someone slapping me in my face. Blackness set in and lights flashed. I could hear them talking, but it was muffled. I felt my body being picked up and then it would slam to the floor. I remembered looking up and I could see the three of them carrying me. My feet were dragging on the ground. I felt my feet bounce off what felt like stairs. I would come to for a moment and then drift back out. The next thing I remembered was my body slamming off the asphalt in the parking lot. I could feel my body being picked up and then dropped. They were trying to throw me into a dumpster to get rid of the evidence. I felt the warm asphalt on my face. The voices stopped and so did the violent crashes to the ground. I was finally able to pick my head up off the ground. I was gasping for air. It felt like someone was standing on my throat cutting off my airway. I could see a road with cars going by and a large metal dumpster. I remember crawling across the asphalt and then everything going black.

The next memory that I had was in an ambulance. I guess some lady had seen me laying in the parking lot and called 911. The ambulance crew administered Naloxone and saved my life. Naloxone is a drug that, when administered in time, reverses an opioid overdose. When I overdosed, the friends from whom I scored the drugs tried to throw me in a dumpster to get rid of me like a piece of trash. I was admitted to the hospital for observation. I guess my head received some damage from being dropped onto the asphalt. I dodged another bullet.

The hospital staff wasn't very helpful. I was scared and I had no clue where I was at in Denver. I only went to Denver to score drugs every once in a while. I always struggled with direction in the big city. I lost my wallet, but even worse my drugs were gone as well. Probably a good thing because if I still had them on me, I would be talking to the cops. I wasn't cooperating with the hospital staff. Let's just say that I was being an ass. I wouldn't give them any personal information because, if I did, I knew that my mom would find out with my insurance. I couldn't have anyone find out about this. I was embarrassed that I was such a lightweight that I overdosed.

I was discharged from the hospital and put in a taxi with a taxi voucher. The taxi took me about ten minutes from the hospital and pulled the car over, told me that this was as far as the voucher was good for, and if I wanted to go any farther, I would need money. I was broke so I got out of the taxi and started walking. I was in the downtown district. I talked to different people trying to figure out how I was going to get back to my apartment in Boulder, which was about forty minutes away. I was given enough money from a nice guy who showed me to the bus that went to Boulder.

I rode the bus back to my apartment and the only thing that I could think about was getting high. The Jones was intense. Once I was back in Boulder, I found my other dealer, scored heroin and coke, went back to my apartment, and got high. Thirty minutes after I was home, I was doing the same drugs that had just about killed me and almost got me thrown into a dumpster to die. It didn't faze me. It didn't even register in my mind the danger that I was putting myself in. I didn't care that I just overdosed. I didn't care that I almost lost my life. The only thing that mattered was making The Jones go away. The only thing that ever mattered to me was getting high.

I get it. I get that they had to try and get rid of me in a dumpster. This was a sad fact about the drug world. When I was high, my judgment was questionable. My judgment didn't line up with who I was as a person. I had even thought about throwing someone out to the wolves to die about a year before. A few of my friends and I had been at my trailer house smoking coke off tin foil. We all were kneeling and sitting on my living room floor around a step stool that we were using to set our drugs on when Rocco took a big hit of coke. He sat straight up, his eyes rolled into the back of his head, and then he fell face first into the stool, knocking it over.

His now convulsing body fell onto my lap. I could feel Rocco's body shaking as it thrashed around. I pushed him to the floor. I remember looking at him and thinking that he was dying and there was nothing that I could do. He was dying because he overdosed. I was high and the consequences that came into my mind outweighed the consequences of losing my friend. My mind raced and I thought about where we were going to get rid of him once he was dead. I thought about throwing his dead body in a park or in front of the hospital and then driving away. Rocco finally came out of it, but the thoughts that raced through my mind that day cut me deep because I liked Rocco and he was my friend. On a good day I would have died for him, but not that day.

Neither one of these overdoses slowed me down. This was part of my life. We were supposed to die when we were getting that high. Bad things were supposed to happen and, to be completely honest, it would have been a blessing at this time in my life to get snuffed out from an overdose because the pain and the vicious cycle of addiction would have stopped.

Tommy used to say to me, "Ty, we do drugs to get high and you do drugs to die."

I took great pride in being a drug pig and I would gobble up whatever was in front of me at the time, no matter the consequences. I wasn't afraid to die. I made peace with death, because no matter what I did I couldn't stop using drugs. I used to pray at night for God to not let me wake up.

CHAPTER 29

Drugs 1, Love 0

I was in a relationship with this girl after my Colorado experience. I loved her and she loved me. I was selling some pot here and there to help fuel my addiction. Let's just say her name is Britta. Britta had one of her friends from college come over to the house and let's just say his name was Brian. Brian was an IV drug user that would buy a bag of pot from me occasionally. I remember the first time that he asked me if he could use my bathroom to shoot up. Whoa, Brian, let's put on the brakes. Nobody is shooting up in my bathroom. I didn't want anybody dying in my house.

"No, you can't shoot up in my bathroom."

Get out Brian, not my deal. I always judged people that used IV drugs because I thought that I would never be that bad of a drug addict where I would shoot up my drugs. I wasn't that bad. I used it as a justification so I wouldn't have to look at my own problem which was just as bad as Brian's. In fact, it was much worse. Brian was telling me about the high that I was missing out on from not shooting up.

"Tyler, have you ever tried Oxy?"

"No, what are they?"

"They're awesome, dude. I can get a couple for you from Britta if you want to try them?"

"Sure, why not. Let's do it."

I bought a couple twenty milligram OxyContin from Brian that day. Later on, that evening, Britta and I sat on the couch and each popped one twenty milligram Oxy and swallowed. One hour went by and we weren't feeling anything.

"Britta these Oxy suck. I don't know what he was talking these up so big for."

Let's just say we were very disappointed. The next time Brian came over to the house to buy a bag of weed, I told him how shitty the pills that he sold us were and that we didn't feel anything.

"Did you chew 'em up, Tyler?"

"No, why?"

"You dumb ass, there is a time release on them and you have to break the time release to get high all at once.

"Really? That sucks that we wasted them."

"Money down the drain. Your loss."

Britta chimed in and said, "My dad has a bottle of OxyContin under his sink out at our house."

This perked up Brian's ears.

"Do you know how much money you can get for those?" Britta questioned.

"Lots of money. Oxy is like gold."

Later that afternoon, when Britta's parents were gone, we went out to her parents' house and found the bottle of OxyContin under the sink. The prescription was her dad's and it was for 140/20mg OxyContin. I grabbed the bottle and dumped about half the bottle in my hand and then straight into my pocket. We sat on her mom and dad's bed, each popped a pill in our mouth and made damn sure to chew it up this time and swallowed. Five minutes later it started to hit us. I looked at Britta and instantly felt that our connection was way stronger than it was five minutes ago.

"Oh my God, I want to spend the rest of my life with you. I love you, Britta."

This time, when I said "I love you," it meant a whole lot more than ever before. She leaned over and put her lips to my ear and whispered. "I love you too, Tyler. Fuck me now. Please!"

Holy shit these OxyContin pills makes this girl freaky. She wanted me to take her in her mom and dad's bed and have sex with her. We got naked fast and proceeded to live out her fantasy and my newfound fantasy. I am not sure if it was the drugs or if I fantasized since the day that I met Britta's mother. I often thought about having sex with her mother. This was awesome, I was banging her daughter in the spot where she slept. This turned me on, and I was hooked.

We had some of the best sex that we had ever had in her mother's spot on the bed. It felt so wrong that I was doing horrible kinky shit to their daughter in their bed. That OxyContin high lasted twelve hours. Twelve hours of pure heaven. I think that we had sex on every surface in her parents' house that day. This was just the beginning of the end. Nothing this good can ever last. Over the next few days, we took the rest of the OxyContin that we stole from her dad. We were hooked instantly. I had done a lot of drugs over my life up to this point, but this had me right by the balls and wouldn't let go for years.

The next time that Brian came over to buy some pot, I bought more Oxy from him. They were expensive. It cost me about a hundred per high. Some real special shit. It was like gold, just more expensive. The urge to get high every single day plagued me.

CHAPTER 30

Oscar Nomination In My Future

Brian told me that I need to go see my doctor and make some shit up to get my own prescription. I called up to my doctor's office and set up an appointment for my bad knee. I remember that day clearly. I knew exactly what I wanted, hydrocodone and OxyContin. I got out of my truck and started limping bad as I walked into the doctor's office. I needed to play the part if I wanted to get the drugs. I was not quite sure how this was all going to work, but I knew that I was very ambitious and that I needed these drugs so bad that I was willing to do anything for however long to maintain this high.

I met with the doctor and played everything out perfectly that I had planned. One thing that I had going for me was that I had two prior knee surgeries on this knee. The doc pulled out his prescription pad and started scribbling. The anticipation was running through me. I could hardly wait to see what he was going to give me. I was praying that I was going to get what I ordered. Hell, if my knee wasn't jacked up, I would have gotten down and prayed. He handed me the prescription and had me scheduled to see him again in one month. My eyes gazed at the pad as he was writing. I struggled to resist looking out of fear of getting caught. No suspicions. He handed me the prescription paper. I kept eye contact with him, forcing my eyes to not look down.

"I prescribed you something for your pain. I wrote you a prescription for two hundred hydrocodone 10/650s and one hundred and twenty, 20 milligram OxyContin. These prescriptions will last you a month until your next appointment." Boom, exactly what I went in looking for.

"Thank you. I will see you in a month."

I limped my way out of that doctor's office that day not quite knowing what I had just started. It was so innocent and fun in the beginning. Just give me my Oscar now please. No, I don't have my speech prepared. Trust me, I knocked this one out of the park. Well, it was fun until the pills turned viciously on me. The sickness and desperation set in fast. Constantly chasing the high to make the sickness go away suddenly became a nightmare.

Over the next twelve years of my life, I was living out my acting career as a full-blown drug addict. I was winning Oscars year after year. I was being praised for my commitment to the role. My face was featured on 'Addict of the Year' journal and if I don't mess this up it will be a miracle.

Britta couldn't handle my fame. She became jealous of my commitment to my characters that were constantly changing. Wild sex in her mom and dad's bed and on their kitchen counters was not enough to sustain the relationship. We tried hard, but it was not meant to be. I heard that she met a guy. Poor girl missed out on all of this. Nothing ever was as good as that first day that we chewed up those Oxys. No regrets, we used to say. Looking back on it today, it was just lies that we told ourselves to make all our shit look okay. I should've known that the relationship was not going to last. Sometimes you do not know until after the fact and the false sense that everything is going to be okay is in fact a false sense and nothing is even close to being okay. I had a nice run with Britta, lots of memories made and lost. She was not the kind of girl that forever was in our future. While I was losing Britta, I was gaining a new lover named drug addiction. This relationship trumped all other relationships for years to come. A lover that took me to levels that I never thought were possible.

I was all in, believing all the lies that the drugs were telling me. The sicker that I made myself look to obtain the drugs from the doctors, the sicker I became in real life. Juggling all my lies and chasing the high that I fell in love with became a real challenge. I was spinning fast through the ranks of opiate addiction. No drug dealers' houses for me. I could walk out of the doctor's office with my prescription for my drugs in my hand, walk into a pharmacy, stand there out in the open in front of everybody and get some of the strongest drugs known to man and woman and walk through the parking lot with that little white bag with the receipt stapled to the front of it.

I didn't have to hide it under my shirt or in my pocket. I got in my vehicle and set it right next to me for the world to see and accept. Most of the drugs that I consumed in my life had to be hidden from society. When I would get my heroin, it always had to be hidden. Pills are accepted in our society. Quick fix Pillville. Prescribed from an individual who had a lot of schooling and then dealt to a nice individual who never thought about pistol whipping you or ripping you off.

No one ever explained the dangers of narcotic pain medication to me. I am not sure if it would have made much difference if they would have. I would have never believed them anyway. Drug addicts always think that it is never going to happen to them. My teeth won't fall out from meth. I won't be the one that ODs. My life is secure, drugs won't affect me. All my dreams will come true. Never once as a child did I say that I wanted to be a drug addict. I got this shit. I can quit at any time. This is the last time I promise. All lies, every single one of them.

CHAPTER 31

Insanity

Losing the use of my right hand from meth was heartbreaking. Nerve damage, the doctors said that it was from my landscaping career and the repetitive work that I did with my hands. Yeah doc, you knocked that diagnosis out of the park. Whatever you say. I Googled all the symptoms for nerve damage so I could play my part to the best of my ability. I could feel another Oscar nomination in my near future. Back to reality, Tyler. Don't you remember? Yes, I remember it clearly. Meth did it you dumb ass. Remember watching the muscle in your hand disappear right in front of your eyes, while you were all gawked out. No! It was from my repetitive landscaping career. That's what the doc said. You are in denial you dumb ass. No! Your doctors suck dude. No, they don't. I am an Oscar winner, want to see the trophy case?

One beautiful thing about nerve damage is that it caused a lot of pain. I used my research about nerve damage to my advantage and narcotic pain medication just kept pumping into my pocket. I was seeing specialists at the Mayo Clinic in Rochester, Minnesota. They believed me because I had nerve damage, but little did they know that I was acting out all the symptoms and lying about the pain. I had no pain in the beginning, but once I was in full character, the pain became real and so did the symptoms. I could not believe that some of the smartest people in the world were believing my lies. Why wouldn't they? I was making myself sick from all the acting that I was doing. My workload was horrendous. Professional acting is tough.

The acting continued even when no one was looking. I was doctor shopping. There were different times in my life that I had doctors in small towns that surrounded our community and multiple doctors in my own community. They were all prescribing me narcotic pain medication and none of them knew about one another. What a beautiful racket. So, I thought! I was dying and I couldn't see it.

Thousands and thousands of dollars' worth of medical procedures done, all for that little pill. Back and forth from the two hospitals in Bismarck. I would go to the ER one day at one hospital and then to the other ER a few blocks away. ER shopping. Different doctors, different shifts. It was all pre-planned. Things became so desperate that I would punch the wall outside of the ER, breaking my hand to make it more believable. Some of the doctors in the emergency room would give me pain medication and then there were some who wouldn't. I would even call ahead to see which doctors were working and this would determine what emergency room that I went to. I avoided the doctors who wouldn't prescribe.

I would bash my head on a wall so it would swell up and say that I fell off a ladder. I had back issues, shoulder issues, broken bone issues. One time, I was so sick from not having any narcotic pain medication and was withdrawing so bad that I went out on my mountain bike and wiped out on purpose and messed myself all up. Then I went into the ER and scored some dope. Crazy, right? Desperate? You could say that. Brilliant? Beyond brilliant. Everyone around me was believing me, even the person looking back in the mirror.

I once worked at Bobcat as a forklift driver and I was pill sick. The brilliant idea of faking a seizure started to ruminate in my cloudy brain. I had it all planned out to fall face first into the garage door bashing my face and my head before smashing off the cement floor. I planned out that I was going to lay there and fake seize until the ambulance was called so I could get pills. I gave myself a little pep talk because it takes a lot of balls to physically harm yourself. Instinct is something that I needed to fight the most, so I made it look believable without catching myself with my arms. I needed to take the blows in a limp position.

I got into my role and went for it. I was all in, no hesitation. I limped up, smashed face first into that garage before my head bounced off the cement. It hurt really bad. Best actor on the face of the earth. I could feel the swelling start on my face. My now open wounds were stinging. I could feel the blood, running out of my head and face. People came running from all directions. I played the part, my body convulsed. I forced my eyeballs into the back of my head. The noises were something out of a horror movie. Everybody was tuned into the Tyler show. Hook line and sinker. Nothing but net and he scores. The crowd goes wild. Oscar please. My boss stood over me; he was trying his best to comfort me.

"The ambulance is on its way, Tyler. Hang in there, buddy, you're going to be okay."

I muttered, "What happened?"

"You had a seizure. It's going to be okay. Help is on the way."

The ambulance crew showed up and rushed me to the ER where I spent that night and the next day under close watch with a multitude of tests. I was given an IV for fluids and pain meds, a morphine pump that I could press the red button every ten minutes to get my fix. I played it well. My plan was playing out to a T. Friends and family rushed to the hospital to see me and give me their best wishes. I was in heaven. Just a little vacation to Drugville. Cute nurses and drugs by the syringe. A trip to the emergency room to make sure that Tyler was okay. This was heaven for me. Major medical issues going on with Tyler and he needs medical help. Yes, I do, I needed more than medical help, but will get to that later in the story.

CHAPTER 32

No Rock Bottom For Me

Over an eleven-year span, I had twelve or thirteen surgeries. Out of these twelve to thirteen surgeries, only two of the surgeries were needed. I was getting cut open on a regular basis so I could keep getting narcotic pain medication. This worked great; everyone around me believed that there was something wrong with me and I had the stitches to prove it. What a horrible messy cycle to be stuck in. The pain medications were making me sick and I was being admitted to the hospital for up to fourteen days straight. Over these fourteen days, I was throwing up stomach bile and blood. Doctors were constantly scoping me and burning the ulcers inside of my stomach shut to make them stop leaking blood. None of this scared me. The ambulance rides didn't scare me. Overdoses? Bring them on. I begged God to check me out of this earth daily.

"Please God, don't let me wake up. Please take my life. Please!"

What scared me the most was running out of pain medication and having to go through the sickness that comes along with a habit as great as mine. Most would call me a pig. That was a fair assessment at the rate I was shoveling pills into my system. Withdrawing from narcotic pain medication felt like I was dying. Five days of cold sweats. You know, the kind of cold sweats that wreck a bed because of the nasty stench and the gallons of sweat that poured out of my body.

I would throw up on myself because I could not sit up fast enough to realize what was happening. Sometimes when I was on my last pills after a long binge I would throw up and then I would dig through my puke and find what was left of the pills and pick them out of my puke and eat them so they wouldn't go to waste. I would crawl to the bathroom and lie next to the toilet shivering. Death was knocking at my door and I was letting it in. After shitting myself for three days straight, I swore I would never do pills again. I promised myself that this was the last time. Bullshit. I wasn't done, not even close. The pain was unbearable. Everything hurt.

On day five, the misery started to lift. The curtain of hell shed life on my rotting body. Everything felt like it was going to be okay. You would think after enduring the withdrawal symptoms that I would stop. Nope, not me. I couldn't do that. It was not possible. The disease of addiction was even stronger than it was before, tricking me into thinking that I was only going to do a few pills at a time. I am done taking six hundred milligrams of OxyContin at one time. I will never take forty hydrocodone 10/650s in three gulps. This time when I get my prescription, I will make it last the whole month just like it is supposed to. What a crock of shit. I had a hard time making a thirty-day prescription for six days. Man, I hated day five because I believed all of my lies again.

"This time I am not going to get sick. This time I am not going to steal shit from the people that I love to buy pills when I run out. This time is going to be different. This is the last time that I will go see the vet." This time, this time, fuck this time! Hours were spent hiding pills when I was high trying to make them last longer, then I would spend days looking for them tearing apart our house.

I had everyone convinced that I was still sick from my damn gallbladder. My gallbladder had everyone fooled including myself. I was even doing gallbladder flushes, because I believed that's why I was sick. It couldn't be the pills. No.

This was pure hell and my relationships were feeling it. I was not worth a crap at work or at home. I am grateful for the withdrawals that I went through over my lifetime, because today this makes me not want to ever go back to the hell and misery that I escaped. I never want to make myself believe that so many things are wrong with me when there's nothing wrong. The mind is a powerful weapon of mass destruction if used by the wrong person.

I went to every length possible to fuel my addiction. Get this shit, I was even getting pain medication from the veterinarian clinics in town. Yes, I was taking puppy drugs and horse drugs. High grade animal pills. You're probably wondering why the veterinarian clinic gave me all of these different drugs when I only had a dog. Well, I lied to the veterinarian clinics. The vets were unsuspecting of the wrecking ball that was smashing through my life. I was getting drugs from the veterinarian clinic that were out of this world. My friend was a horse guy, so he supplied me with the knowledge and the photos of sick horses that I used as bait. It worked. Some vets were just handing me drugs when I showed them the pictures of the horses that were seeing a vet across the state for their issues.

These drugs were used for sedation and pain relief for my horses. As you can see, I am not a horse so figuring out how much of each of these drugs I need to take was a very dangerous balancing act. Tada, I am still alive. I always took just enough to get really high. Let's be real, sometimes I would take too much. Too much, was perfect. Anything to knock me out for a long period of time. I would make sure that if I was going to take more than intended, I would do it at night before I went to bed so it didn't look suspicious why I was passed out during the day. The side effects from some of the drugs were horrible. Not meant for consumption by humans. Yeah, Yeah, Yeah.

Tramadol is a non-narcotic pain medication. I would take thirty Tramadol at one time and then spend the next three hours sick, trying to hold my guts down inside of me while they tried their hardest to come up through my throat. Once the three hours of hell was over, it was twelve hours of the best high that you could get from a non-narcotic pain med. It was pure heaven. This med was prescribed to my dog, Keetah. Veterinarians really weren't up on the human consumption of their drugs, so it was easy to manipulate these systems and I did. Friends of mine would think I was crazy for taking veterinarian drugs. The words were muttered on many occasions "What the fuck is wrong with you?" This was the last time that I told anyone that I was getting drugs from the veterinarian clinic. This was my little secret. I often wondered if I was going to start barking like a dog.

My judgment was definitely distorted. My business was very much appreciated and the fact that I paid large tabs with cash was a plus. I thought it would be a good idea to ask one of the vets if he would extract a couple of my teeth in the back room of his clinic for cash. Shit, I shouldn't have shown him my hand quite yet. He definitely said he could not perform a tooth extraction on a human in his veterinarian clinic. That was the end of that connection, no more veterinarian drugs from him. Vet drugs were always a nice supplement when I struggled to get narcotic pain medication.

Some of the doctors in town started to catch on to my little game. The pharmacists definitely were on to me. They were actually the ones who gave me the hardest time. They knew what I was doing. My doctor would believe me when I told him that my truck fell through the ice and my pain meds were inside of my truck or that my bag got lost by the airlines on my trip to Nashville. I didn't ice fish and I did not go to Nashville, but I was able to present this information, so it worked for me. When I was desperate the lies flowed out of me like I had spent months making them up.

CHAPTER 33

God Who? Looks Good In Love

My first wife and I were married in a Catholic Church. I had to jump through all the hoops that go along with marrying a Catholic girl. I was okay with jumping through all these hoops because I was in love. I also was carrying a very deep secret and that secret was that I was using drugs daily for many years. In this Catholic Church, the message that my ears heard was that I would be forgiven for my sins if I just showed up to a building on Sunday, knelt down on some weird benches that pulled out, and prayed to be forgiven. Oh, yeah, and give some money. I lied to the priest and told him that we were not living together before we were getting married. Looking back on this today, our marriage started out with a bunch of lies that I chose to tell. I even overdosed at our wedding only making it to the second dance. But, I guess this seemed to be the thing to do in my eyes and that is to deny everything.

For over eleven years I went to church. Off and on, I have thought back on my first church experience. All the times that

I went to church service under the influence of every drug you could imagine. I would sit in the pew, singing along with the songs wondering if I would be forgiven since I was participating in a church service, even though I was blasted out of my mind on drugs. I would kneel when everyone else did. I would look down the row checking out all the pretty girls' butts as they were leaning forward praying. One particular Sunday I was so high on meth that I felt like God was staring down upon me judging me for the nasty thoughts that I was having in church. But then again, in my eyes, God was a long-haired hippie who wore sandals. I thought that he would have smoked a joint before the service just like me, and he would have gazed at all the nice butts. I was really hoping that what they were telling me wasn't true, because if God could see everything that I was doing and thinking, oh, boy, I would be on my way to hell.

This went on for years and I started to get a great feeling from going. I was really enjoying myself. Sometimes I even went to church because I craved it. I even thought that God could help me defeat my demons of addiction. I did not crave the message; I craved the feeling. Once I separated people from God, God was beautiful to me. People were the ones that always messed up the nice feeling. I guess if you sit in the front row and give the church lots of money, the pearly gates of heaven will open for you.

I struggled over the years with the whole God thing. Between my addiction and the negative people in my life, I pushed God further away each day.

CHAPTER 34

Reality Is Slipping Away

The meth was taking over. It was suffocating my life. I officially couldn't control what happened when I was high. You can say I was out of control. But, for me to say that is crazy, so I won't. My reality had been distorted for about four years, but I felt in control. That's what the drugs do, they give you a false sense that everything is good, when in reality, everything in my life was burning to the ground all around me. The flames were burning high and I was walking around dumping gas on them. I would always get paranoid from the meth. There is paranoia and then there is actually living out the delusions, following them through the shit and taking stereo equipment apart to make the voices inside of them stop.

The first time I called 911 was during a heavy meth binge. What the hell? Are you serious Tyler? You don't call the police while you are high on meth. Now, this is what I am talking about when I say I was following my delusions through the shit and the shit was getting deep. I had been up for three days. My deer rifle was propped up on a bookshelf so I could watch everything that was happening in my neighborhood out a small opening in my blinds. I watched people through my scope for hours, actually a whole day and a night. Little did the people who went by know that someone was aiming a gun at them. I wasn't going to shoot anyone. Well, let me clarify this, I was only going to shoot someone if they deserved it. After sitting for so long, I was getting sore and my muscles were cramping. My .270 Weatherby deer rifle was pulled up tight to my shoulder for hours, my left eye was shut with my right eye looking through the Nikon 10x40 scope. I could see everything through this baby.

Day turned into night. I started seeing people running through the houses to the west of my house. I could see cops chasing them with their flashlights lighting up the yards. These people were fast, I couldn't even get them dialed in to the cross hairs on my scope. I could feel the rush from the excitement. This was an overwhelming feeling watching cops run to your house when you are high. It didn't help that I had a bunch of drugs on me. The lights started getting closer. I laid the gun down on the bed that was in my living room at the time and ran to the kitchen window and looked out. I could see a man run into my dog kennel and then crawled into the doghouse. I grabbed my rifle off the bed and moved it to the kitchen window just in case this guy in the doghouse gave me trouble. I grabbed the phone and called 911.

"911, what is your emergency?"

"Hi, I saw the cops chasing someone through my neighborhood and the man they are chasing just went into my dog kennel and crawled into the doghouse."

"What is your name, sir?"

"Tyler Auck. I could see flashlights going through the yards looking for the guy that's in my doghouse."

"Do you have a dog?"

"Yes, she's in the house with me."

"Okay, we have officers on their way over now."

"I can see two patrol cars pull up on 16th street."

"Okay, Tyler. I would like you to hang up the phone so you can talk with the officers."

"Thank you, ma'am."

I watched two officers get out of their cars and start walking towards my house. I could see an officer shining his flashlight in my driveway. I opened the shade, slid the window open and stuck my face up the screen.

"He's in the doghouse."

"This one here?" His flashlight light beam shone at the entrance to the dog kennel.

"Yes, I saw him crawl in." The officer entered the kennel and walked up to the doghouse, crouched down and shined his flashlight through the opening.

"No one is in here."

"Officer, I watched him go in there. He must have run away."

I asked the officer who they have been chasing over the last hour through the houses.

"No one."

I was blown away and thought that he was lying to me. I could see the other officers' flashlight beam shining through my yard on the other side of the house. The two officers were talking. The officer that looked in the doghouse came back to the window.

"If you see anyone, make sure to call 911 and stay in your house for the rest of the night."

"I will, officer. I will call if the guy comes back through my yard. I watched the officers walk back to their patrol cars and drive away.

I sat in front of the window looking through the scope, and it seemed like the traffic on my street had increased. I saw patrol cars roll by one street over. Everything started to fail me both physically and mentally. It was 3:00 a.m. I started questioning myself wondering if there were actual people running through my neighborhood? I changed my mind back to the idea that the cops were lying. This must be some kind of cover up.

See what I mean about following the delusion. Reality was slipping away. Everything that wasn't real became my reality.

Three and a half years gone, $800 per week worth of meth up my nose or into my lungs. I was buying ounces of meth from lots of different people and hiding it from the people who were the closest to me. My plan was to sell the meth and make some money, but once I dipped into the bag it was over. I was doing more of it than I was selling, I got to the point where an ounce became personal stash. I was smoking up to two and a half grams per day just so I could function and go through the motions of life. My pockets were full of money from all the marijuana and cocaine that I was selling. Having lots of money for a meth addict is a recipe for disaster and that's what was happening. Craziness became my normal. My life was on fire and it was about to burn out of control.

CHAPTER 35

Another Loss

November 29, 2006, I was in the loader on the south east side of the Capitol grounds waiting for my dad to drive by on his way to work so I could flash my lights and lift the bucket of the loader to say hello. I was excited about my new job as a groundskeeper at the Capitol and so was my dad. He watched me struggle to find myself over the years and now I had a good job with good benefits. This morning he took a different way to work because he needed to put gas in his car. I was a little disappointed that dad didn't get to see me in the loader moving snow.

I went into the shop for my break. I was sitting on my chair in the corner of the break room getting to know the guys who I had recently started working with when the break room phone rang.

My boss answered the phone and instantly looked at me and said, "It's for you. It's your aunt, and it's not good."

My heart sank into my guts as I reached across the desk and grabbed the phone. It was my aunt and she informed me that I needed to go to the hospital immediately because something happened to my dad. She told me that it was bad. I hung up the phone and asked my boss if I could leave and he told me to go. I went up to my vehicle with a sick feeling in my stomach. On my way to the hospital, I knew that dad was dead. I knew something bad happened. The drive to the hospital was surreal. The trees were covered with a beautiful frost. It was a winter wonderland. My dad always loved it when the frost covered the trees. I thought that this was fitting for his departure from this earth.

Once I arrived at the ER, I went in and was instantly met by my mom and my brothers. They told me dad had died. We all went into the room where he was laying. I grabbed his hand and held it. I leaned down and hugged him and kissed his forehead. I was in shock. I hugged my mom and my little brothers as we all prepared for the next steps that needed to be taken. Dad died from a blood clot that went to his heart. We all decided that we would meet out at Mom and Dad's house.

I hurried out of the ER and drove as fast as I could out to the rock house. The pain was too much for me to handle at this time and I was withdrawing from the pain pills that I took over the last week. I went straight into the house before anyone else got there and took my dad's drugs that he had locked in his safe. I took a handful of hydros, broke them all in half and swallowed twenty of them in hopes of making the pain go away. Everything was a blur. I figured that he didn't need any of his pain meds anymore. I justified my actions because I didn't want to look at the fact that I stole my dad's pain meds before his body had time to cool. My drug addiction trumped everything. The pain was still there. We spent the rest of the day calling people letting them know that my dad was no longer with us.

The day of my dad's funeral was a hard day and a beautiful day all at the same time. My dad had done a lot of bad things in his life, but who hasn't? The four hundred plus people who attended his funeral was a testament to the man he was when he wasn't consumed by his demons. People loved my dad and showed it by honoring him as he traveled to heaven. I truly feel that my dad went to heaven because he continued to change the bad in his life for good. The changes that my dad made in his lifetime were hard to see because the damage was so great. But, there were changes, because I felt them and saw them.

My dad, Rick Auck, was a hard-working man. He worked at Bobcat for over thirty years of his life as an assembler to provide for his family and he died on the floor of that building. He tried his best to raise his family with the tools that he was given. He sometimes fell short and other times touched all of our hearts. Nothing is perfect in this life, but he did his best to undo his wrongs by changing. My dad taught me a lot about broken gifts and grit. He taught me that we need to be tough in this life to survive because there are bad people who surround us. My mom and dad stood through the tests of life and survived. My mom was his girl who believed in him when he didn't believe in himself.

PART IV

More Fucked Up

After my dad's death, I continued to dig my hole deeper until I stopped looking up for the light. I made peace with myself that my life would end soon. I thought that the only things that I was good at were the illegal acts that could have put me away for years. My heart was breaking and I felt alone inside. I not only did drugs to get high, I did drugs to stay alive. Every breath I took was for the next high. I felt all of my dreams going up in smoke. My life, as I knew it, was over. My identity was being stripped away one high at a time.

CHAPTER 36

The Big Drift

There was a shit ton of snow that had fallen in the winter of 2009, and everything was difficult living out in the middle of nowhere. We had moved from Bismarck to Baldwin. Most days my driveway was completely blocked in with five-foot-tall drifts of hard packed snow. I had to ram the drifts daily with my V-plow that was hooked to the front of a F250 Super-Duty. I went through transmissions, motors, windows, and vehicles that winter. I had a $6,000 towing bill that the insurance company paid through my towing plan. Let's just say that the insurance company dropped me after this particular winter. I was fucking shit up daily.

One morning, I got the truck stuck on our driveway, so I had to walk back to the trailer to have my wife bring our brand-new Jeep Grand Cherokee Limited down to pull me out. This Jeep was a beautiful white, fully-loaded luxury machine. I had a giant tow rope with a chain hooked on to the end of it so it would reach the top of the driveway from where I had slid down. The truck was down a slope, so it was in an awkward position off the road. I had my wife back the Jeep up to the tow strap that I already had laid out on the snow. I jumped out and hooked it up to the Jeep. I told her to back up a few more feet. Then I told her that when I gave her the signal she was to nail the gas pedal and give me a good yank. She did her best backing up and pushing the gas pedal to the floor. The truck wasn't moving. She was out of position. Every time she would tighten the strap and push on the gas pedal the Jeep would hit the end of the rope and it would whip the Jeep sideways bouncing her head off the side window (not funny).

She opened the door and stepped out. She yelled at me that she was done. I calmed her down and made sure her head was okay. I had her get in the truck and put it in reverse. I instructed her to give it gas once I gave her the signal. I jumped into the Jeep, backed up a good twelve feet, gave her the signal and hit the gas, slamming the rope tight. The truck moved about a foot. I continued to do this over and over again until finally the chain snapped, and the rope slammed against the tailgate and then right through the back window of the truck, shattering the window to pieces. I will never forget the look on her face as her head was twisted around looking back through the busted window at me. I think from that instant the plan to divorce me started to form. I guess this isn't too funny. No, it's funny because the look said it all. It didn't help that a week later I smashed her Jeep into the ditch, smashing up the passenger side. After that was fixed, ten days later, I blew up the engine and left it on the side of Highway 83 for the dealership to pick up. Get this shit, none of this was my fault.

I met up with some people at the Pride of Dakota show at the Capitol building. I had known them for some time. We planned on going out to eat after they were done working the show. These were good people. People of God. Hard working people. These people, who had no clue what was going on in my life wouldn't have allowed it to happen around them. But, clearly, if they were around me it was happening whether they could see it or not.

The week had been hell. I was putting in lots of hours moving snow at the Capitol. I was smoking meth daily and I was struggling in the evenings to lay my head down so I could rest my eyes. That's all I did was rest my eyes. No sleeping for me. Oh, man, did my eyes hurt. I couldn't stop taking hits of meth. Shit was always strange, but I started to chase the paranoia and participate in the delusions. I stopped talking to most of the people who were in my life. I was paranoid that I was being watched and that people were constantly following me.

I would even occasionally chase them in my truck through my neighbor's farmyard. I would look out my trailer house's windows and see people poking their heads over the buttes in the distance aiming guns at me. This terrified me and it was hard to function in my daily life thinking people were trying to kill me. I was always carrying guns and shooting at these people to scare them off. I was in a war zone popping rounds off daily at people who weren't there. I prepared daily to shoot it out with these people, fully intent on killing them. I was unraveling fast.

Let's just say it was a Thursday evening, because I have no clue what day it really was. All I remember is that I had worked earlier in that day moving snow at the Capitol and I knew that I needed to go back to work at four a.m. the following morning. I made up some bullshit excuse again that I was not feeling well. I wasn't lying, I was sick. I hadn't eaten in days; dehydration was sucking the life out of me and the only thing that was helping me put one foot in front of the other was the meth. I needed to pull myself together for dinner that evening so I figured that I would get off early. I didn't want to go, but I respected these people and they seemed so excited to see me.

I left the Capitol grounds and made my way up State Street until it turned into Highway 83. My patience was running thin and the paranoia was setting in from the day, making my mind race. I came up behind two semis that were next to each other on the two-lane highway. They were not moving as fast as I wanted them to so I thought it would be a good idea to pass them both on the inside median. I stepped on the gas and steered my vehicle up alongside the semi's. I had two tires on the asphalt and the driver's side tires on the top side of the ditch. The vehicle started bouncing off the uneven snow. I was two feet away from the semi's trailer. I could feel my driver side tires start to get sucked down into the snow, the steering wheel jerked to the left, sucking my vehicle into the ditch.

My speed was hitting eighty-five miles per hour or more. Snow was shooting in all directions. Then, my vehicle hit an approach, launched ten feet into the air before slamming down into the middle of the ditch about eighty feet from where I had left the ground. My head slammed off the steering wheel then hit the windshield busting my forehead wide open. I felt the blood run down my face. The momentum from the speed and the jump helped me plow through the snow back up onto the road. I could tell instantly that my vehicle was damaged badly. It was wobbling. It felt like it was bent in half.

As I drove up the road, the reality of just what just happened sunk in. I turned down the gravel road heading to my house, pulled into my yard, got out and looked over the vehicle. The vehicle was in fact bent in half and there were wires and plastic pieces hanging from the bottom of the vehicle. The windshield was cracked. I knew I messed it up really bad. I hadn't even made the first payment on this thing yet. I went in the house and sat down feeling dazed. I spent the next two hours peeking out the blinds and smoking meth.

I showered and cleaned the wounds on my head, then put on some nice clothes. I felt like I was as ready as I was going to be. I needed to get this over with so I could get back home and into my routine. I jumped into the F250 Super Duty and drove to town. Once I pulled into the parking lot of Applebee's, I looked at myself in the mirror preparing to go inside. I looked like shit. I walked in and the lights instantly hurt my eyes. I gazed across all the tables until I could see Lara waving me over to their table. I walked over and sat down. Bill took one look at me and said, "What happened to your head, Tyler?"

I could see the concern on their faces. I made up some bullshit story about a semi running me off the road and me hitting a small approach. I told them that the semi kept going so I was not able to get a license plate.

The dinner was painful. I struggled to eat. When I Looked down at my plate, the burger and fries were staring right at me. They knew that I was too high and that I couldn't eat. Stop staring at me, you are making me nauseous. I struggled with every single bite trying to make it look like I was enjoying myself and the food. The conversation was hard to follow with my racing mind and the constant paranoia. I nodded my head a lot and kept reminding them of my head injury to throw off any suspicions that I was on drugs. We finished up dinner and went our separate ways.

I went back out to the scene of the accident after dinner armed with a video camera. I pressed record as I walked off the steps to see how far I flew through the air. It was easy to do because I could see the tracks that went into the ditch and hit the approach. And then there was nothing that touched the snow for eighty feet until my tires slammed into the earth. I stood there in the center median of Highway 83 looking at my near death experience, feeling proud that I had flown so far in the air and landed on on my wheels, and still managed to not get stuck in the snow.

On the way back out to the house that night, I could see snowmobiles chasing me and the men on the sleds were shooting at me trying to kill me. I rolled down the window of the truck, stuck my 9 mm pistol out the window and pulled the trigger emptying clip after clip into the side hills. I sped into the driveway and slammed on the brakes. I grabbed my pistol and two boxes of shells, jumped out of the vehicle, and prepared to shoot it out with these motherfuckers. I hunkered down next to my truck, using it as a shield. I reloaded my clips. I listened for the sound of the sleds, but there was no noise. Just the crunching of the snow under my shoes and my breathing. Where did they go? They were just right behind me. I don't hear a fucking thing!

I ran into the house, slammed the door behind me and locked it. I could feel the goosebumps and the adrenaline surging through my body at the thought of bullets flying through the side of the trailer at any minute. I started to panic. I shut off all the lights, grabbed my shotgun, deer rifle, pistol, and multiple boxes of shells. I sat on the floor with my back to the wall aiming my shotgun at the door. Then I waited. I spent most of the night sitting on the floor with my dog Keetah, smoking meth in the dark, preparing to have a shootout. I heard lots of different noises outside throughout the night. But, none of the noises made me respond with bullets.

My alarm started to go off in the back room. This startled me until I figured out what was going on. Shit, it was time to go to work. The paranoia started to dissipate and everything went back to business as usual. I had to go to work at 4:00 a.m. to meet my boss in the J Wing parking lot to haul snow. I jumped in the shower to refresh myself and try and wash off this horrible feeling. I spent twenty minutes before work smoking meth just so I could make it through the first three hours of work. I was not feeling well.

I went to work and punched in at 3:45 a.m., just like I had done a hundred times before. I pulled the loader out of the shop, hooked up the bucket and went upstairs and started the dump truck for my coworkers. I got in my Bobcat, put the bucket on and went over to the J Wing and started to push the snow off the berms. Ten minutes later, I could see the loader lights coming over the hill, followed by the dump truck. The dump truck pulled up to the first snow pile. The loader started to load it until it was heaping full of snow. The loads were taken out to the field and dumped. I pushed the snow off the berms into the pile that they were loading. When the pile was small, I would push the remaining snow into the loader bucket and then the loader would dump it into the truck. We moved through each parking lot until we finished hauling snow for the day. We all met back at the shop for break. Once in the break room I started to feel paranoid and sick to my stomach. I asked my boss if I could go home and get some rest. My boss let me leave early since we were caught up and I had a bunch of overtime for the week.

Once I returned to the property, my driveway was drifted over from the snow that had blown in over the course of the morning. I spent the next few hours moving snow and getting high. I was struggling to move the snow. Nothing was making much sense to me. I kept pushing the snow around and around, not really accomplishing much. I was way too high. The paranoia started back up again. My vision was compromised from the bright sun that was reflecting off the white snow. I started to see groups of people on the surrounding buttes looking at me through binoculars. I would randomly jump out of my truck and shoot some rounds from my pistol towards the people to scare them away. Then I would jump back into my truck, reload, and move some more snow.

I could feel the stress and the anxiety mounting. The people were getting closer and my shots were no longer making them duck for cover. I was unsure who these people were and why they were coming after me. I knew that I needed to protect myself. I jumped out of the truck with my dog and ran into the house. I continued to glance back over my shoulder watching them get closer. As I was running, I could see seven people, they were two hundred feet away from my trailer door. They were darting back and forth in the trees right down the hill. I turned around and emptied my clip into the trees.

I ran into the house and grabbed my deer rifle. I needed to look at them through the scope. As I looked through the scope,

I could see the group walking towards the trailer. I put the cross hairs of the scope right on one of the men and pulled the trigger, he kept walking so I shot again. I started to scream out.

"If you come closer, I am going to kill you." I leaned the deer rife up against the wall and sat down on the floor, aiming the shotgun right at the door, waiting. I loaded my weapons making sure I was prepared. I opened one of the windows in the living room, stuck my deer rifle out the window, and fired off five rounds into the group of people. I retreated down the hallway to position myself at the door of the back bedroom. I was trembling with fear. I started to think that the people outside were cops and they were coming to arrest me for my drug dealings. I hid the drugs that I had in the house in the bedroom closet. I grabbed the phone and called 911.

"911, what is your emergency?"

"I need to know if it's the police that are coming out to get me. I don't want to shoot a cop. Is it cops or the drug dealers?"

I spent some time on the phone telling the 911 dispatcher what was happening. She asked me to put my guns down. I refused.

"Officers are on their way. You should be seeing a couple of vehicles in your driveway any minute." The first two units came speeding up the driveway positioning themselves on the backside of my trailer house. They were soon followed by more Burleigh County Sheriff units. I stood there talking on the phone with the 911 dispatcher. My shotgun leaned against the wall along with my deer rifle. In my left hand I had the phone up to my ear and in my right hand I had my 9-millimeter pistol. I peeked my head around the wall and looked out the window at all the deputies who had shown up. I could see some guns aiming at me. The officers were positioned behind their vehicles with some of their doors opened for protection.

I was in a panic, not quite sure who to trust. What was real? Was this really happening? By now, the 911 dispatcher had me on a three-way call with my Addison. I hadn't seen her in three days due to our work schedules. She was begging me to put the guns down and come out. Just hearing Addison's voice made reality sink in. All the deputies in my yard aiming guns at me wasn't enough to help me find reality. Shit! What did I just do? I wanted to walk out and tell them there was a terrible misunderstanding and that everything was okay so they could just leave. I just called the cops on myself. I had thousands of dollars in drug money in my shed. I had pounds of pot and kilos of coke in white coolers buried in the snow drifts on the other side of the hill and one ounce of meth stuffed in a shoe in my closet in the back room.

I was screwed. I paused for a moment standing in front of the window looking at the deputies thinking that it would be easier to shoot myself in the head to make this all go away. The talking continued for some time until I finally made the decision to go out and face my nightmare. I told the dispatcher and Addison that I was coming out and I was setting my guns down on the floor. The dispatcher let me know that she would be getting off the phone with me so I could leave the trailer.

I hung up the phone. I set the pistol on the floor and motioned to the deputies with my hands in the air that I was coming out. I walked out the back door feeling some relief that this was almost over. Once outside, I was instructed to not make any sudden movements. Guns were aimed at me. I was met by two deputies with their weapons drawn, aimed at my chest.

"Kneel on the ground and keep your hands in the air." I kneeled down in the snow. The next thing I knew, I was pushed face first down in it. The two deputies were kneeling on my back and neck holding me down, twisting my arms behind my back.

Click! Click!

I could feel the handcuffs tighten against my wrists. I was helped up from the ground and patted down. The questioning started instantly and so did the explaining. By now, some of the deputies were in my house securing the weapons and going through my vehicle that was sitting in the middle of the yard with the doors open, parked on top of the snow ridges that I was pushing around earlier. I made sure to let them know that my dog was nice and begged them not to hurt her. The one deputy did all the questioning as we stood in the yard.

"Where did you see these people?"

I pointed with a head nod in the direction that I saw the group.

"How many people did you see?"

"Seven to ten, they were here earlier, too."

"Do you use drugs?"

"Yes, I smoke pot daily for my anxiety."

"Do you see people all the time?"

"Not all the time."

He then noticed the cut and lump on my head.

"What happened to your head?"

"A semi ran me off the road yesterday. I hit an approach and jumped my Yukon. I busted my head off the windshield."

"What vehicle were you driving?"

"The green Yukon sitting right over there. There is still blood on the windshield and the thing is bent in half."

He walked me over to the Yukon and looked over the damage.

"You're lucky to be alive."

"I know, man."

"I can take you out to the trees where the people were hiding and show you their footprints in the snow."

He loaded me in his SUV and we drove close to the spot before the snow became too deep to go any further. We got out and walked the rest of the way, trudging through the deep snow.

"Right here is the spot they were standing."

"Where are the tracks?"

"Shit, the tracks are gone." I was confused. We went back up to the house and by now my Addison showed up. Shit, how am I going to explain this one to her? The well of lies was all dried up. We stood in the yard talking with the deputies. Well, they were talking. I was being questioned. The deputy kept looking at my head.

"You better get to the hospital and have your head injury looked at. You might have bleeding in your brain. This could be the reason you are seeing people." My eyes lit up. Is this really happening?

"I have a head injury? This is why I am seeing people?"

None of this had anything to do with the meth. I started to believe that it was my head injury. The deputy took the cuffs off me. Addison locked up the house. I rode with my wife to town. It was a quiet, awkward drive to town. We were escorted to the hospital by one of the deputies. I was seen in the ER for head trauma. I had everyone convinced that this was all from the vehicle accident. I did have some head trauma, but that was the least of my worries. The lies worked, or so I thought. I must be the luckiest human on the face of the earth or am I just that manipulating?

I dodged another bullet.

CHAPTER 37

Not The Father

Never in my life did I ever think that I would go through this much pain. Never did I ever think that after giving someone my heart that it would hurt this bad when it was breaking. The years of trying everything to have babies and failing after each attempt devastated me. Little did I know my drug abuse played a giant role in my ability to reproduce.

After finishing up drug and alcohol treatment for the day, I had planned to meet with Addison to get some things straightened out with the bills that needed to be paid on the property that we had together. We had been living apart for three weeks now and it was tough. She had left and told me that she wanted a divorce. So, I did what I needed to do to try to get her back. I checked myself into drug and alcohol treatment, believing that there was a possibility of us getting back together if I received the help that I so badly needed. That afternoon we had planned to meet. I had some time to kill because I am always early for everything. I drove around town before our planned meeting on the south side of the Capitol building.

She showed up at the time that we were scheduled to meet. She met me with a big hug. We walked and sat in the nice green grass on the state Capitol grounds. We sat across from each other and talked about the land and the bills that needed to be paid. Financially, I was struggling to stay afloat. We talked about possibly selling the land and getting out from under it, but at this time it wasn't an option. I wasn't ready to give up our beautiful property. My heart was shattering in a million pieces with the thought that someone else might be in love with my wife. My mind was evil, and it was trying to kill me. My mind always takes things way too far.

She seemed very concerned about my treatment and my well-being. We talked about possibly getting back together once I successfully completed my drug and alcohol treatment. In my mind, she made it seem like there was a big chance that we were going to get back together.

We parted ways that day with a plan of how we were going to possibly move forward with our relationship and the financial situation that we were in together. She told me that she was going to hold off on seeing an attorney for a divorce to see how this played out. I let her know that I still loved her a lot and I wanted our relationship to work out. I told her that I was willing to do whatever it took to make this happen. It was a big lie that I was telling myself, because I was still up to my old ways. I guess in my mind I was willing to make it look like I was willing to do whatever it took, while still selling drugs.

I showed up to treatment the next day. I made sure to let Brita, my counselor, know about the suspicions that I was having. My counselor talked with me about my gut feelings and how I should wait until I have facts before I start having suspicions. In my twisted mind I thought she was cheating on me for some time and that's why she wanted a divorce. It was because of an affair and not because of all the damage that I had caused to our lives. This is what my twisted, warped mind was telling me without any hard evidence of anything at all. I continued to not take responsibility for my part and that part was big and scary.

Brita said, "Tyler, just concentrate on yourself and keep coming to treatment every day and stay sober in between."

My counselor basically told me that I was full of shit, but in a more clinical, acceptable way. I loved Addison and I wanted her in my life so bad that my heart was completely broken in half. She had been my everything over the last eleven years and I couldn't see my life without her.

I wanted babies so bad. I thought that they would fix everything. I thought that if I could make our dreams come true, my drug addiction would just magically disappear, and I would stop doing all of the bad things that I was doing in my life. The problem was that it just wasn't working out on my end of it. We had names picked out and a nursery designed. We knew in our hearts that we would be good parents together. I knew that if I got my shit together that I could be an amazing husband and one of the best dads on this planet. This is why I was going to treatment to get my wife back and to keep moving forward with our dreams.

I talked to Addison on the phone daily to make sure that she was okay and to see if she needed anything. Over time, our phone conversations went from daily to one time per week. Every time I talked to her my mind plagued me with thoughts of my dreams being shattered. The images of her and another man being intimate kept flashing through my mind over and over. What does this mean? Is there a reason these images keep haunting me or is it that I am just that messed up?

Six weeks of treatment complete. I did it. I made it through treatment without using. Six weeks of sobriety has been the longest stretch since my first use at the age of fifteen. I can't believe that I had finished treatment and that I was continuing to work on myself daily, even if it was just to get Addison back. I kept thinking that there was possibly a chance that we were going to get back together. In the back of my mind the suspicion of another man was still running strong and the thoughts continued to get stronger and stronger. To be completely honest, I was embarrassed that my brain did that to me without any evidence at all, and on top of the embassament it was painful.

I felt that she was full of life and I was completely broken and devastated. They always say that one heart breaks more than another and I was the one with the heart that was more broken.

We continued to talk on the phone, but then the talks became less intimate and more about business. I knew that something was happening. I started to become very resentful towards her because she was able to grab her clothes and just leave. She left me with everything, all of the responsibilities to clean up the mess of our life. I often wished that I would have been the one who had grabbed my clothes and just left.

Everything in my life reminded me of her, because everything in my life over the last eleven years was her. I was confused and now back to using the drugs that I was selling. The pain was too much, and the drugs helped me cope with my life.

I met with her one day on the south side of the Capitol building. We sat in the grass across from each other like we had done many times before. We were both happy to see each other. We hugged and it always felt like something might change in our relationship, even though the divorce still loomed in the distant future. I was losing all of the material things in my life and one thing that I didn't want to lose was her. But, I didn't want her, and yet I didn't think that I could live without her.

Sitting across from her on this beautiful spring afternoon I noticed the trees that were blooming and the birds that were chirping. As we were sitting there I had a gut feeling that she was pregnant, but I kept my mouth shut in fear of being wrong and pissing her off.

Many weeks had passed and I had not texted Addison or talked to her by phone. The next contact was when she called me up and told me that she needed to talk with me about something. I knew instantly what it was, she was going to tell me that she was pregnant. Sure as shit. She told me she was pregnant. I instantly started crying. I felt horrible for her because she sounded scared. I felt bad for her because I thought that she was going to be alone raising a baby. I let her know that I was there for her if she needed any help.

This tugged at my heartstrings. I wanted to have babies with her so bad and now she is having babies with someone else. She told me that she still loved me and that she wished things would be different. We said our goodbyes and hung up the phone.

My brain went in a million different directions. Within seconds I thought about taking her back if this guy didn't want her or the baby. I thought about raising the baby with Addison, even if it wasn't mine. I know all about mistakes because I made lots of mistakes throughout my life. I was scared and confused. I felt horrible because my drug addiction was the reason we were apart. My actions were the reason we were losing our land.

My selfish choices were the reason our dreams were falling apart. The problem was that I still loved her, and I was breaking down daily trying to cope with the thought of losing her.

I started to pull away at this time. Addison and I were only communicating by text message. I knew in my gut that the guy who got her pregnant would come around and hopefully love her half as much as I did, because no one will ever love her as much as I did!

I was going to my community support groups and reaching out to people in those groups trying to get guidance on what to do and how to stay sober during this difficult time. My mind was consumed daily with the thoughts of trying to make it work with Addison and helping her however I could. But, could I actually pull myself together to be in a relationship and raise someone else's baby? I had a lady at one of the community support groups tell me that "any dumb son of a bitch can make a baby, but it takes a damn good man to raise someone else's." These words gave me hope that I could actually do this if I was given the chance. I knew in my heart that she was going to be ok.

As the days went by, my feelings for her started to change. I no longer obsessed over the thoughts of getting her back. Now, I wanted the divorce and I wanted it right then. I couldn't do this any longer. It was completely over. There was no chance that this relationship was ever going to be. We're selling the land and moving forward with the divorce. I made a list of everything that we had and proceeded to split it up equally to the best of my ability.

One afternoon, Addison came out on the property to grab some more clothes and look over everything that we had. I gave her the list of all of our belongings that I had split up. I watched Addison get more of her things and her pregnancy was now showing. This completely took me off my feet again, but this time I didn't use drugs. I went to my home community support group after she left and talked about my feelings and I actually worked through it, but I was closer to relapsing than I thought.

CHAPTER 38

Late Fall Harvest

The tedious work was done, and now we prepared for the fruits of our labor. This was my first outdoor marijuana harvest. I had learned a lot over the last couple of summers about soil preparation, pest control, mold, nosy neighbors, pruning, and the scare of the occasional plane that flies too low over the patch. I also learned how to find serenity in a life-changing high-consequence stress zone. Our friendship was growing stronger. I looked up to Booker like a father figure. Everything was going well and my heart was full, finally finding my place. The leaves were changing on the trees and starting to drop. The bright reds, yellows, and oranges covered the hills and the mountains with a magical beauty.

I was promised $10,000 in cash for three days' worth of hard labor and some marijuana for my personal use for the rest of the year. I was putting my ass on the line.

I got a call on the non-traceable flip phone the week before, letting me know that the "girls" were ready to be harvested. I planned on leaving early Thursday morning and getting to the farm late that night to begin our work early that next morning.

There was no turning back at this point. I was committed to getting this job done and getting the fuck back home. After driving late into the night, I finally arrived at the farm. I could see the door open and the silhouette of my good friend standing outside waiting to greet me. I stepped out of the truck, stretching, and groaning from the long drive. My dog jumped out right behind me.

I heard the voice greet my dog, "Hi Keetah! You pretty girl, it's good to see you, girl." I walked around the backside of the truck and met Booker.

We hugged and shook hands as he said, "Dammit, it's good to see you, Ty."

We stood there shooting the shit for a couple minutes. "Let's go up to the house and find you your bed, buddy."

As we walked up to the house the screen door swung open squeaking loudly.

I was greeted with a big hug from Booker's sister Jill. Jill is a tiny little lady with a mouth dirtier than a drunken sailor. I sat down at the round kitchen table and we passed the bong around until the kitchen was filled with smoke and I couldn't smoke anymore.

"I'm good," I said.

I kneeled on the floor next to my bag, unzipped it, and pulled out the pile of cash that was neatly packaged. I had the cash wrapped with rubber bands, neatly stacked in two one-gallon Ziploc baggies, $1,000 per band. $20,000 per baggie.

Booker rolled a joint and said, "This is Bubba Kush. It will help you sleep."

Honestly, I didn't need anything to sleep, my eyes were heavy and already half closed. We spent the next fifteen minutes passing the joint around until I had to finally pass it up. Jill went to bed.

"I need to get to sleep," I said.

He showed me out to the camper that was parked next to the house.

We planned to get up at sunrise to get started.

The next morning my eyes struggled to open. I was exhausted. I could see the sun peeking through the curtains. With my head still on my pillow I reached over and felt around to find my gun that was resting on the bag next to my bed and Keetah. I needed to make sure that the two things that were important to me were still where I had left them when I fell asleep. I greeted my dog, "Good morning, girl." I could hear her tail wagging as it banged against the table leg. The more I talked to her the louder the banging of her tail got.

Booker met me in the yard next to the camper with a smile on his face, "Good morning, Ty."

I replied, "Good morning, buddy."

He offered me some coffee.

"No, thank you. I have a cooler in my truck with my Diet Dew."

He said, "Come inside when you're done and have some donuts."

I walked down the driveway to my truck, reached into the cooler full of ice water and grabbed a sixteen-ounce bottle of ice-cold Diet Dew. I instantly leaned against the truck and cracked opened the bottle and took a drink. It was so cold that it took my breath away for a moment as I gulped it until the bottle was gone. I could smell the plants that surrounded me. It was ten times stronger than the last time I was out to visit. The smell was amazing.

This made me a little nervous, because if I could smell it, anyone else who had been out to the farm could smell it, too. I went into the truck and pulled out the small Ziploc baggie of pills that I had hidden under the fabric on the driver's seat and grabbed fifteen Oxycodone. I folded up the bag and slid it back under the fabric. I popped them all in my mouth crushing all fifteen of them with my teeth tasting the bitter burn. I crushed all my pills so the high would hit me faster. I walked over to the cooler and grabbed another Dew out of the cooler, opened it, and took a big swig chasing the chewed up pills down my throat, washing out the bitter taste from my mouth. I grabbed another Dew, walked up to the house, and knocked on the door.

"Come in," Jill said.

I walked in and sat down at the table. There was the same box of donuts sitting on the table next to the bong. Jill and her daughter, Sam, were sitting at the table surrounded by boxes of untrimmed buds that they were pruning by hand with scissors.

Jill looked up at me and said, "Have a donut and there is orange juice in the fridge."

Sam looked up at me and said, "Hi, Tyler."

"Hi, Sam."

I felt horrible looking at this fourteen-year-old girl trimming buds on an illegal marijuana grow. The whole kid thing always fucked me up and I didn't like it one bit.

I had boundaries when it came to kids and women. Don't mess with them when I am in the room or I will drag you far away so they can't see what I will do to you. There is honor in my heart for the women and children, and that will never change.

I finished up my Diet Dew, went into the bathroom and took care of my business before meeting Booker out in the driveway in front of the house. We walked out to the out building and sat down in the office. He pulled out a jar of THC oil; it was a beautiful golden color, nice and syrupy. He had a jar of suckers on his desk, so I grabbed one, took the wrapper off, jammed the sucker into the oil, and then straight into my mouth.

"Holy crap. That was a lot." He giggled and leaned back in his chair.

The taste of the oil was sweet, I could feel it coat my tongue and the top of my mouth.

"How many licks does it take to get to the center of a Tootsie Pop?"

Two and that little sucker was chomped and crushed in my mouth. No matter how hard I tried, I couldn't suck on a sucker even with THC oil on it, I always had to bite them. We continued to smoke the joint until I could not take any more hits. We came up with a plan for the day. He showed me the bud-trimming machine that was loaded in a wheelbarrow. This thing was fantastic. It was an eighteen-inch stand motor driven trimmer in stainless steel. This thing looked just like a grill without the lid. It had stainless-steel razor-sharp blades placed under the grates.

"This is the one we will take out to the patches," he said.

We climbed the stairs in the out building up to the second-floor loft. We entered a room with wood racks nicely stacked and covered with screens.

This was a beautiful set up. I was always impressed by my friend's ability to take it to the next level and what he did with everything. He is a very talented man. Once he was done showing me the drying room, we went back outside.

"Let's get to work".

We each grabbed a wheelbarrow; my wheelbarrow had the trimming machine, a water jug, and some plastic cups. His wheelbarrow was full of empty boxes stacked five feet high, pruners and a chainsaw. We pushed the wheelbarrows down the dirt path. He led the way, because you always let the lead grower enter his patch first out of respect. There were extension cords laying on the ground all the way back to a pop-up canopy surrounded by trees about sixty feet away from the big patch. We unloaded the trimmer and placed it in the middle of the canopy and stacked the boxes on the ground. He grabbed the end of the extension cord and plugged in the trimmer. Turning on the power switch, we watched the blades spin and listened to the motor hum. We both stood there smiling until he bent over and shut it off.

"The canopy is so no planes can see you. What do you think?"

"This looks like a good spot to me."

"Let's go look at the patch. You have to see the beautiful girls."

We walked through the trees until we came to an opening in the field. There they were, beautiful giant plants. Some were leaning over from the weight of the main buds. These things looked like small fire extinguishers on the A-train plants and the sativa plants lined the back of the patch, some standing ten feet tall and had stalks that were five inches in diameter. Now I knew what the chainsaw was for. The smell at this point was so powerful that my mouth began to water. We just stood there like little kids in a candy shop, staring, touching, and smelling.

Fully-budded plants are beautiful, so full of deep colors and textures. The Purple Kush plants were such a dark purple that they looked black, until you were close enough to see the rich purple colors that popped out from the deep green color of the leaves. The main buds were covered in little crystals that glistened in the sun. The leaves were green and purple. The colors were outstanding. Other plants had orange and white colors throughout the buds. For this brief moment, I forgot that we were totally breaking the law and we could go to jail for a long time.

My luxurious moment with the flowers was met with the reality of what needed to be done.

"Well, let's do this," I said. "Let's go! I'm ready to bust my ass."

I walked back over to my station and grabbed the boxes and started to carry them over to the plants. Soon, we were both chopping the main buds and putting them into boxes. I carried the boxes that were full of untrimmed buds over and sat them down under the canopy. Booker came over and turned on the bud-trimming machine. He took one of the big branches of the plant with buds on it and ran it across the top of the grates, back and forth, back and forth as he rotated the plant making sure to hit all the sides. This thing chewed through all the protruding fan leaves and the stems. This machine was badass and I couldn't wait to get started. I started grabbing the big buds and ran them back and forth over the grates as fast as I could go, placing the trimmed buds in the empty boxes. I stopped for a moment, to look around.

Fuck it, let's do this! I am already here and if they are going to get me, they are going to get me. I had my pistol hid in one of the boxes with my Dew. We went to work. I worked my ass off hour after hour. I stood in the same place trimming buds and filling boxes over the next twelve hours, only stopping to take a piss, eat some THC oil, or spark up the pipe that I continued to stuff with the hash that was on the table under the canopy. Right at dusk, we started loading up the remaining boxes into the wheelbarrow and pushed them up the dirt trail carefully stacking them up in the building out of sight. We made trip after trip until all the boxes were hauled.

My hands were sore and covered in sticky resin. My hands were so sticky that everything that I touched would stick for a moment. My shirt and shorts were covered in sweat. As the sun went down, it made me feel safe. I felt like no one was watching me anymore. We went into the office and plopped down in exhaustion. Booker lit up another big joint. We sat passing the joint back and forth until it was a little roach, my fingers had nothing else to hold on to. I set it in the ashtray on the desk.

He praised me over and over on the work that I did that day. He knew that I was a hard worker and he knew that praise was something that I craved. I always wanted to give my best. Hard work was instilled in me growing up from my mom, dad, and grandpa. Praise wasn't something that was often said to me. And, if it was, then there seemed to always be forty negative things that were said to me that countered the one positive.

"Ty, I have never seen anyone do the amount of work that you did today."

"Thanks, buddy. I'm glad that I can help you out."

Everyone who was going to help backed out on him at the last minute. Finding reliable people to do this work is tough. Even the most seasoned miscreants thought twice about putting themselves around such large operations. People were scared to stand in a pot patch this size. The pay wasn't that good and the consequences were high to place themselves in a situation where you were a sitting duck. All the control was taken away and we like to be in control.

Booker stood up and said, "Let's go see how Jill and Sam are doing, run down the road to a burger place, and eat."

After eating at the burger place we drove back to the farm. Once back at the farm, we took more THC oil and I took a few hits off the bong. "Let's go out to the building and I'll show you my other toy."

Booker turned on the lights, "Grab a box and let's go upstairs to the dry room."

In this room there was another work table with a machine set up at one end. We both stood in front of the work bench and set our boxes down. There sat another smaller machine that looked like a big pressure cooker, this thing had a grate, and rubber arms that tumbled the buds over the blades. A Trimpro Rotator Leaf Trimmer could do four pounds per hour. This machine was used for the final stages of the pruning and once the buds have gone through this machine they would be dried and put into vacuumed sealed bags ready for sale.

The machine was caked with hashish from all the resin and trichomes that built up. He had a Tupperware container that was full of balls of hash that he had cleaned off the machine from the buds from the indoor winter hydroponics grow. Booker opened the lid and handed me the Tupperware that was full of hash balls.

"Smell this shit," he said.

It smelled so good. I love hash. I always have, so, I was super excited about this process.

"You can take some hash home with you when you leave." We stood there, smoking hash, and watching the arms tumble the buds around and around in the machine.

"Looks like it's done," he said as he shut off the machine.

Then he opened the door and poured the buds out onto a drying rack. We could no longer do anymore work that evening, we were done. We walked up to the house after closing up the barn.

I called Keetah and we went back to the camper. I was exhausted from all of the THC that I put into my body, the stress, the labor, and the handfuls of pills that I took earlier in the day. Once I sat on the edge of the bed, I was done. Keetah climbed up onto the bed and licked my face.

Once my head hit the pillow, I could feel my body trembling from exhaustion. I had a brief moment of wondering if this was the right thing to be doing. I made sure my gun was next to me. My thoughts started getting stirred up in my mind and I began tracing the shapes of the dark camper, mentally tracing fingers over shapes for what seemed like hours. I wanted the thoughts to stop because I needed to rest, but my mind had a different plan. I screamed in silence to stop the madness in my brain that I thought was trying to kill me. I finally fell asleep.

Over the next two days, we continued this process of getting high, barely eating, and working ourselves to death until we had 90 percent of the harvest complete. We harvested A-Train, Purple Kush, Lemon Kush, Bubba Kush, White Widow, and Sour Diesel. I was completely blown away by the amounts of pot we just harvested.

The last morning I was there I said my goodbyes to Jill and Sam. Booker walked me out to the building and handed me two black duffle bags with sixty pounds of mid-grade pot that I had been selling for him and he told me, "This will be the last of the mid-grade pot, we will have to sell the pot we just harvested from now on." He handed me $500, a small baggie with some hash and one ounce of some good pot. I instantly was pissed as he explained that was the only cash that he had at the time.

If he could have heard my thoughts, he would have been afraid, and our friendship would have ended right there.

They went a little something like this, "Are you kidding, me you motherfucker? I should take my gun out of my bag and shoot you in the fucking ass and take all your pot and the $40,000 that we fucking counted out on my first night that I was here, fucker!

One-ounce, asshole? I wouldn't have even driven twelve fucking hours for an ounce of pot! Over the last three days work I had ten ounces that was stuck to the bottom of my fucking shoes while working in the building, prick, and you only give me one ounce!

"I paid almost one hundred twenty-five fucking dollars in gas, to get here and I still have to drive home, you son of a bitch! I could have pocketed all the hash when I was cleaning your machine and I didn't! I could have snuck out at night and carried ten fucking boxes of weed and hid it along the road and picked it up when I left and you would have never known, but I didn't you son of a bitch! This is the last of the mid-grade pot? Are you kidding me? I know there are warehouses full of this shit! Don't be such a selfish dick! You're a selfish motherfucker!

"I knew you and your partner would screw me! My fucking system has been working for years, you prick! And now, you are changing it? Fuck you and your partner! I risked everything for you! I want to punch you, now!"

But, instead, what actually came out my mouth was, "Pay me when you can. Thank you for the hash and pot. I'll sell your mid-grade pot and meet you for breakfast with your money next month. I had a lot of fun with you over the last couple days, my friend."

I really thought that I was going to get paid, but I didn't. I thought that everything was going to play out in my favor, but it didn't. This moment changed everything in our relationship.

I continued to jump through their hoops and play their game all while this festered inside of me making my resentments boil. The drive home was miserable. My brain raced with anger over the next twelve hours, plotting horrible plans. But, the reality was that I was broken inside and another father figure in my life had just hurt me. Once again, I would have died for this person and he would have left me to die if it benefited him. Yeah, nerves were hit and a giant crevice was cut in my heart. I can't believe that I let this happen again. Fuck it. I guess I am the one that should always get hurt.

This kind of shit had been brewing for over a couple years. He told me that he and The Boss were going to cut me in on some more of the dealings.

I should have seen this coming, but instead, I had trusted Booker and now he pulled this shit on me!

CHAPTER 39

North Dakota Pot Grow

Soon after my nuts were dipped into the black market pot-growing industry, it was time to step up my own grow. If I wanted to change my life financially, I needed to take the next step. And, honestly, with the predicament that I was in, I had no choice but to take the next step. I didn't just dip my nuts; I was going all in before I lost everything in my life. I had balls of steel, a hell of a work ethic, and nothing to lose. This made me the perfect candidate to dive deeper into their organization.

"Let's do it!"

After making many trips to Colorado during previous summers to work on the illegal pot grows, my preparation was complete. Booker had groomed me for the next step in my much bigger role that they had been planning. I say this because Booker had a lifetime criminal partner whom I hadn't met yet. I knew everything about The Boss, or so I thought anyway. I had been selling and transporting large amounts of pot for these guys for a few years. The trust was damaged on my end due to these guys jerking me around every chance they could. Now, it was my time to be in control of my future. It was my time to do the screwing!

I didn't trust The Boss, and I hadn't even met him, yet. We all had a plan, but there was their plan and then there was my plan.

I was living north of Bismarck on a beautiful piece of property that I was about to lose. I didn't want to lose it. This property was located in the middle of beautiful rocky buttes and had a million-dollar view. The gullies were loaded with natural springs that would sometimes run like a creek to a dugout that held thousands of gallons of clean water. This property was tucked away from the views of most roads. This was my little piece of heaven and I was willing to do whatever it took to not lose it. It felt like this new opportunity being presented to me was going to be the golden ticket to help me keep my land.

I was super excited about getting this going and was willing to take all the risks that were involved in order to have all the profits for myself. Booker and I set up a plan to have him and The Boss travel to North Dakota to visit my property on a Friday afternoon in the fall. We were going to prepare the prospected grow sites for the following pot-growing season. The week before their planned visit, I prepared everything that Booker asked me to. I went up the road to my neighbors and had him load two-year-old sheep shit onto my car trailer. I had gathered all of the tools that would be needed to get the job done for when they arrived. I had sold all of the pot and had all of their money ready for the next deal. Everything was complete!

I knew that they would have some coke and they were going to bring me a couple bales of pot so I wouldn't have to make the ten-hour drive to pick it-up. I had around ninety thousand dollars in cash for them as well. I was Jonesing, bad, for some coke and a little nervous to finally meet the Boss, because, in my mind, I had pictured this big, badass man because of all the trafficking stories and of him being a fugitive from the law for so many years. I could hear the vehicle coming over the hill in the early afternoon on this particular Friday. It's funny how we envision people into something that they are not even close to.

The truck stopped in front of my trailer. Both of the doors on the blue Chevy opened up at the same time as I rounded the corner on the outside of the trailer house. I was greeted with a big hug from Booker and then introduced to The Boss. He was a short little man with gray hair. I could have picked him up with one hand and threw him. This was a far cry from the badass that I had dreamed up in my mind. Don't get me wrong, he was a badass in his own right. The Boss stuck his hand out and I shook it. They spent the next ten minutes standing out by the truck petting Keetah and stretching off the twelve-hour drive. I had the trailer hooked to my truck with the sheep shit piled on the back. This impressed them that I was ready.

"Well, let's get to work boys!"

They both laughed. Booker said, "I told you he doesn't mess around!"

The Boss said, "Let me take a piss at least!"

He walked over to the light pole in the yard and took a piss behind it. I spent the next ten minutes explaining the lay of my land and let them know where all the neighbors were located. They asked me if anyone was expected to come out to the property that day, and I let them know that we were the only ones who would be there. I jumped on my four wheeler, drove down to the gate, shut it, and locked it to reassure them that no one would surprise us. Driving the four wheeler back up to the trailer, all I could think about was doing some coke.

Once I returned, we went into the trailer house and sat down in the living room. I went to the back room and got the ninety thousand in cash. I handed it to Booker and said, "It's all here, but count it!"

I watched them count out their money to make sure it was all there. It's a beautiful sight to see ninety thousand dollars covering the living room floor. It's always good practice when dealing with this kind of cash for everyone to come to an understanding that it's all there. During this time, The Boss had pulled out a glass vial with a couple grams of coke inside it. He also had a copper spoon that was shaped perfectly to fit inside the vial. It was used as a scooper to snort the coke. We all took some snorts.

Once the money was all counted and put away, The Boss said, "I have something for you."

We went out to the truck. He opened the tailgate and propped the topper door up with a wood stick. He climbed into the back of the pickup truck and slid two cardboard boxes towards Booker and me. We each grabbed a box and walked over to my outbuilding located behind my trailer house. This is where I kept all my illegal shit. We went inside and set the boxes down on the floor. I grabbed a box cutter off the workbench and cut them both open. Inside the boxes were five bales of marijuana that weighed about fifty pounds each. He let me know that four of the bales were for me to sell and the other bale The Boss would be back in a week to pick up.

During this whole time, the only thing that I could think about was the coke that was in his pocket. Two hundred and fifty pounds of pot sitting in front of me and the only thing that I cared about was snorting more coke. I did not want to look like too much of a drug addict, because I had an image to uphold. I tried my best to hide the fact that I was a coke pig. I put the bales of pot in my hiding spot in the rafters before we all walked out of the building. I locked the door behind me. The Boss pulled out the vial of coke and gave us each a couple more snorts before we started working. There was excitement and a little bit of fear running through me. The Boss climbed back into the truck and stuffed the ninety thousand dollars into another box that was positioned right behind the cab of the truck and sealed the box up tight with packaging tape. Booker and I walked over to the trailer that had the manure on it. He reached out and grabbed a handful of it and crumbled it up onto the trailer.

He was examining it and said, "This is some good shit, Ty."

We laughed at the pun. Booker pulled out a nice size joint and lit it up. He took five hits before passing it to me. I hit the joint a few times before passing it to The Boss. We all walked over to his truck and grabbed one bag of iron sulfate, a bag of lime, and four bales of sphagnum peat moss and set them on the back of the trailer with the manure. I went over to the trailer house and grabbed three shovels and a rake that I had lying next to my flower beds. Booker pulled his electronic Ph reader and stuck it in the soil. The Boss opened the peat moss and spread the bales over the manure as I mixed it in with a shovel. We continued to add the bags a little at a time as Booker continued to use his tester until the soil was to his liking. Booker was a master grower, so I always watched him with amazement, trying to learn each step of the process.

I went into the house, got a big water jug, and filled it with ice and water. It was ninety degrees out and not a cloud in sight. We all climbed into my truck that had the trailer with the manure hooked to the back. Booker and my dog Keetah were in the back seat. The Boss sat in the front seat and I drove. The Boss pulled out the vial of coke and passed it around. I stopped the truck in the bottom of a ravine to take my snorts. I was trying to control myself and not let them see me Jones for the coke. They both made it look glamorous when they would take their couple of snorts and stop. I wanted all the coke to myself and, if they weren't with me, I would have snorted the whole vial by now. They were both cocaine smugglers back in the seventies, making many trips by small plane to Columbia to pick up the product and bringing it back to the United States for distribution. It amazed me that they could stop after a couple snorts. We drove back through the fields and sat on top of the hill right above the water source on my property.

Booker said, "Looks like you have water, Ty. That's good."

The ravine that ran along the water source was covered with steep slopes, trees, and all kinds of thickets that you couldn't see through. We drove the truck down the side of the hill closer to the trees and stopped. We all climbed out of the truck. They both agreed that this was beautiful and that it was a perfect spot to set up a large-scale pot grow. They weren't wrong, it was the perfect set up that no one would ever expect.

Booker said, "This is going to make you a lot of money, Ty! So, how many plants do you want to shoot for?"

"I don't know. What do you think?"

"You could easily put a thousand plants or more on this property, but that would be pretty hard to take care of without a crew."

"I don't want anyone else out here on my property, so definitely a thousand is way too many to start out with."

The Boss let me know that he would be able to come to North Dakota throughout the season to assist me with the operation. I let them know that I would be willing to do a couple hundred plants to start out with. They both agreed that would be perfect.

We spent the next hour walking through the ravine scanning the ground looking at the different areas where the plants would go. The only thing that was a concern was how to keep the wildlife away from the plants. Booker said that we could get big cat urine from a company out of state, spray it all around the plants, and this would help with keeping the deer and rabbits away from the plants. We made our way back up to the truck and came up with our plan on how we were going to dig the holes. The Boss pulled out a clipboard with a blank piece of paper attached and made a quick drawing of the landscape so we could document where all the plants would go the following year.

The Boss pulled out the vial of coke and handed it to Booker. As he leaned his head into the truck, I could hear him take a couple snorts before handing it back to The Boss. He then walked over to the truck and leaned his head in and took a couple snorts. Then he walked back over and handed it to me. Booker had lit up a joint that they were passing back and forth. I went over to the truck, leaned into the door and took spoonful after spoonful as fast as I could shovel the coke into my nose. I handed the vial back to The Boss.

He held it up into the air and looked at it through the sun and said, "What the hell, Ty! Did you spill it?"

"No, I didn't spill it. I did it. You have more, right?"

"Well, of course we have more, but holy shit, you just snorted over a gram in like twenty-five seconds?"

"Yes, I did and is it wrong of me to already want more? I can't help it!"

We all sat there on the side of that hill laughing about all of the coke that I just did. The Boss handed me the vial and said, "You, mis' well finish it off."

They both watched me with amazement as I shoveled the rest of the coke up my nose. Then I took the vial and dumped the little bit into my mouth.

We each grabbed a shovel and went to work. We walked right down the hill from where the truck was parked. Booker was giving out orders on how far apart we needed to make the holes and how deep each hole had to be before we mixed in the manure. We hit some really nice dirt that was underneath the prairie grass, so it was easy to mix the manure in with the rich soil. We were about a hundred holes into it when all of a sudden we could hear an airplane approaching through the ravine to the west of us.

They both looked at me like, what the hell is this? We all stood on the hillside with shovels in our hand. Over the hill popped a small engine plane coming right at us through the ravine we were standing in. The Boss and Booker both ran down the hill into the trees and threw their shovels down and covered their faces. I didn't run because really this was my place and I was screwed no matter what. The plane flew back and forth through the ravine only about fifty feet off the ground. This didn't look good for me at all.

Booker said, "What the fuck, Ty! Do you know who this is?"

"No, I don't! I have never seen a plane fly through like this before!"

I stood there full of fear and uncertainty. My mind was picturing a SWAT team swarming my trailer and shed over the hill. Booker and The Boss hid in the trees until the plane finally flew away. The mood changed instantly. The look on these guys' faces was horror. Our plan for the day was over. I was already coming up with a plan to cover what we're doing. We were getting ready to plant trees to make the habitat for the wildlife better. Yeah that's it! Give me a trophy for doing my part in taking care of the earth. But then again, there was no way I could explain the ninety thousand in cash in the back of their truck and the two hundred and fifty pounds of pot in my shed.

Once the plane was out of sight, they came out of the trees, walked up to me, and asked me what that was at all about. I tried to reassure them that I had no clue what just happened and that I had never seen a plane fly over my property in all the years that I had lived here. They looked at me and asked me what I wanted to do. I said that I needed to be done for the day. The paranoia was running through me and I started to wonder if these two were being watched. I needed time to figure out what the hell was going on. I am sure they thought that I set them up and I was thinking, did someone follow them here because we were being investigated?

We got back into my truck and drove up to the trailer house and parked on the backside. You could cut the silence with a knife on that bumpy trail leading back up to the trailer house. The only thing that you could hear was the metal ramps bouncing around on the trailer. Once we were back at the house, I could see that their paranoia starting to set in.

The Boss climbed into the back of their truck to make sure that the cash was still there.

I looked at Booker and said, "Well this was an awkward first meeting for me and The Boss!"

Booker kind of chuckled. The two of them decided it was best if they left. I asked The Boss for some more of the coke since he just gave me enough to tease me. He went into their truck and came out and handed me an ounce of coke and said, "This is on me!"

"Thanks man! I really appreciate it, and I have no clue who was in that plane."

"That was messed up man, really messed up."

"It was nice to meet you, Boss Man."

"Same here, Ty. I'll call you in a week so I can pick up that extra bale of pot."

They got into Booker's truck and left. A few minutes later I could see them backing up over the hill. Booker's arm was hanging out the window waving me to come over to them.

Booker yelled, "The gate is locked."

I grabbed my keys, jumped on the four wheeler, sped down the driveway, unlocked the gate, and opened it. They drove out as fast as I could swing the gate open. I left the gate open to make it look as normal as possible. I drove the four wheeler back up the hill, past the trailer house, and back out to the trees. I picked up the shovels and rake that were left out there in all of the commotion. I returned to the trailer house and sat down on the couch wondering what just happened. I pulled the bag of coke out and snorted four giant lines. Finally, I was able to do as much coke as I wanted without being judged. I got a phone call from a number that I have never seen before, so I answered and it was Booker. He was calling me from a phone he just bought at Wal-Mart because he destroyed the other one that we communicated on. We went through twenty-five phones a year when we were at the peak of drug dealing. He asked me if everything was okay and if anything happened since they left. I told him no and that I haven't seen the plane or anyone else. He let me know that they would be leaving town and that we would be in touch.

This ended my chances of growing pot and saving my property. I lost everything and our relationship was back to these two being in full control. I later found out that the plane that flew over was a Game and Fish plane and they were probably counting the mule deer population for their records.

We were struggling to sell our land. I had talked with my neighbor up the road quite a few different times about buying the land. He continued to offer me less than what we were selling it for. He knew the predicament we were in and he intended on getting the best deal, but who wouldn't. It was getting down to the end where I thought we were going to have to declare bankruptcy and let the bank take the land back. I tried everything legal and illegal to make it work with no results. I thought what the hell, I may as well throw a Hail Mary, so I went up the road and pulled into my neighbor's yard.

"Hey, are you still interested in the land?"

"I'm always interested in that land."

"Well, we have some people who are putting an offer in on it this evening and their offer is ten thousand dollars more than what we are asking. But, they are from out of state and they are planning on putting up a housing development."

"We don't need a damn housing development out here."

"I agree! It's too nice out here for a development!"

"This is farmland and grazing pasture out here, not yuppy town."

"If you pay me what we are asking, I will decline their offer. It will be worth it to me to sell it to someone for less just so it doesn't get developed and ruined!"

"It's a deal, Tyler! I will buy it for your asking price. I will go to the bank tomorrow and get everything in order. "

"Ok. It's a deal."

I was super pissed off and sad that this day had come, but relieved that we now wouldn't have to let it go back to the bank. I made the whole story up. There was never anyone who was putting an offer in on the property. I threw the Hail Mary and he caught it. I can't believe my plan worked. I called up Addison and let her know what I did. I could hear the relief in her voice that this battle was finally over.

CHAPTER 40

The Move To Slipping

Once the sale of our land was complete and the divorce was finalized, I desperately needed a place to live. My mom always had her door open for me to move back in like I had done time after time over my life when things fell apart. I didn't want to move in with her because I always felt like a failure and a burden. Everything that I was part of went good for a while then it would crumble before my eyes. My mom never made me feel like a failure. She supported me and showed me love, even when the world was crashing down around me and everyone else was running from me.

My dog Keetah was my biggest priority. I knew that she was always welcome at my mom and dad's house. When my dad was alive, he loved my dog. This was a crazy thing to watch because my dad didn't care for dogs all that much. He would always want Keetah by his side. He would rock in his recliner for hours with her sitting next to his chair. He would pet her with every rock of the chair.

"If all dogs were like Keetah I would get three of them." My dad and mom had a special bond with her. Keetah girl was a great dog, one of a kind.

I decided to move into my mom's shop right to the north of the house. The shop was a 30'x 40' shop with two garage doors and one walk-in door. The shop was a blue and white metal building with a cement floor. My mom was in the process of trying to sell her house. The shop was the best place for me. I was still struggling each day, fighting my disease of addiction, and trying to cope with losing my wife and our land. Most days I was losing. I was a complete wreck. I was working at the Capitol building taking care of the Capitol grounds. I commuted to work daily. My mom's place was closer to town than the place that we just sold by ten miles, so the shorter commute was welcomed, and it also saved on gas.

I stayed in the shop most of the summer. I was really working hard at trying to remain sober, but I was failing miserably most days. I was not quite ready to give up the things that meant the most to me. These things were my friends, drug dealing, pot, my negative attitude, and my love for excitement. I was barely surviving. My heart was broken, and the pain was overwhelming most days.

I moved all my belongings into the shop. I placed my box spring and mattress on top of a piece of plastic to protect them from the dirty cement floor. I placed all the boxes of my belongings inside and placed them around my bed. I was just happy that I was able to get all my things after the divorce. Well, most of my things anyway. I had to leave a lot of shit out on that property, because I was not able to find a place to store it. I had all the things that meant the most to me. I had a mini fridge that I kept my soda and some food in. I had a microwave set up on the floor next to my bed that I cooked my boxed meals in. I was living the bachelor's life. I would wake up in the morning and hit the button on the garage door opener and I had a beautiful view of country life. In the evenings, I would hang out in the garage tinkering around with different projects that I was helping my mom out with. I moved all of the boulders that I had been collecting over the years to the tree rows behind the shop.

My rocks were something that I could never have left behind. There was this one rock that I once could lift, but at this time in my life I was defeated and broken. The strength that I once had was depleted. This rock was in my flower bed in front of my trailer house. It weighed about three hundred pounds. This thing was a beautiful piece of granite with a quartz ring that protruded out of the tip. It was filled with greys, greens, and pinks. It still breaks my heart that I couldn't pick it up to bring with me. I think about this rock often and it still hurts my heart today. I fell in love with it years prior on a job site. I just had to have it, so instead of placing it in the yard we were working at, I picked it up with the skid steer and drove over to my truck and tried to slowly dump this rock into the box as carefully as I could before my boss saw me. Yes, I was stealing the rock. As I was dumping it in the box of my truck it slid out of the bucket faster than I intended and it bounced off the bottom of the box and slammed into the top of the bed rail, crushing it. I was sick to my stomach looking at my truck, but happy that I was able to get the rock. Screw the damage, it was only a truck.

Looking back on it, I regret stealing this rock and cursing something so beautiful. I know now that I should have never stolen anything so beautiful and sacred. First things first, I deserved the damage done to my truck. Second, Karma is a bastard. Third, the rock was never meant to be, and finally don't ever cloud up the mojo of your garden with stolen rocks. It's not worth the pain and suffering that comes with it. Images of that rock will always pass through my mind as a reminder of a valuable life lesson. There were so many hard life lessons.

I was still making my forty-five day runs back and forth. Dropping money off, picking up drugs, selling drugs, collecting money, driving, and starting the whole cycle over again. I had to deal drugs because I needed the money to stay afloat and my drug addiction was out of control at times. This was my identity. I thought this was the only way of life for my future. I was smoking pot daily and taking large amounts of THC oil to cope with all my pain, both physically and emotionally. If I could only just smoke pot and stay away from all the other drugs, I would be fine, life would be perfect. I was wrong. It was harder than hell to stay sober when I had a hundred pounds of pot stuffed in boxes that surrounded my bed. It's difficult to stay away from drugs when you deal with addicted people daily. It's a heck of a time to remain sober when you have unresolved issues that you didn't even know existed.

CHAPTER 41

The Governor And The Deep Freeze

I had a 2002 Jeep Wrangler at the time, and it was giving me troubles. I could not afford to pay someone to fix it. The ignition switch was broken inside the steering column. I had been up for about a week straight, high on meth. I had my Jeep pulled into the garage. I had all my tools lined up on the floor. I was going to fix this ignition switch myself. One thing about meth is that it sure helps you take shit apart, but the struggle is real when you try putting it back together.

I had worked on it for two days straight. On day two I had the seats out. I managed to put a new alternator on. I had most of the steering column out. Shit was getting really confusing. I was going a million miles per hour, but I was going backwards. Nothing was making sense. I was paranoid. I was hearing voices talk to me. I thought people were sneaking up on the house to harm me. I was convinced that the SWAT team would kick in my door any time now. My anxiety was running high. I still couldn't figure out how to fix the ignition switch. I figured out that if I used a screwdriver, I didn't need a key.

"Screw it."

Screwdriver it is! I was isolating from people so they wouldn't see that I was high again. I had spent those two days and three nights scrambling around in that garage spinning my wheels trying to put the Jeep back together again. This was a struggle. I had so many nuts and bolts left over when I was done that I just put them in a gallon Ziplock baggie for another day to deal with.

My mom had given me a heads-up earlier in the week letting me know that someone might be coming out this particular weekend to buy a used deep freeze that she had in the basement. I cleared a path through the snow around to the backside of the house to the patio door for easy access to the freezer. I was prepared so whoever came out could get this deep freezer deal over with as quickly as possible. I didn't want to deal with anyone for too long of a period because of the drugs and paranoia.

My phone rang. This startled me. I struggled to answer it. I was too high to answer the phone. Okay, I have to answer the phone. The caller ID says Mom. Here I go.

"Hello."

"Tyler, it's Mom."

"Hi, Mom."

"Tyler, I sold the deep freeze. They are going to pick it up in an hour. Are you out at the house?"

"I am working on the Jeep in your garage, so I will be here."

"The Governor is going to be coming out with his son. They will help you load it. They will be paying with a check for $50."

"Okay, I'll be here."

"Love you, Tyler."

"Love you, too, Mom."

I hung up the phone and started to panic for a moment until I pulled myself together. I thought that my mom was just being funny. My dad used to always say that "It was the Governor" whenever someone would call. It was always funny when he would say stuff like that, so I thought my mom was just making a joke. No big deal. I will hold my shit together when they show up and get this deep freezer deal done, loaded up, and then they can leave.

I had not slept for five days. No showering in at least three days and I was still wearing my work clothes under my coveralls. I looked rough. I had black rings around my eyes. My face was sunken in from not eating, except for two bites of a cheeseburger from Mc Donald's that I had to force down with soda. Just looking at me screamed drug addict. I continued to work on my Jeep over the next hour.

I heard a vehicle pull into the yard and then heard a knock on the door. I had a million different scenarios of who it might be.

"Is it the cops?" I composed myself before I went to open the door. I unlocked the door and pulled it open. There were three men who were very nicely dressed standing outside of the door. I walked out and shut the door behind me to hide the chaos that was in the garage. What the hell? It was Governor John Hoeven. I was instantly met with handshakes and introductions.

"This is my son, Jack." He introduced the third guy, but his name slips my mind at this time.

"We are here to pick up the deep freeze that we are buying from Cindy."

"I am Tyler, Cindy's son."

"Nice to meet you," the Governor said.

"I have met you before."

"You have?"

"Yes, I work on the grounds crew at the Capitol. I take care of your snow in the winter and your lawn and yard in the summer. You walk by me a couple times per week." Awkward silence.

"I will have to pay better attention next time I leave the house."

The only time this guy ever said hi to any of us on the grounds crew was around re-election time. A couple other guys from the grounds crew and I were working on sprinkler lines in front of the Governor's residence and John walked over and said, "Looks nice guys," and tried to shake our hands, but none of us were having it. We knew he was just playing the politician role to get a vote for re-election. I kind of felt bad that we all gave him the cold shoulder. I voted for him and thought that he was a good governor. He had walked by me a hundred times never saying a word to me. But, I guess, why did I think that I was that special. He was a busy man.

"The freezer's in the basement. We have to go around back to the patio door and haul it out that way."

"We'll help you."

My brain was tripping out. I couldn't believe that it was the Governor. I couldn't believe that the Governor was buying a used freezer from my mom.

We walked around the back of the house to the patio door. They helped me carry the deep freeze up around the backside of the house and then we loaded it in the back of their Suburban. They wanted to take pictures with me. This really freaked me out. The paranoia was too much. I thought that this was a set up. The cops and the Governor are here to get information on me. Was I being watched by the FBI? Holy shit! I was hallucinating that drones were hovering above us taking pictures. Everything was really strange.

I posed for the pictures standing next to the Governor. What I wouldn't give for that picture today. To see my dumb ass all strung out on meth posing with the governor. We said our goodbyes and they left. I was really pissed off at my mom because she didn't tell me that it was the actual Governor. Well she did tell me. I just thought it was the fake governor that my dad talked about all the time. Holy shit. Talk about screw my high up.

I went into the house, and I sat by the window for the next five hours straight. I was smoking meth with my pistol by my side thinking someone was going to be coming out to get me any time now because the Governor told them what I was up to. I called my mom up and chewed her ass out for not clarifying that it was actually the real Governor who was coming out to buy the freezer. I spent the rest of the day trying to put my Jeep back together. Seeing the Governor show up to my doorstep was very traumatic and caused paranoia over the next two weeks. Let's clarify this, the Governor didn't cause paranoia, it was actually the meth that I was consuming that caused the paranoia. I was convinced that I was being watched. I was telling people that he was out at my house watching me. I can't imagine what they thought. I am sure they thought that I was lying and that the Governor was not at my house. I was not lying; he was there and there was a picture floating around somewhere to prove it. The FBI probably has my photo on a board somewhere tying me to all of the other drug dealings that I was involved in. Shit!

PART V

Lost

At this point in my life, I was lost. I had lost everything. And, the things that I did have felt like I would lose them at any moment. Everything was up in the air and I wasn't quite sure if I wanted to give up or start over again. My heart was breaking and my identity that I had come to know was changing. I had heard a saying that you either feel enough pain and decide to change or you die, and I was right on the edge. Pain wasn't something that I could handle anymore. But, I slowly began to listen to my pain and the changes did start to come.

CHAPTER 42

Due Date

Addison's due date was getting closer.

I got a call from her telling me that she would be having her twins the following day. I offered to come up and support her, but she declined my offer and said that she will do this on her own with her family there. I went to the flower shop and I ordered some roses that she could have in her room next to her while she had her babies. I was a bundle of nerves because the woman whom I still loved was having someone else's babies. I was not able to be there for her and walk this path with this girl who I once called my soul mate. I was not able to stand next to her bed and hold her hand as she gave birth to our babies that we had dreamt about for years.

She called me up and let me know that she had her babies. I congratulated her and she thanked me for the beautiful flowers.

"Tyler, will you please come to the hospital?"

"Yes, I can come to the hospital. What do you need?"

"I need you to come and sign a form to relinquish all of your parental rights for the twins so Tim can sign the birth certificate."

Silence.

"Ok, I will come down."

"The sooner the better, Tyler!"

This Tim guy was at the hospital with her supporting her. He was getting ready to sign the birth certificate, but he couldn't because there is a law in North Dakota that says you have to be divorced for a certain amount of time before parental rights don't have to be signed away. This birth happened to fall in this time frame, so this signature needed to happen. Now, I needed to find the strength to go to the hospital and sign over my parental rights. I knew from doing the math in my head from the last time that we had sex that the kids were not even close to being mine. My brain kept telling me that these kids were mine and that now by signing these papers I was abandoning my kids. My brain was trying to kill me once again. I wanted kids so bad. This was one of the hardest things that I have ever had to do in my entire life. I drove around that hospital for an hour crying uncontrollably racing every scenario through my mind. I was feeling all of the hurt from the last nine months.

Finally, I got up the nerve to walk into the hospital and ask for the nurse. She came down to the lobby. We sat on one of the couches by the reception desk. She had a brown clipboard with a piece of paper hooked to it with a blue pen in her hand.

"You must be Tyler?"

"Yes, I'm Tyler."

She stuck her hand out to shake mine. The tears started pouring out of my eyes.

"Are you okay, Tyler?"

"I'm okay! This is just the hardest thing that I have ever had to do in my entire life. Me and this girl were once in love, actually madly in love, and we had giant dreams to have a family of our own!"

"I'm so sorry, Tyler."

"It's okay. Hand me that pen and show me where to sign."

She handed me the pen and pointed to the line.

"Sign here."

I took a deep breath and wiped the tears from my eyes with my forearm and I signed my name and the date. I handed the nurse the pen and the clipboard back and said, "Thank you."

"I hope you are okay, Tyler. It takes a strong man to do something like this."

"Thank you. I don't feel strong right now. I feel broken and weak!"

"Well, I see a strong man that deserves a beautiful life in his future."

"Thank you so much for your kind words! Have a beautiful day."

I walked out of that hospital not quite sure of what I did, but I knew that I had to do it. Now Addison and Tim can move on with their lives. I went through many different emotions that evening. I did feel a little bit free, but only for a moment. I wondered what Tim thought about the flowers on the ledge in her room from her ex-husband while she was having his babies. I felt horrible that I sent flowers. I wouldn't have if I would have known that he was in her life.

Maybe I was not man enough to give her babies. This really hurt me because I was confused and trying to figure out who I was as a person. I felt like a failure that I was not able to give her the one thing that she wanted.

Over the course of that year, I was tested and failed daily, but I was starting to put some of my pain and personal issues in the past. This was definitely the year of closure for many things. They all hurt, but there was some healing that came out of all of it. I stopped pointing the finger and started to take the blame for my part in all of this mess. No matter how hard the things were that I went through, there was always good in everything if I slowed down and opened my eyes. I tried my best to send positive energy to those I had hurt in the past. I was owning up to the fact that this was the year for me to hurt and change.

CHAPTER 43

I Survived For This Miracle

Once I started to finally get some sobriety under my belt, I experienced a summer of flowers consuming me. I spent that whole summer out in the open not afraid of pulling out the gift of discovering beauty in flowers, a gift I had stuffed away for many years. Being able to be myself and loving flowers was life changing. During this time, I was working at the state Capitol grounds as a grounds crew worker. In the springtime, the Capitol grounds were in full bloom. I had spent previous years on these same grounds and had never seen the miracle like I witnessed that summer.

There was life bursting with beauty all around me. For some reason, during this growth in my many attempts at sobriety, I started to notice it all happening. From the littlest buds on the branches to the green shoots of the day lilies that were poking out of the dirty leaves after the long, cold winter. I watched the flowers grow every minute of every day. I was able to see the miracle that was snuffed out by drugs and alcohol addiction.

I was on top of the world, surrounded by the most magical, beautiful feelings that I have ever felt in my entire life.

I was racing back and forth through the Capitol grounds checking on each plant as if it was going to be the last day I would ever get to see that flower. I cherished every moment with all of the plants and bushes on the grounds. We hired summer help each year to assist with the care of the grounds. Some of the summer help got dragged into my flower obsession. I remember the look on their faces of, "Wow, dude. Are you ok?" when I would point out all the beauty that was happening around us. But, they just weren't ready to see the beauty that I was experiencing. I pushed it on them anyway. I think they thought maybe that I was a little crazy! In fact, I know they thought I was crazy, because I am. They would tell me daily, "There is something wrong with you, Tyler!"

The flowers on flowering crabapple trees are definitely a life changer for me. I love the white ones; the light pink ones and the dark purple ones are my favorite. The Capitol grounds are covered with pinks, purples, and whites for a few weeks in the spring. There is a bigger grove of mostly purples and pinks with one or two whites to the east of the Capitol building. You can smell their sweet aroma from blocks away. I loved it when the grass would get long so I had a great reason to spend a whole hour under their beauty mowing the lawn. I could spend hours under those trees. I have had some life changing moments under those trees, looking at their beauty and watching them change. The best is when these trees are at their fullest bloom and the colorful petals start to fall. There is nothing more magical to me than watching it rain pink, purple, and white flower petals. The ground is covered in color. I would stand under these trees and watch in silence as the petals fell to the ground all around me. I loved how they would catch the different wind currents as they spun and floated to the ground.

Sometimes, I couldn't even wait until the flowers would fall. I would take the backpack blower, start it up, put it over my shoulders, stand under the trees and aim the blower spout up at the trees. I would blow the flowers off the trees and then I would shut off the blower and watch it rain pink flowers all around me. I felt like I was in heaven. It made me feel like that little kid again who dreamed of finding a valley in the mountains that was covered in wildflowers and spending the rest of my life there. I would even run into the smaller trees with the riding lawn mower to knock the flowers loose just so I could see them float to the ground. When I would tell people about these experiences that I was having, I would burst out with excitement. I couldn't take my eyes off these trees during their time of blooming.

One day, I was blowing the entrance to one of the main doors of the Capitol building clean of debris like I had done almost every day during the summers. The area was full of pink and white trees that were in full bloom. I started the backpack blower up and I blew it up into one of the pink flowering trees, knocking the petals off the tree just to watch the beautiful flowers fall out of the sky, raining down on top of me. There was a lady walking into the building. She was a fancy lady who was wearing high heeled shoes and she was dressed very nicely. I stopped blowing the flowers off the tree when I saw her, in fear of getting turned in for messing around.

She stopped on the sidewalk and watched me. I was not sure what she was thinking until she pointed at me and waved in a gesture that suggested that she wanted to come stand by me under the tree that was full of pink flowers and the ground blanketed with petals. I nodded my head in a yes-come-here motion. She walked over and stood shoulder to shoulder with me on the grass and dirt. I thought that she was going to sink in with her heels, but she didn't. We looked at each other as the blower was idling and she said "Do it!" I hit the gas button on the blower, revving it to full force then aimed the blower spout up into the tree, knocking the beautiful pink petals off of the branches. I shut the blower off and we watched the pink petals rain down on top of us. The smile that was on her face is one that I will never forget.

She looked at me and said, "Thank you!" She walked away into the building.

I have never seen that lady since that day, but we will always have that moment in common that bonds us forever. I think she was an angel sent to me to show me that other people cared, even the fancy ones.

I used to cry when the rains would come during the crabapple blooming season, because I knew that it would be the end of them. The raindrops would suck the life right out of the big beautiful blooms. I would pray that the rain would miss us so I could see the blooms one more time. Today, when I look at a flowering crabapple tree I am not afraid of the rain because I cherish every second like it's my last moment on this earth. Nothing lasts forever. That is why we need to grab life with both hands and love it like it's our last chance to do so.

During my lunch hours and on my breaks, I would take a five-gallon pail out to the peonies patch when they were blooming. I would turn the pail upside down and sit down on it in the middle of the patch. The smell was stunning and the colors were breathtaking. Pinks, purples, and whites. Each bloom was the size of a small paper plate. I would lose myself during this time. It was better than doing drugs. I was feeling high and it wasn't messing up my life. People would drive by and I didn't care about the voices that still haunt me today about how a man should be. If someone called me a little queer pussy for loving flowers, I would think about punching them in the head! Actually, I would get up from my bucket and drag them away from the flowers so when I open-hand slapped them, they wouldn't hurt the blooms when they hit the ground. I was taking it all in and the real me was showing up to my life and I liked it.

The Governor's residence always had the most beautiful flowers. I used to love it when there was a job to do over at the Governor's house so that way I could take the opportunity to look at the beautiful flowers in the backyard. I was in love with every single flower that bloomed. In the springtime, along the stacked sandstone wall, the tulips would bloom. This was the first sign that flower season was here. These tulips were the brightest reds, yellows, whites, and purples that I had ever seen. They were huge.

I loved to look into the center of these tulips. The ovary was green with the pistil that shot straight up in a translucent creamy color which was topped with the black furry looking stigma. The smallest, most intricate details popped out at me. I wish that I could crawl inside of the tulip and go for a walk. The Asiatic lilies were amazing, actually one of my favorites. I love the orange ones the best. You know, the ones with the black spots. The begonias were breathtaking and made my heart melt every time I would get down onto my knees to take a closer look. The Governor's yard was under constant surveillance, but I didn't care. And, honestly, I couldn't help myself. There was no holding back this excitement.

On the south side of the highway building, there was a yellow rose bush that was the most brilliant yellow that I had ever laid eyes on. The yellow was so bright that it hurt my eyes, but I still looked every chance that I got. Different rose bushes surrounded two sides of the highway building. I have spent a lot of time looking at these beautiful roses and smelling them. I had brilliant and amazing feelings when I stuck my nose in a rose and took a big whiff! I felt serenity and a peace that everything was going to be okay, even though my life was shattering all around me. I can't even explain using words what these flowers did for me, but it was a change in my life that I never thought was possible.

I hated God at this time and flowers made me look at this hate in a different way. I no longer looked at God through the eyes of other humans, because most of them really wrecked it for me. But, instead I looked at God through a spiritual sense and the wonder and amazement came rushing back when I let myself go completely into flowers.

I was completely addicted to flowers. Cross addiction is when you quit one drug and switch to another drug. It was always easy for me to quit coke when I could switch to meth. This time was different. This time I switched to flowers and there was nothing easy about this switch, but it was definitely the most rewarding. Throughout my life, I have gardened at all my different homes. The bad thing about flowers is that it takes years to establish beautiful plants and most of the time I didn't have years. I have had to walk away from two different gardens because of poor decisions on my part and that has always been a big regret of mine. It is difficult to walk away from my flower gardens because I was in love with them. My heart aches just thinking about the plants that I started and had to abandon.

CHAPTER 44

Mending My Broken Heart

My life was in shambles and my understanding of a healthy relationship was consumed with negative experiences. The role models in my life struggled at relationships. They actually could have written a book on what not to do in a relationship. I was following the trend that was being set all around me. I swear everyone thought that divorce was the answer to their marital problems. I was grasping at straws. My heart wanted so much more, but I couldn't give it at this time without help.

During my drug and alcohol treatment at Saint Alexius, I was put into a dual diagnosis treatment program for my many disorders and diagnoses. My counselor, Brita, could see the turmoil that I was going through daily. The turmoil wasn't just from the drugs and alcohol, it was also coming from my broken heart. Brita suggested that I sign up for Beginning Experience in the fall. Beginning Experience is a group for people with a broken heart. People who suffered a loss to death, divorce, or separation. The program focused on how to love one's self after going through such losses, in hopes that we can come through our pain and love ourselves.

"Tyler, you should attend Beginning Experience this fall to help you with the grieving process from your losses."

"Brita, I'm good."

"Tyler, it will help you, but if you sleep with anyone in this group it will wreck everything."

I heard through the grapevine that people slept around with one another in these different grief groups for broken hearts. I guess if your bike gets stolen, the only way to get over your loss is to go buy a new bike. Brilliant, this might actually work. This definitely piqued my interest. I was lonely, broken, and I thought what the hell, sleeping around sounds kind of fun. The only problem was that they met at a church and it was a God program. I wasn't ready for this, but living with a broken heart was a lot scarier than the whole God thing.

Daily I cried, sobbing about how bad I missed my ex-wife and telling everyone about my broken heart.

My heart was shattered in a million different pieces. Once Brita planted the seed of Beginning Experience it started to grow. Something had to change if I would have any chance at remaining sober. I signed up for the group and went to the church that evening and walked through the doors not quite knowing what was in store for me over the next two years. Once I found a seat, I started looking at all the faces. I could see the brokenness in each person. We all had different reasons why our hearts were broken, but we all decided that it was time to pick up the pieces again. Everyone in the room was much older than me except for two gals who instantly caught my eye. They were pretty and about my age. My counselor Brita's words of wisdom instantly popped in my head: "Tyler, it won't help you if you sleep with anyone in this group. It will wreck everything."

Brita was right. I was here for help, not to cause any more issues in my life. I wanted the help and desperately needed it more than I knew. We all sat around in a big circle. There were about thirty of us. We introduced ourselves and told the group why we were there. Most of us were there because of divorce and some were there due to losing a loved one to death.

I scanned the room wondering which women were there just for some sex. I really didn't want to have sex with anyone at this time. My confidence was at an all-time low. My brain was thinking about having sex with some of these women to better cope with my fears. If I thought about inappropriate things, and I did, I wouldn't have to look at my issues, and my issues ran deep. I just used the sex thing as a coping mechanism to deal with all the hurt that I was feeling inside.

I walked out of the church that evening feeling a little bit better than when I walked in. I realized that my heart was not alone and that there were a bunch of people just like me who were going through the same kind of pain. I started my journey alone and now I had a group of people whom I didn't know personally, but I did know their hurt. We bonded that first night.

Over the following weeks, I made friendships that were bonded for life. Pain is a beautiful thing when it is brought together in a safe environment.

One night we were separated into smaller groups to work on our broken hearts. One woman I recognized from the hospital, but I didn't know her name. She was one of the younger girls who I noticed that first night at BE. She was a nurse at one of the local hospitals. Years prior, I had ended up having to go to the hospital because I took too many drugs. I tested positive for everything under the sun. If it was an illegal substance, I tested positive for it. This tiny brunette nurse came in. She was wearing a white doctor's coat. She had a clip board with all of my information on it and the drug screen results. She stood next to my bed where I was laying, and she chewed me out, up and down.

"Tyler, you are positive for cocaine, methamphetamine, heroin, benzodiazepines, alcohol, and marijuana."

I looked her in her eyes and said, "No, that has to be wrong. I only had a couple beers and a tiny line of coke. The heroin and meth must have been cut in with the coke. Yeah, I smoke pot to deal with anxiety."

I could see the fear she had in her eyes as she looked at me with disbelief.

"You are going to die, Tyler. If you continue down this path, you will die."

I knew that there was a good chance that I was going to die. This had been my reality for a long time, but for a brief moment in time I believed her when she said it to me. She made a huge difference in my life. Sometimes, people do things for other people and you don't see the effects for years. I knew that I needed to stop. I tried. I just couldn't.

That night at BE when we separated into smaller groups, the tiny brunette that chewed my ass up and down sat in my group, sitting across the table from me. I looked at her with amazement that our paths had crossed in a much different setting. I told her how much of a difference she made in my life by doing what she did that day in the hospital. We ended up becoming friends and healthy supports for one another.

The time came to participate in the weekend retreat that BE offered. It was an action-packed weekend full of healing and releasing all of the negative energy that we were carrying around inside. I hated God during this time in my life, but I tolerated people around me who were believers. The Richardton Abbey is a beautiful facility that is breathtaking. The beautiful architecture and the stained glass blew me away. I felt some things that weekend that truly changed my life forever. I can look back on it today and I am able to see that it was a God thing. God was with me even when I hated him and pushed him away.

I shed many tears and released anger that had been built up for years. I didn't understand the pain that I was carrying around with me my whole life. From this moment forward was when the healing started. On one of the days we wrote letters to the people who had hurt us. The people who had affected us in a negative way. I wrote a letter to my ex-wife and my dad. I wrote in the letters how I really felt inside and the damage they had caused me. My words were real and raw. I was able to say things that I never thought were possible. Once our letters were complete, we read them out loud to the people in our groups.

That evening in the chapel of the abbey we made our peace with the feelings that we wrote down on those pieces of paper. We then placed these letters in metal buckets and discarded them forever. I felt a lot of things change at that moment. I felt like I took some of my power back. I had an out-of-body experience. I felt light, as if all my pain was gone for a moment. I allowed God to enter me for a moment, or should I say that God was always with me. I just pushed him away with everything that I had because I was not ready.

The weekend was over and we were all exhausted. Our bond was stronger than ever. I continued to work on myself and progress through the groups that BE offered. I felt myself getting stronger and more confident. My relationships were getting stronger with some people and with others relationships were ending. I set my bar higher and let people into my life who were healthier. I was learning what I needed in my friendships and who I was as a person for future intimate relationships. I went from hating myself to slowly learning to love myself. I was learning to accept other people and allow them into my life. I learned how to be a friend and the different levels of friendship. Setting healthy limits and boundaries became my norm. I treated myself with respect. I started this process full of ego, grandiose ideas, and self-hatred. I blossomed into something beautiful even though it only lasted for a short period of time before my demons came creeping back into my life.

CHAPTER 45

Enough Is Enough

Will I ever figure this out?! I couldn't stay sober if my life depended on it. And, my life did depend on it. I was dying and I couldn't stop. Meth and pain pills were strangling me and I was hoping they would just put me out of my misery. Treatment after treatment, I could have written the book on how to not stay sober. I was feeling broken enough to give this sobriety thing another chance. I needed to go all in and all out on a lot of things in my life that were keeping me stuck. I had felt enough pain to make the change. The look on people's faces who are in recovery are beautiful and peaceful. And I wanted that so bad.

I decided to go all in on the whole recovery thing. The two years prior I hadn't been ready. I thought that I could get high occasionally and be okay. I thought that I could sell drugs and not do them. That's a lie that I was telling myself. I was a drug addict and my life was completely out of control. The pain was too much. I was dope sick daily, even when I was on drugs. After many failed attempts to normalize my drug use, I was finally broken enough to give up on the thought that I could control my drug use. I was no longer in control of my out-of-control normal life. I no longer did drugs, I was drugs. Drugs were my everything, they stripped me of my soul, both physically and emotionally. I was shattered into pieces. Even the broken pieces were gone.

I was able to string together two months of sobriety and maybe three months, if I fudged the truth by a day or two. I was so miserable that I thought about dying daily. I was unsure if I wanted to go through this life any longer. I attended a community support group on a regular basis over the previous year, so I was doing one thing right anyway. I wasn't able to see any of the changes in my life that were happening and I sure didn't feel any of the things that the program promised.

The people at the meetings bugged me when they would talk about gratitude and serenity and how wonderful their lives were now without drugs and alcohol. The whole "God thing" really pissed me off and some days if the topic was going to be on a God step, I would leave the meeting. I would find every way possible to sabotage any chances that I had at making changes in my life to find happiness. It was scary to change and to face all the shit from my past that haunted me. Drugs helped me stuff all that hurt deep down inside. My recovery sucked because when you only put in half of the work, you only get out half of the rewards. I just needed to show up, sit down, and listen. Then I needed to leave the meeting and practice the principles in all of my affairs. Yeah, yeah, yeah, sounds easy, but it's not.

Pot has never caused any problems in my life, even though I was risking my freedom daily by moving large amounts of pot and some occasional coke. No big deal. Pot was the only coping skill that I had, and I was using it daily to cope with all of my underlying issues. I was even getting high and going to my community support group. I had a few different people at the meetings who started to believe in me even though I didn't believe in myself. My family's long-time friend, Scott, started to support me and help me figure this crazy-ass life out. Scott and his wife, Marvis, were my only sober friends at the time. Our friendship grew stronger and Scott and I supported each other through our attempts at this whole sobriety thing. I was keeping a big secret from them and I needed to keep it sealed up tight, but it was starting to weigh on me.

I wanted to tell Scott that I was deep in the black market, but I was afraid of the possibility that our friendship would be lost if I said anything. I was living a double life and it was making me sick. They say that our secrets keep us sick and that is so true.

CHAPTER 46

The Truth Comes Out

Scott was helping me out one day with getting my Jeep to the shop to get fixed. He met me at the shop and gave me a ride out to my mom's house where I was staying. I made sure to clean my pot out of my Jeep when I left it at the shop. I had my wooden dugout and a one hitter shoved in my pocket. My dugout was a dark walnut piece of wood that had a slide off lid with two holes, one for pot and the other hole for the metal pipe that only held one hit of pot. The dugout was a little smaller than an iPhone 6. Scott and I drove out to mom's house in Scott's vehicle. We parked in the driveway. I grabbed my gloves and hat and, as I was getting ready to get out of his vehicle, my dugout fell out of my pocket into his cup holder. I heard the wood hit the plastic and I panicked. But, before I could reach for it, Scott grabbed it and held it up into the air and looked at me and said, "What's this?"

My mind thought of a hundred different lies and they all made perfectly good sense to me. I wanted to tell him that it had a match box car inside of it or a knife, but instead of relying on all of my lies I told him the truth.

"You know what it is, Scott."

He handed it back to me.

"How long have you been smoking this shit, Tyler?"

"Twenty-three years."

"So, you haven't been sober?"

"Kind of. It's just a little bit of pot. I haven't been doing pills or meth."

"Tyler, this shit is going to keep you stuck."

Scott was right. It was keeping me stuck. I felt so ashamed that I had been lying to the one person who had my back. I felt little and broken at this moment, so I took the opportunity to come clean all the way.

"Scott, I have been selling pot and coke to stay alive financially."

"How much pot are you selling?"

"Hundreds of pounds."

"Holy shit, Tyler. Don't tell me anymore. I don't need to know about any of that shit."

"Sorry, buddy. I'll stop smoking it and give the sobriety thing a real chance."

"I'm here for you, Tyler."

"Sorry I have been lying to you and everyone else."

"I forgive you! Now get that shit out of my vehicle!"

"Thanks for the ride. I'll call you later."

Scott drove away and I went into the house, sat down on the floor and tried to process the disappointment that I was feeling inside. Now what? I was caught. I felt horrible that I let Scott down. I needed to do something different. I got up off the floor and went out to the garage. I grabbed a hammer out of my toolbox and went outside to the driveway. I pulled my dugout out of my pocket and set it on the snow packed driveway and beat it into tiny pieces with the hammer until it was unrecognizable. I grabbed the snow shovel and scooped up the broken wood pieces and the metal one hitter and walked across the road to the field and tossed it. I went back into the house and called Scott and let him know that I was going to be done smoking pot.

I am grateful for that moment because the pain and embarrassment helped me change. I never wanted to let anyone down, especially the people who believed in me when everyone else ran away from me. Changes come in the smallest steps and now there was a change I could see and feel. Change was happening my whole life. I just wasn't ready to accept it or acknowledge it.

CHAPTER 47

Longest Stretch Of My Life

During the next eleven months I went all in on the whole sobriety thing. No pot. No nothing. All in. I was so miserable. I was hungry, angry, lonely, and tired. This was the perfect recipe for failure in the recovery world. HALT, stands for hungry, angry, lonely, and tired. HALT is an acronym that I have adopted and use as an identifier to judge where I am in the key areas of my life. If I was hungry, I'd better eat. If I was angry, I'd better check myself and reach out to talk with someone. If I was lonely, I'd better get my ass to a meeting or reach out to a friend to talk. And, if I am tired, well, you know the drill, I'd better get some rest.

I didn't feel any type of serenity or gratitude that was promised with recovery. I used drugs to escape my emotions and once I took my coping tool out of the equation, I was left with a big pile of shit from my past! My OCD, PTSD and all of my other issues shifted into another gear and haunted me daily. The drugs and alcohol made all of my issues bearable until the drugs stopped working. They just stopped working. It was like a lifetime friend that just disappeared and left everything in my life in a big old pile of shit. My life was a blur when I used drugs, but once I stopped, everything became clear and painful. I didn't think that I could stay sober. I wasn't quite sure if I wanted to be sober. The only thing that I knew is that I couldn't live with all of this pain.

My using friends started distancing themselves from me once they found out that I was trying to stay clean and sober. I had a few people from community support groups who were positive supports in my life. Scott and Marvis were always my constant support no matter what. My life sucked. I was going through the motions one day at a time and sometimes even one second at a time. Everything in my life was different without drugs and alcohol. It was like I was standing on a spinning top just hoping to find some balance so I wouldn't crash and burn again.

I was still hanging around a lot of my old friends, because I didn't see the need to make that change in my life at this time. I was stronger than that. I thought that I could be around people who were doing drugs and not do them. People from the program said that I needed to clean my side of the street and that means don't go to my old playing grounds and play with the same people who are doing drugs. This was much easier said than done. How could I get rid of my friends? How could I walk away from my only support, even if they were all negative? How could I get rid of my family just because it was full of unhealthy people who abused drugs and alcohol? I loved these people and now they told me I needed to stay away from them. Shit, this sounded impossible. They were everywhere. I thought that everyone did drugs and drank alcohol! Everyone who I knew did.

I was so deep into the black market that it would make me cry at night when I thought about how I might find my way out of this mess without the potential negative consequences. I needed to come up with a plan.

I was screwed. They were going to kill me if I left. This was the giant hurdle that stood in front of me. I never thought about getting out. I have always fought my way in, trying to find the biggest drug dealers who I could work for and my hard work usually paid off. I found some hard hitters and I never thought that I would need an exit plan. I was scared. Not only was I looking at changing careers, but I was looking at changing everything in my life. I thought it would just be easier to die. But, shit, I couldn't even get that done.

Many of my dreams were lost. The dream of having kids slipped away. I lost my dream piece of real estate. This chunk of land had wildlife everywhere with a creek that ran through it in the spring and a million-dollar view. I lost the love of my life and that was drugs. I didn't even want to sell drugs anymore and that had been my identity for years. Even with all the losses, one thing stayed constant in my life and that was the community support groups.

I was slowly getting better. I wasn't able to see any of the changes in my life, but other people would tell me that there were changes happening. I was no longer carrying a gun and I was no longer having violent thoughts about hurting people. I was reaching out for help and I was trying to do the next right thing. I was working a full-time job at the Capitol. Miracles were happening all around me. I started to have a spiritual awakening. I reached out to psychologists and started to do a little bit of work on my issues. This time was a pleasant time in my sobriety. I found comfort and something beautiful with flowers. Life was slowly getting better just because I was giving it a chance and not messing it up with drugs, but I had many lessons yet to learn. But, for now I was okay.

Eleven months of sobriety. I still remember the evening that I received my eleven-month coin and all the praise that I was getting from the people in my life. I went to the 6:00 p.m. happy-hour meeting at Serenity Place like I had done hundreds of times before. This evening was special because it was birthday night. Birthday night comes once a month on the last Friday of the month to celebrate people's sobriety. This was always a big meeting. Seventy plus people filled the rooms.

The chairperson started out with, "Who in here has twenty-four hours of sobriety?"

This was always the most emotional call out for me because I have been through many of my first twenty-four hours of sobriety. Making it through the first twenty-four hours of sobriety was a miracle. There is nothing easy about the first twenty-four hours of sobriety because at this point, we are all teetering on life or death. I loved seeing the fear in people's eyes because I understood it and it was raw and real. I didn't like that they were hurting, but I liked that I had something in common with them that I understood. Seeing that pain helped me remember that I never wanted to go back to the first twenty-four hours and relive that misery. The chairperson continued going through the months of birthdays until he called out, "Who in here has eleven months of sobriety?"

I stood up and everyone in the room cheered. I hated this part because getting recognition was hard to accept, but I needed this part so much to keep fighting. The people who supported me were the reason that I was putting together any time of sobriety. I stood up and walked across the room and got a big hug and an eleven-month sobriety coin.

The chairperson said, "Tyler, if you put this coin in your mouth and make it dissolve you can drink again!"

The wheels were turning as I looked down at the beautiful red anodized coin and thought about putting it in my mouth and giving it a try so I could use again. I always had an angle. This was a beautiful night and a tough night because I made it to eleven months, but I was slipping back into my old ways and I was preparing to relapse and I didn't even see it coming. I was hiding many different demons and they were starting to win.

It was the end of November. Winter was always tough on me and so were the holidays.

This time of year, my drug abuse would increase significantly due to the pressures and the traumas of my past. Eleven months! I did it! The one year of sobriety mark scared the hell out of me because it had always seemed impossible for me to reach. I was close and then where does it go? This felt way too good and it scared me because I might just screw it up. The season was changing and the flowers were no longer blooming all around me. I needed to go back and try it again to see if this time I could control the drugs. This time will be different after eleven-months of sobriety. This little stint of sobriety taught me how to control my usage. I got this. This time it would be different.

The pressures all around me and my poor choices in the people who I was surrounding myself with were starting to catch up to me. The depression of the winter started to smother me. I was lonely, I missed Addison bad. I missed our life together and it was killing me knowing my family of eleven years was no longer my support. It was difficult to understand the pain inside of me and know that just across town their lives were still moving forward while mine felt like it was at a dead end. I couldn't take it any longer. I started slipping back into my old ways and my disease of addiction had me right where it wanted me. I still thought that I could sell pot and not get high. It worked for eleven-months until my world crashed down all around me once again.

CHAPTER 48

I Feel Trapped

By this time in my life, my drug dealing career had come to a screeching halt. I wanted out for some time now, but between the good money and the fear of the people who I was working for, I felt stuck. I was nuts deep and it felt like if I stepped away the slightest bit, I would get my nuts cut off or worse. Being in so deep was scary, so many things could go wrong and they did.

I had been dealing large quantities of pot for years and it always had its ups and downs. I had worked on large scale grow operations. I was even transporting kilos of coke for my partner's friend, Butcher. Butcher went behind our friend Booker's back and said, "Tyler, since Booker and The Boss are not paying you what you deserve, you should stop off and meet me while you are down here picking up the load of pot and pick up some coke and drop it off for me." I was all in because the carrot he was waving in front of my face was big and I was already taking the risk. I just couldn't let Booker and The Boss know that we were doing business behind their back. Butcher and these guys had been friends for years, so it was a slippery slope to be doing business this way. But, screw it, Booker and The Boss had been looking out for their best interests for years and I was the third wheel.

I was loyal to these guys to a fault, until they cut me to my core and stepped on my pride and went back on their word. I didn't need a written contract. I needed you to look me in the eye, shake my hand and you had my word just like my Dad and Grandpa taught me. What do they say, "honor among thieves?" This is true until someone goes back on their word. We were brothers and I trusted them with my life for a moment. I would have died for these guys, but I am afraid that they wouldn't have reciprocated the same actions for me and they didn't. Greed runs deep, "among thieves." When the times are good, they are good, but at the slightest crack, it crumbles fast. I struggled because I am a loyal person and once I felt like Booker and The Boss were screwing me, I started to go back on my word and this was an internal battle. I was definitely losing my way fast. My moral compass was spinning out of control from my drug addiction and the hurt that I was feeling inside.

When I look back a year I can see that the biggest crack started when The Boss found out that I was getting a divorce. He called me up and questioned me in the most caring and self-serving way that he knew. He had concerns that I might have told Addison information about what we were doing. I reassured him that she didn't know anything. He didn't believe me. This was his own issues surfacing. I guess years back he had a few different women whom he had loved turn him in to the cops while he was a fugitive from justice. I understood why he was concerned, but I was telling the truth. Addison didn't know anything.

I hid this from her so she would never be put in danger. I told him too much about the internal dealings of the divorce and the possible fight over finances.

I had two partners who were greedy. Once the pot started coming in from the illegal marijuana grow, that was the only pot that was available. It was tough to make a lot of money on this because it was a lot stronger and this meant a higher price. My profits were shrinking because I was selling the high-grade pot. I couldn't move the quantity that I had been moving with the mid-grade pot. I received a call from The Boss one day and he told me, "Tyler, the pot I was getting for you is done. My guy got busted. You will have to strictly sell the high-grade pot."

"Can you just introduce me to your guy so I can go get it without you?"

"No, I can't do that."

"This is going to hurt my business."

"We will work with you and drop our price."

"I can't sell pounds of the high grade. My guys love the mid-grade."

"You need to stick to the plan, Tyler. This is what's happening, and you need to adapt. We can have you make runs for us to California and Seattle to make up for what you will lose."

Getting the pot at a cheap price was no longer available and now they wanted me to do even more work for the same price. These bastards were pinching me out. I was promised a lot of shit over the years that did not come true. During the divorce I received a phone call from The Boss.

"Tyler, how is everything on your end?"

"I'm hanging in there."

"Has Addison said anything?"

"No, but the divorce is in the works."

"Tyler, don't fight her. Just let her have whatever she is asking for and we can move forward with our business. You will make way more money."

"Fifty percent of everything is mine."

"It doesn't matter, Tyler. She could make your life hell and mess things up for us. Just sign the papers and let's move on."

"I'll get this over without a fight over money. I'll sign the papers."

"Good. Tyler, we're glad you're thinking straight. You're going to make so much money over the next year that you will be financially stable for years to come."

I believed my partners. I really thought that they were going to let me all the way in. I thought that all their promises were going to come true. I was proving to them that I was a team player. I felt like I would be okay financially.

Sure, this sounded great. Everyone at this point was promising the world, but no one wanted to sign on the bottom line. Being the good little people pleaser that I was, I listened to my partner and I walked away from the divorce without much of a fight. I was stuck with lots of promises that didn't come true. I felt hurt and betrayed by the people who I once trusted with my life.

The money on the black-market side of things was not as plentiful as was promised. These punks were just looking out for themselves. It was apparent that I was on the bottom of this food chain and I was tired of it. I had put in my work and proved that I was trustworthy.

I thought about robbing my partners at the end of the grow season when they had lots of pot and money, but I didn't want to hurt my friend Booker. He was like a father figure to me and my heart was involved. The Boss, on the other hand, was a punk and I would have punched him in the face if I had the chance. The Boss was the one who was leading me astray.

I finally got up enough nerve to make my move and get mine. They promised me the world and wouldn't even give me a cracker. I was bitter. My life was crumbling around me and I started to obsess, thinking about the times they screwed me over while working on the illegal marijuana grows just enraged me. I thought about it and decided I was just going to take mine. To hell with them. I didn't care if I lived or died so the consequences didn't scare me.

I made up a big story in my mind that the storage units where I kept the pot were robbed and the $25,000 worth of marijuana was gone. I called Booker to give him the bad news. I picked up my work phone and dialed the number. The phone rang.

"Hey, Ty."

"Hey, buddy."

"How are things going, Ty?"

"Not so good." I made my attitude sound really depressed to make him believe that I was bummed out.

"What's up, buddy?"

"The storage units that I was using were robbed."

Silence

"How bad is it, Ty?"

"They only got $25,000 in pot."

"Where is the rest of the money?"

"I have it. They didn't get that."

"Shit, Shit, Shit."

"I will make it up to you buddy, I promise." I had no intention of ever making anything up to them. I told him that I would try to find the people who did this and make them pay. That pot was mine now. Booker reassured me that this is all part of doing business and that we would work something out. He really tried his best to keep my spirits up so I would keep working hard. I was finally getting mine. I slept with my pistol next to me and carried it daily just in case they sent someone to get me. I was prepared for the worst.

I had been trying to stay sober over this time while still dealing drugs. This time it was different. I started to go against the people who could ultimately ruin my life and I really didn't give a shit. I looked up to these people. I once considered them my best friends. Things started to change and, honestly, I was tired of the game. I knew that I couldn't continue to deal and stay sober. I knew that if I didn't make a change the drugs were going to take my life. I just ripped these bad dudes off $25,000.

I used this opportunity to pull back a little bit. I slowed way down. I still had an obligation to uphold. I still was making my trips to get the marijuana and the kilos of coke. I would bring it back to North Dakota and unload it. I would spend hours counting their money and maybe twenty minutes counting mine, if I was lucky. I would haul all the money back to them and like a good little boy, hand it over. No one ever mentioned the $25,000 and I sure wasn't going to bring it up. They knew that I was trying to stay sober. They were kind of happy about this because I was not a very good drug addict.

I had eleven months of sobriety under my belt and things were starting to look up. With each new day of sobriety under my belt, the further away from the black-market I wanted to be. I was starting to really believe in myself. I started to want a different life.

PART VI

Survivor

It's surprising that I had made it this far in this whirlwind of a life. I am a survivor. I'm proof that no matter what we go through in life, there is always hope. No matter how far down the hole of addiction we fall, there is a light. From this moment in my life, I no longer felt that bad luck had anything to do with my journey. It was all about choices and doing the next right thing. Hope began to start finding its way back into my life. The question that haunted me during this time was, "Tyler, why are you not dead?"

CHAPTER 49

Yes Or No

I finally felt enough pain. All the years of people caring about me and believing in me even when I continued to fail started to pay off. The positive supports in my life had been leaving me messages and expressing their concerns that I had dropped off the recovery radar. I reached out to Scott and let him know what was happening in my life. I reached out to Booker and let him know that I was not sure if I could go on living anymore. Scott made a call to The Heartview Foundation and put my name in line for an evaluation and for a residential bed at their inpatient drug and alcohol treatment facility. Scott called me up and said, "They have a bed for you on January 5. Three days from today, Tyler. It's up to you if you want to go get help."

"No! I can't go into treatment again! I'll lose my job!"

"They'll hold the bed for three days, so think about it."

"I'll think about it, but at this time it's a no!"

"I love you buddy and I am here for you!"

"I love you, my friend!"

I hung up the phone and broke down. I was pissed that Scott cared about me so much. He should just let me die. I knew in my heart that he was right and that I needed help to get out of this giant hole that I had dug over the last three weeks. The next three days were pure misery. I was sticking my gun in my mouth every hour of the day trying to find enough nerve to pull the trigger.

Nothing was working anymore. I felt like a puddle of water on a table. I just wanted someone to push me over the edge into a glass and stand me back up and help me. I was completely broken. More broken than I had ever felt in my entire life. Scott called me on January 4, 2011, to tell me that he loved me and supported me. He reminded me of the bed that would be open on the 5th. Scott even called a guy in upper management at the Capitol and asked if I would lose my job if I went in for help again. The guy in upper management was also in recovery so he had my back. He told Scott that if I needed help that I should get in there and that there would be no negative consequences with my employment. Shit. Hearing those words come out of Scott's mouth was a relief, but it pissed me off because that excuse was no longer on the table for me to use to back out.

I told Scott to pick me up in the morning to take me to treatment. I called my boss at the Capitol to let him know that I would be going into treatment for drug and alcohol abuse. He was supportive and reassured me that my job would be there when I was done. That night I contemplated suicide, but I couldn't even pick my gun up and put it in my mouth. This was the longest night of my life. I didn't sleep much. I was filled with fear of the unknown. I wanted to back out so badly, but I knew that my life depended on this. I knew that if I didn't get help, I would die soon. I still had a bunch of pot to sell and kilos of coke to transport and drop off for my business partners.

I called up Booker and told him that I was going into treatment the next morning. He was supportive of me going to treatment because my substance use wasn't good for his business. I called Butcher and let him know that I wouldn't be available to drop off the coke for at least a month. Butcher wasn't so understanding and threatened me. I understood where he was coming from! No one wanted to wait on coke, but now they had no choice. I told Butcher that he needed to wait or I was going to go outside and dump gas on his coke and set it on fire. He agreed to wait because he knew that I would do it and he didn't want to lose his product! All my loose ends were tied up and I was as ready as I was going to be to go to treatment.

The next morning Scott picked me up from my mom's house where I was staying and took me out to the rock house where I had all of my belongings. Scott gave me some space to get my things gathered up. He waited outside smoking a cigarette while I gathered what I needed. I grabbed a black garbage bag and stuffed it half full of my clothes. I had 40 milliliters of pure THC oil in the bedroom closet. Once I was alone, I pulled out the syringe and took the duct tape off the tip. I thought about walking over to the bathroom and squirting it down the toilet, but my hand pulled it up to my mouth. I was nervous that Scott was going to walk in and catch me so I pushed on the plunger and squirted the whole syringe down my throat. 40 Milliliters is equivalent to 12 ounces of high-grade pot. Let's just say that this should have rocked my world, but with all of the nerves and all of the scenarios that were running through my mind, I had a hell of a tolerance, so I didn't even notice the high. The car ride to town was the longest fifteen minutes of my life. Scott tried his best to let me know that I was doing the next right thing by going to treatment. I was afraid, but ready to do something different.

We pulled into the parking lot of The Heartview Foundation. I started to have second thoughts. Everything inside me felt broken and hopeless. I struggled to breathe. My arms and legs felt like a ton of bricks. It was snowing and this triggered my brain to start thinking about my job and leaving the guys shorthanded at the Capitol building moving the snow without me. I was trying to sabotage this moment. I wanted out.

CHAPTER 50

The Healing Begins

We walked into the building together. Once inside, Scott was greeted with lots of hellos and nice-to-see-yous. He had been to treatment here a few times, so he knew the process. I was carrying my black garbage bag with my belongings. I walked up to the front desk and dropped my bag to the floor.

"Hi, I guess I am here for treatment."

"Welcome! We are glad that you are here and everything is going to be okay, Tyler."

"I sure hope so. Nothing feels okay now."

"We need you to fill out some paperwork and our nurse will be out to visit with you soon."

"Thank you."

Scott and I sat in the waiting room trying to fill out the paperwork. I was struggling to write because my hands were shaky. My brain was spinning in circles with a continuous loop of reasons to say screw it, and get up and leave. I filled out my paperwork and handed the clipboard back to the business office, sat back down, and waited. People were coming in and out of the building. Everyone was carrying three ring binders full of paperwork. Scott did his best to hang with me. I could tell he was afraid for me. I started to trace all the shapes in the room. The TV was on with the morning news playing. I struggled to understand what they were talking about. I was tracing the words that would pop up on the screen.

Scott was talking to me. I felt numb as my body slouched down in the chair. My physical body needed rest, but my brain was scrambling and doing its best at trying to kill me. I was full of anxiety and fear. A lady came out and took us on a walk through the facility giving us a quick rundown of the facility. She took me over to the residential unit and showed me my room. She had me set my garbage bag down on the floor and let me know that they needed to go through it before I could put it in my room. I looked into the room. There were two single beds on opposite sides of the room. Next to each bed was a nightstand. I could see that I had a roommate and his belongings were nicely arranged on his nightstand. There was a Bible on the nightstand and an Alcoholics Anonymous book next to it. I was introduced to the residential staff. I looked over at Scott and could tell that he was getting fidgety and looked like he needed to leave.

"Scott, you can go, buddy. I'll be okay now."

"Are you sure? I can stay if you need me to."

"Thanks for giving me a ride. but there is nothing else you can do so you can go."

"Okay, buddy. I'll call you later."

I gave Scott a big hug and watched him walk out the door. I wanted to follow him, but I stayed instead. I was scared and alone now. The staff did their best to comfort me and make me feel welcome. I sat down on the bed in my room, looked out the window, and watched the people going into the auto parts store across the street. The snow had stopped falling and the sun was shining. I tried to tell myself that everything was going to be okay and that I needed to do this. I looked out the door of my room and watched the staff going through my bag and checking everything carefully and then folded my clothes up nicely and stacked them on the counter in the office. Shit, I forgot shampoo, deodorant, and my toothbrush. I walked out of my room over to the office and told them that I needed to go home and get my toiletries. They told me that I couldn't go home right now and that they had all of the items that I had forgotten. I went back to my bed and sat down and waited.

I heard a knock at my door and a white-haired lady with a big smile was standing outside of my door.

"Hello, Tyler. I'm Judy, one of the nurses who will be taking care of you."

"Hi, Judy. I'm Tyler, but I guess you probably already knew that."

I knew instantly that Judy was a kind soul and that I would be safe in her care. She took me back and did an exam on me to determine my withdrawal potential. She also had me pee in a cup. I told her that I had been using everything under the sun when it came to drugs. Surprisingly enough, I only tested positive for meth and pot. I thought for sure that there would be heroin and some Oxy in my system. Judy told me that they would be sending it off to the lab for further testing. Once she thought that I was fit to move on to the drug and alcohol evaluation, she walked me down a hallway.

There was construction going on in the facility at the time so there were construction workers in each section. I looked over and a guy I went to school with was carrying some duct work for the furnace system. We made eye contact and nodded our heads at one another to say hi. I was vulnerable, broken, and a little bit embarrassed for him to see me. I lowered my head and followed Judy to an office at the end of the hallway. Judy knocked on the door and said, "Good morning, Violet. I have a nice gentleman, Tyler Auck, here for you."

"Good morning. Tyler. Come in and have a seat."

She pointed over to two chairs on the opposite side of her desk. I sat down.

Judy said, "I will see you in a bit, Tyler. Violet will take good care of you."

Violet had blonde hair and blue eyes. I could tell that she was different. She gave off a confident, strong, brilliant, and a don't-mess-with-me attitude. I was a wreck. I struggled to hold a conversation. My OCD was out of control. I was tracing everything in her office with my mind. My brain was manic and my body was limp and slouched over in the chair.

"Are you okay, Tyler?"

"No."

"What can I do for you?"

"Can I please get some water?"

"Would you like some Gatorade?"

"Yes, please."

She left the office and came back with an orange and blue Gatorade and sat them down in front of me. I thanked her and slammed the blue one and threw the empty bottle in the garbage. Violet went over what would be happening next. She told me it would be about ninety minutes of questions on my substance use and my life. I told her that I had a few evaluations done in the past so I was prepared. She started out asking me questions about my demographics and then moved on to questions about my substance use.

My anxiety was out of control and I struggled to not chew on my fingers. My brain was struggling to keep up with the tracing and trying to follow all of the questions that were coming at me. Violet stopped asking questions and asked me if I was okay. I told her that I was good and we trudged on. I was open and honest about all of the drugs that I had used from the first time that I used to the last time that I used. I lied about the amounts that I had been using. I didn't want her to think that I was a pig, so I minimized all of my substance use. It was still a lot of drug and alcohol use. I spent the next ninety minutes answering her questions, tracing everything in her office with my mind and trying to stop my racing thoughts. If she could have seen what was going on in my brain, I think they would have put me in a straitjacket and hauled me off to the loony bin.

I was struggling and every part inside of me was trying to talk me out of going through this treatment. I wanted to run and get high. She finished up the evaluation and walked me back to the residential unit and let me know that she needed to staff my case with her team and would be back. I sat down on the couch in front of the TV in the main living room. There was an office with a half door and some other workers behind it. There was a giant bowl of candy on the end table next to me. I reached over and grabbed a handful and went to my room and sat on the edge of my bed. I opened the mini candy bars and shoved the Reese's peanut butter cups into my mouth faster than I could chew and swallow them. I made work of ten individual peanut butter cups and walked out to the candy bowel and when no one was looking I grabbed two more handfuls and went back to my room and devoured them.

I fought to hold back the tears until they finally came pouring out of my eyes. I had chocolate and tears covering my face. I grabbed a Kleenex off the nightstand and wiped the tears from my eyes and the chocolate that was running down my chin. I thought about the last two years of my life. I thought about all of my losses and my broken heart. I was overwhelmed with sadness. I looked around the room for a place to tie the bed sheet to hang myself. I wanted these feelings to go away. I wanted out so bad. I heard a knock at the door. I was startled from my trance of self pity. It was Violet. She let me know that I would be starting a group the following morning with Otis. She let me know that I would like Otis and that the nurse will be in to see me shortly to take my vital signs.

I laid on my bed for the remainder of the day in a fetal position. The reality of the situation had sunken in and I was scared. Judy came in to check on me and brought me another

Gatorade. I was miserable and tired, but my mind wouldn't stop trying to kill me with intrusive twisted thoughts. It felt like my brain was torturing me. I was trapped and I couldn't get out. The residential staff offered me supper, but I declined to eat. I was still stuffing my face with chocolate. My garbage can had over eighty empty Reese's wrappers that were starting to almost fill it. I was withdrawing from the drugs. This had been the longest time period that I had been without drugs in the last month.

My feelings felt like they were broken power lines sparking off everything that they touched. I felt like I was going to die. I was covered in sweat and shaking uncontrollably. Judy would come in and make me drink Gatorade and cover me up. Later that evening I heard my roommate come into our room and turn on the nightstand light. I didn't move besides the adjustments that I needed to make it through my misery. I rolled over so I was facing him. I pulled the covers over my head with only my eyes peeking out. I could see my roommate sitting on his bed reading the Bible. He looked over at me and said, "Welcome! I'm Ed and if you need anything let me know!"

"Hi, Ed. I'm Tyler and I'm sick."

"We are going to be in the same group tomorrow so get some rest, buddy."

"Sounds good, Ed."

"Good night, Tyler."

I struggled to sleep. I was covered in sweat and my mind was racing all night. Every noise was distracting and the thoughts of grabbing my belongings and running out the door was an option. The next morning was a Thursday morning. I woke up after spinning all night long. My clothes and bedding were soaked from sweat. I rolled over in bed and put my feet on the floor. Everything at this moment was real. The tears ran down my face. I wiped them away as fast as they poured out. I stood up, put the rubber flip flops on that they gave me the day before and stripped my bed, grabbed all my bedding, and headed out to the office. My roommate was still sound asleep. Once I hit the lights in the living room everything hurt. I walked over to the office and asked where the washing machine and dryer were.

There was a young girl behind the half door in the office doing her schoolwork. She paused what she was doing and asked me if I was okay because it was 5:00 a.m. I told her that I need to shower and wash my bedding. She took me down the hallway and showed me where the washing machine was. She opened the lid and helped me load my clothes inside and started it for me. I forgot clothes in my room. She told me that my clothes were stacked in the office after the search. I followed her into the office and grabbed a pair of shorts, underwear, socks, and a tee shirt. She asked me if I had any toiletries? I told her that I had forgotten all of my things at my house. She grabbed me a bag of mini toiletries out of an office cupboard, handed them to me, took me down the hallway, and showed me the bathroom with the shower. I felt myself getting sick. Once she showed me the bathroom, I thanked her and shut the door. The room was spinning, and I knelt down next to the toilet and threw up for the next thirty minutes. My anxiety was high. I looked down into the toilet after each time I flushed and cried uncontrollably.

I was shaking and the cold sweats were pouring out of me. The flooring was cold and hard on my body. After throwing up I laid on the bathroom floor freezing. I couldn't get up. I needed to pull myself together and get into the shower. My skin felt like it was crawling. I frantically scratched my chest. I looked down at my fingers and they were covered in blood from chewing on them throughout the night. Once I saw the blood on my fingers, I stood up from the fetal position where I was laying on the floor and looked in the mirror. My lips were covered in blood from chewing on them during my anxiety-filled night. My eyes were black and I struggled to see their green color. My cheeks were sunken in from malnutrition while on my meth binge.

This was the first time in a month that I actually looked at myself and that I could see myself. I was disgusted with what I saw. I looked horrifying and the girl from the office didn't even tell me I had blood on my lips. I was in so much physical pain. I turned on the shower to extra hot because I was freezing. I stripped my clothes that I had slept in and dropped them to the floor. I opened the curtain and went into the shower and positioned my head so the water hit it. I could feel all the nastiness run off my body and down the drain. I started to cry again when my thoughts went to my ex-wife. I thought about her and her new family and all of our dreams that were no more.

It's crazy to think that when I was sober for those eleven months, I was moving on from my sad feeling of losing her, but once I used drugs all of the pain came rushing back like it was day one when I was kneeling on my kitchen floor with that gun in my mouth. Suicide was definitely an option. I washed up with the soap and got out of the shower. I dried off with the towel and got dressed. By the time I was done getting dressed, my clothes were soaked in sweat again. It was running off my face and I was struggling to not throw up. I started to Jones meth and pot. I walked out of the bathroom and looked down the hallway at the exit sign above the door and thought about running out the door and going to score some drugs. Then I thought that I would have to go into my room and get my coat and shoes, but I didn't want to wake up Ed, my new roommate, so I was stuck. I walked to my bedroom door and dropped my clothes to the floor and went over and sat on the couch. I could hear the lights in the ceiling humming and the heating system turning off and on.

The noises within the silence were too much to handle. My brain was racing. I was full of negative self-talk. It was like a record that was playing in my head telling me that I am a piece of shit. Kill yourself, Tyler. More drugs. I missed my dad who had passed away and my best friend Kimmo Slurpie who committed sucide. I thought about all of the pain my dad went through in his lifetime and the changes that he made trying to fix the things that he had done wrong to our family. I thought about Kimmo Slurpie sitting at that bar all broken and alone when he wrote his last words down on a piece of paper before sticking a gun in his mouth and pulling the trigger. This pain was too much, and the tears were falling out of my eyes onto my lap.

This needed to stop. The girl in the office came out and asked me if I wanted the TV on and I told her no. I just needed to sit here and think. She told me if I needed anything that she was here for me. I sat on the couch counting ceiling tiles and tracing every shape in the room with my mind. I was able to soothe myself so at least the tears stopped running. I started to hear noises from the room behind me. It was almost 7:00 a.m. and the other patients were getting up.

My roommate Ed was the first to get up. He came out of our room and put his hand on my shoulder and told me to stay strong and that he had my back. He invited me into the kitchen for breakfast, but I declined. The thought of food made me nauseous, so I grabbed two handfuls of chocolate out of the bowl and went to my bed and sat down. My bed had new bedding on it and it was made. Ed must have got new bedding out of the closet and made my bed for me. I looked over at his side of the room and I was pleasantly surprised that he had everything in order. He looked like a nice man who was clean and I needed that. I didn't have time to deal with a slob and my OCD couldn't handle one at this stressful time.

CHAPTER 51

Group

Judy came into my room and took my vitals and cleared me to attend the group. I was sick to my stomach and nervous about attending the group. Ed came into our room and helped me find my way to the group room. Our counselor's name was Otis. Otis was an old iron worker that had many run-ins with the law over his years of struggling with addiction. We all sat around in a circle of chairs. There were eight of us. Four boys and four girls. This first day was a blur and it was over before I knew it. I liked Otis because he was raw, real, and had a good understanding of what it was like to be in our shoes.

He kept talking about this Slick fella. Slick wasn't a person. Slick was a reference to our addiction. Slick is the little guy that sits on my shoulder and tries to talk me into doing stupid stuff. Slick is my addiction and Slick wanted me to fail. I liked this analogy and it stuck. It made a lot of sense to me and if I could picture something that I was fighting against, I could fight better. I had been to addiction groups many times in my life, but this time felt different. During group Otis talked about the statistics with addiction and he told us that one out of nine people recover from this disease and the other eight either end up in jail, institutions, or dead. I looked around the room that day and thought that I was going to be the one in this room who is going to make it. I liked a challenge and a challenge is what I was in for. I felt a little bit stronger when the group ended that day.

I followed Ed back to the residential unit and talked with him for some time in our room. He told me about what got him here and his life of addiction and pain. I opened up to Ed about my struggles. We both agreed that sobriety was our only choice or death because that was always an option with addiction. Ed gave me a quick rundown on the facility and how things worked. Ed told me that we get to go bowling and to movies on Saturdays and we can have visitors on Sundays.

During the week, staff will give us rides to the gas station and Walmart to shop while under close supervision. We had three meals a day that we had to help with preparation and clean up. We all were assigned to a chore list. Ed took me out and showed me the list, but my name wasn't on it yet, probably because I was so sick. Later that evening, after supper, I saw a man that I had recognized from AA. His name was Oscar and he apparently worked at the center.

Oscar tried to help me when I was struggling in the past, but I didn't like this guy. I thought that he was an arrogant prick. Oscar let everyone know that the van that everyone called the druggie buggy would be leaving for a trip to Walmart, but I wasn't cleared to go due to my vitals and the fact that I was still consistently throwing up. Ed asked me if I needed anything so I gave him some cash and had him get me a twelve pack of Diet Dew and some toiletries. I sat in my room the rest of the evening until I finally fell asleep and rested through the night.

I woke up the following morning and I didn't have to change my bedding and I made it longer than two hours without throwing up. I felt like I had a little bit of energy and my attitude was not as shitty as it was the first day. It was Friday and I guess we only had a group until 11:00 am on Fridays. Everyone was talking about going bowling that afternoon. I wasn't quite sure that I could go. Judy came in and took my vitals and let me know that I was cleared for passes. Oscar came into my room and talked with me about passes and what was expected of me. He was different than I remembered him. He was actually enjoyable and funny. We hit it off on a good note this time around. He had probably always been the same guy, so it must have been me and my shitty attitude that made me dislike him in the past.

I didn't like people who tried to help me because, honestly, I wasn't ready, but this felt different. This time I knew that I needed the help.

All the patients that wanted to go bowling loaded up into the druggie buggy and went to the bowling alley. Heartview paid for our bowling fees and our shoes. We all sucked really bad at bowling, but one thing about addicts is that we have a lot of try in us. It was fun watching everyone try to throw the ball as hard as they could down the lanes at the pins. Let's just say that there were lots of gutter balls. I needed this distraction so bad.

My brain was able to slow down. I was able to let a smile peek out every once and awhile. It took me a couple days to feel better. The withdrawals stopped and my brain started to work again. The only problem with this was, once the cloud started to clear, all of the pain and traumas of my life started to creep back in. The emotional pain started to get real and raw. I spent my whole life covering this pain up with drugs and alcohol and now I had nothing to hide behind. The only choices that I had was to run or stay and fight these demons.

CHAPTER 52

Second Thoughts

On Saturday morning, I woke up and looked out the window and saw that it had snowed about six inches and it continued to come down in large flakes. I panicked and thought of the work that I needed to do at the Capitol and how I now left my coworkers shorthanded. I felt horrible because we were short handed before I went into treatment. My mind went crazy. I cleaned all the sidewalks and the parking lots on the Capitol grounds in my mind while sitting in my bed. Every detail was racing through my imagination. My anxiety was out of control. I stuck my fingers into my mouth and started to chew the raw wounds, making them start to bleed again. I thought about smoking meth and taking THC oil. I could taste it and feel it. I was in full blown relapse within seconds. The Jones was overwhelming. Slick had me around the throat trying to kill me. I started coming up with lies and excuses so I could leave the facility immediately. I went to the residential office and told them that I will be packing my things and leaving. They did their best to try and talk me into staying, but my mind was made up. I was leaving and that was that. I am out! I went into my room and started throwing my belongings into my black garbage bag when I heard a knock at my door.

"Tyler, we called Otis and he is on his way here now to talk with you. Will you please wait until he gets here before you take off? Please?"

"No! I need to get to work!"

"Please, Tyler. Just twenty minutes. That's all we ask of you and then if you still want to leave that is your choice."

"I have to get to the Capitol grounds and clean my parking lots. My boys need me."

I was looking for any excuse to leave, but my plans weren't to go to work. My plans were to get high and then go to work. These feelings were too much to handle and I wasn't ready to talk about them and honestly, I didn't know how. I felt like a failure because I had lost everything in my life that I needed.

"Tyler, Otis will be here in a few minutes so if you are around, he would like to talk with you."

"Okay, I'll wait."

I sat down on my bed with my black garbage bag on the floor next to my feet full of all my shit. I looked down and thought about what a loser I was to be carrying a garbage bag with my stuff in it. I didn't even have a duffle bag or a suitcase. What a loser I had become. I waited with my arms crossed. I started to boil over with anger and fear. I was ready to tell Otis where to go so I could leave and get on with this killing myself business. I didn't think that I could stay sober for one more day. I needed to finish selling the pot that I had out at the rock house and deliver the coke that was already late, But, what I really needed was to sit down and take five hundred hits of meth. I was deep in thought coming up with my plan when I was startled by a knock at the door. It was Otis.

"Tyler, can I come in?"

"Yes."

"How are you doing, Tyler?"

"I am not worthy of shit, Otis."

"What's going on, Tyler?"

"I want to leave. I can't do this anymore."

"I would like you to stay, Tyler. I need you in group. You're way too valuable to lose, Tyler."

When Otis told me that I was valuable it hit me right in the heart and I couldn't believe that he came in on his day off to listen to me and to talk me into staying. We sat in my room for a good thirty minutes talking. He praised me and told me how much he believed in me. This is exactly what I needed. I have always wanted people to think that I was valuable and that I was worth a shit. Otis left that day not quite knowing the impact that he had on my life. He made me feel like I could do this and that I was going to do this. He made me feel that he had my back and I know that he did. I unpacked my garbage bag and started my day over from that moment. My cravings for the drugs went away for the time being and I felt empowered. I felt like I could stay sober for the day and I did.

Over the next three weeks I worked my butt off and put everything into my sobriety. I was attending groups daily and community support groups in the evenings. I was healing because I was doing everything that was suggested. I was being of service to others in the facility. I was working out at the gym in the mornings. I was all in. The pain was still there, but I was starting to believe in myself. Staff at the Heartview Foundation were empowering me to follow the rules and love myself.

I was finally able to look into the mirror and start to like the person who was looking back. I was able to attend my Beginning Experience meetings and continue to mend my broken heart. I struggled daily, but I was getting through it with grace and respect for others. I had many looming fears that I would have to face once I completed the twenty-eight-day inpatient part of the program.

CHAPTER 53

Damage Continues Even In Sobriety

Once back at the facility, I was called into Judy's office. Otis was also sitting in the room. They had a very concerned look on their faces. Otis said, "Come in and have a seat, Tyler." I could tell instantly that whatever they were about to tell me wasn't going to be good. I thought maybe someone died or something. They talked with me about how well I was doing and how they have enjoyed me being in treatment but, okay here we go, I knew there was something else. Judy told me that my THC levels have been so elevated that their drug tests hadn't been able to get a reading over the last three weeks because the tests don't read that high. My levels finally had dropped over the last week, but on the most recent drug screening my levels had been spiking. This had to mean only one thing, that I had been using pot while in treatment. But, I hadn't used anything. They both told me that this is very alarming and they are not quite sure what to do with me. I broke down in tears.

I told them that my last use was when I took all of my THC oil before I came into the facility. I told them that I have been clean and sober with no slips, but I couldn't argue with their test. I was defeated instantly. I pleaded for them to let me stay. They told me that they have a no drug use policy in their facility and it wouldn't be tolerated. I let them know that I understood. Judy told me she needed to make a call to some specialty doctor to look into this THC oil and that they would talk with me later that day.

I walked out of the office and went back over to the residential unit and sat on my bed and cried. I thought for sure that they would be kicking me out that day. Then what would I do? I needed this place. I wasn't strong enough to be let loose. An hour or so passed when Otis and Judy came knocking on my door. Judy reassured me that she talked with the specialty doctor and said that he said that my levels could continue to fluctuate due to the amount of oil that I took all at once. They let me know that they believed in me and trusted that I hadn't been using drugs in their facility. They told me that they would be doing more drug screens to monitor my levels, but I could stay in the facility and continue my treatment. I stood up and gave them both a big hug and thanked them for believing in me. Judy told me that she has been doing this work for many years and has never seen levels this high and the specialty doctor hadn't either.

Here I thought that I was out of the woods now that I made it into treatment. Everything is supposed to be all wonderful, but I guess when I wreck my body and mind up over the last 20-plus years of my life I should expect some damage. Damage is what I got. Week three of sobriety and the anxiety was too much to handle. My poor fingers were bloody and raw from chewing them with my teeth while I was asleep and when I was awake. I wouldn't even realize until the wounds were so deep and my lips were covered in blood that I would stop myself. My OCD was firing on all ten trillion cylinders and it was getting stronger as each minute passed. I know this because I counted each minute by each second and then I traced all the numbers on the clock and anticipated all of the bad things that were coming my way in the next minute. I see why I self-medicated. The past traumas of my life started to haunt me in my dreams. The roommates that shared my room after Ed left would tell the staff and me that they were concerned and a little bit scared of the horrible things that I was saying when my PTSD was coming out to play in my sleep. "Tyler is having horrible violent dreams," they would tell the staff.

Yeah, sure, they were just dreams. Just violent horrible dreams that were once true and real but I wasn't ready to open that can of worms yet, but that didn't stop the thoughts and feelings that were starting to creep in daily to haunt me. The thoughts of all the people whom I had hurt and the deception that I brought on to the people who I loved the most was starting to flood my mind.

There was this one time in high school when some of my friends and I were walking through the park on the south side of town and we saw two kids sitting on a picnic table. It was dark out, so we walked over to see who it was. The one kid I really didn't like. He was a little smart ass and this night was no different. Let's just say his name was Brad. Brad told us that we should screw off and leave, and when we didn't he started mumbling under his breath. I walked over to Brad and hit him right in the mouth and nose, knocking him to the ground.

His friend started yelling at me, "You're such a dick, Tyler!" I was getting ready to smack his dumb ass, too.

I yelled, "Shut your mouth!"

"What the hell, Tyler! Brad's dad just beat him up and broke his nose and now you hit him!"

I looked down at Brad lying on the ground and my heart broke for this kid because I knew what it was like to feel the pain that he was going through at home. I had a lot in common with Brad.

If I could have taken my punch back, I would have. If I could have helped Brad up from the ground and given him a big hug, I would have. Instead the only thing that I could do was feel the pain that I caused him. This moment changed me forever and it was definitely haunting me while I was in treatment.

Sobriety is beautiful, but now there was no numbing the pains and traumas of the past. I was looking them right in the eye and they were trying to kill me in my mind on a daily basis. I continued to do everything that was suggested to me from my treatment team. I was excelling in my group. I was continuing to utilize community support groups daily. Even with the circus that was playing in my head, I was able to push on.

CHAPTER 54

Stoned

I was coming into what I thought would be my last week of treatment when the bottom fell out. I knew it would, but my sick twisted mind didn't think of what was about to happen next. Oscar took a group of us to a community support group in a basement of a church that was across the street from where I went to high school. Karma's a monkey's uncle, or something like that anyway. I wasn't feeling well physically. I had a horrible headache, my lower back hurt, my kidneys hurt, and the cold sweats were drenching my clothes. I knew that I needed this meeting so I stayed. I figured that the physical pain that I was experiencing was easier to deal with than the emotional pain that I need to deal with at this meeting. We walked down the thirty steps leading down into the basement of the church. I sat down at the table and was clearly in physical distress. People were asking me if I was okay. I reassured them that I had been going through some things, but I was going to be okay.

The sweat was pouring down my face and the pain increased to the point that I couldn't even talk and now I was slouched over in my seat. Once the meeting was over, I struggled to stand up, but I did so we could end the meeting with the Lord's Prayer.

The people who rode on the druggie buggy with me were scared. One of the girls ran up the stairs to get Oscar who had just pulled into the parking lot to pick us up and take us back to the View.

Oscar and the girl came running back into the church to help me. Some of the men from the meeting had helped me up to my feet. The pain was bad and now I needed to make it up the stairs to the druggie buggy. With the help of someone under each of my arms we were able to get me into the van. I was slouched over moaning in pain. Oscar needed to drop everyone else off at the View before he could take me to the ER. Once at the ER, I was loaded onto a rolling stretcher and taken into a room. Oscar did his best to comfort me. I heard his cell phone ring and it was Judy the nurse.

Oscar stepped out of the room to talk with her. All of a sudden, Oscar poked his head through the curtains with a big smile on his face and said "Alright big boy, it's time for your exam!" He walked into the room and grabbed a blue pair of rubber gloves out of a box on the counter and put them on making sure to snap the rubber on his wrists after they were on. He then said, "Trust me! I know what I am doing! This will probably change our relationship forever, but I promise not to tell anyone. Drop your drawer's big boy and spread your cheeks! I am coming in hot and there is no Vaseline in sight so this might hurt right away, but I promise this will get better with the more fingers that I use!"

I busted out laughing, and it hurt so bad that it made me cry, but I couldn't stop laughing. We laughed our asses off and I cried a little but this changed the heinous, scary feelings that I was having. The nurse came into the room and looked at Oscar standing there with the blue rubber gloves on and her reaction was priceless. She looked at Oscar and said, "So, what you are saying is that Tyler will not need an anal exam any longer?" We all busted out laughing, but I couldn't do it anymore because it hurt way too bad.

Oscar told the nurse that Judy from View cleared me for narcotic pain medication if I needed it. The nurse asked me if I would like anything for pain. I had every emotion running through my body. I wanted drugs so bad and now I could have them without any consequences. My brain thought about the million different ways that I could manipulate this system to get more drugs. I looked at Oscar and the nurse and said "No! I don't need any narcotic pain medication. I am in recovery." What the hell did I just say? I had never said those words in my entire life. I just passed up an opportunity to take some of my pain away and I said no. I could handle the physical pain, but not the emotional pain.

Oscar drove me back to the View. Once back at the View I laid in the bathroom on the floor puking in the toilet and trying to piss through a funnel with a screen attached to catch these stones that were trying to come out of my penis. I am not sure what was worse, the pain or the thought of a rock coming out of my penis. Either way, it sucked really bad. I had to throw the funnel away and just piss into the toilet. It hurt too badly and I really didn't care to see the stones that were plaguing me. Maybe I deserve this pain because of the kid that I beat up in the church parking lot where this all started years ago. Karma, that's what this is.

It was easier to take knowing that I deserved this pain. Oscar knocked on the bathroom door checking on me periodically. I pissed one more time and the pain lessened enough that I stopped puking and sweating. I was able to pull myself up off the floor and go to my room. Oscar went home at shift change. I was struggling to rest, thinking about my regrets of not taking the pain medication while I had the chance. It was a rough night and it was about to get stranger.

The following morning at around 4:00 a.m. I was awakened by a loud crash outside my bedroom window. I kneeled on my bed and looked through the shades to see what just happened.

To my surprise, there was a man in a vehicle that hit the building right by my window. I could hear the vehicle revving as he pressed on the gas trying to back up. I could hear him screaming and smashing his hands on his steering wheel. His vehicle was stuck on the cement flower planter and the snow ridges that the plows had just plowed up an hour or so earlier. The man got out of his vehicle to look at the damage.

He was screaming, "Fuck, fuck, fuck," over and over again until he jumped back into his vehicle.

He revved the engine. I could hear the tires spinning as the SUV started rocking back and forth until it finally caught enough traction to back out onto the street. I jumped out of bed. I was still in lots of pain from the stones that I was passing. I ran to the office and told the night staff that a man just hit the building with his vehicle.

"Tyler, no one hit the building."

"Yes, he did. I was looking at the guy out my window and he is still out on the street."

The night staff grabbed his winter jacket and gloves and went outside. I ran back to my room, but the SUV had left. I could see the night staff looking around before coming back into the facility.

He had part of a bumper and part of a headlight in his hands and said, "Tyler, you were right, someone did hit the building," as he held the parts up.

The night staff told me that I should go back into my room and try and get some rest as he picked up the phone and made a call. I went back to my room and counted my blessings. I was thankful for that cement planter for slowing the vehicle down enough so the SUV didn't crash through the wall and kill me in my bed. Wouldn't that be something to die this way in treatment. I wasn't able to get any rest after this ordeal. The next morning around eight the guy had come back to the facility to fess up to what he did. The police were there talking with this man who was nicely dressed in a suit. I heard through the loose lips of a counselor that the guy was drunk and left the scene to go sober up before coming back. This counselor said that the guy was some big shot who worked down the street at the news station and was a large donor to Heartview so no changes were pressed. See how this works, if it would have been me or anyone else in the facility we would have been cuffed and stuffed and charged with leaving the scene.

I was thankful that the guy was okay and a little bit excited that he got away with it. It's kind of brilliant to use your power and influence to get out of trouble or the loose lipped counselor was just making stuff up and the guy fell asleep or had a seizure or something like that. Who knew that treatment was going to be this action packed? I thought it was wild when the crazy girl got us banned from the library for giving blow jobs in the bathroom or the phone that flew across the room and busted right by the staff's head. I like this treatment life. Wildness, art, acupuncture, and yoga. Maybe I will stay forever.

CHAPTER 55

Choices

When everything was stripped away, lost, broken, and rubbed raw, some of the most wonderful things happened in my life. There is beauty in brokenness. No time to focus on the things that don't matter, just time to focus on the small moments in time. It sounds simple from the outside looking in, but once I was in the eye of the storm, I had a gift of seeing the things that matter and the beauty that surrounded me. Just like that day standing in the field watching Larry get beat half to death when I noticed the beauty in the field grass swaying in the wind. This was no different. This was the toughest time in my life and while the storms were raging all around me, I was able to focus on my heart, what it needed, what was right, and what was wrong. I was ready for a change in my life and it was scary and difficult doing it sober.

I had been in treatment for about a month now and I was starting to clear up mentally, physically, and emotionally. I was surrounded by people who were not doing well. We were all sick and when you put a bunch of people together who are broken it's a recipe for silly shit to happen. The Heartview Foundation was a male and female facility so there were women and where there was a woman there are my thoughts that have plagued me my entire life. Or maybe it's a gift. I know one thing for sure and that is it definitely consumed me at times.

The women in treatment didn't help because a couple of them were talking about sexual things with me. I enjoyed the thrill and the excitement of all the possibilities that were in front of me. These were all normal things that some of us experience when we are trying to get sober. These are the things that happened in my previous treatments as well because we're all lonely and we're all looking for something else to make us feel good and to make the pain go away. Sex could do that. Two sickies don't make a welly, but some of us weren't afraid to try it anyway.

There was this one girl in particular. Let's just say her name is Violet. She had it planned out that on Valentine's Day we were going to get a hotel room which I agreed upon at the time. I thought what the hell, she is cute and I'm lonely. I thought it was a good idea to go spend a weekend with her and have sex. It sounded great and it was exciting talking about it with her because it was against the rules and I hadn't done anything stupid in like, thirty days now. When I was thinking with my penis, I was all in. But, this big, stupid heart that was in my chest kept getting in the way.

I started to have second thoughts and change my mind. I thought about all the negative crap that comes along with this girl. She was just as confused as I was and, honestly, what was she thinking wanting to have sex with me since I had all this wonderfulness going on for me being in treatment and my life crumbling all around me. I was coming up with a plan in my mind to back out of our Valentine's weekend sex session.

But, before I could implement my plan to back out, something happened. Violet came back to the residential unit from the nurse's station. She was crying hysterically. During all of her blabbering and mumbling I picked out the words that she was pregnant and that an older gentleman from one of the bars that she frequented before she came into treatment was the dad. She wasn't sure though. Well, there goes Valentine's Day. Shucks! I felt bad for her because now she needed to go out on a pass to find this older gentleman, who was married, and to let him know that she is pregnant with his baby. My heart broke for her because this is not what she had planned or deserved. She needed someone to love her not just screw her. I could see the pain and fear in her eyes.

I felt bad that I was thinking about being one of those guys who was just going to use her. I thought it would be all fun and games until the pregnancy test came back and said, Tyler, you are the father. Not today! I knew that just poking fun at this girl would have been a mistake and my heart never wanted to hurt anyone. This knocked me off my feet. I was somewhat relieved because I just dodged a bullet. I might have actually followed through with our date on Valentine's Day if this new issue had not presented itself. Everything became real and I started to think of the consequences if I was promiscuous. Sometimes the most beautiful gifts are given in the most messed up ways and this one had a lovely little red bow.

CHAPTER 56

Feeling The Change

After my three-week trial period in treatment they decided to keep me another ten days before releasing me back into the wild like a blind leopard. During this time, I continued to work my butt off in my group and I even started to give back to the new people who were coming into treatment. Something inside me was changing and I started to believe in myself. The staff at the Heartview Foundation was completely amazing and provided me something that I was willing to accept this time. I worked on my usage history and during group one day I was allowed to put it on the white board and share it with my group members. Seeing all of the drugs and alcohol that I consumed from the age of fifteen to now was unbelievable, even to my own eyes. I knew that I was a drug addict, but once I wrote it down in a completely honest way it blew me away.

I broke down and cried during the group. I was ashamed that my life had come to this. The consequences from my substance abuse were astounding. The years of pain that I brought onto myself, my family, and my community broke my heart. Looking up at white board after white board filled with drug and alcohol use, consequences, and losses, changed something inside of me. I was sick to my stomach. I was no longer proud of what I thought were my accomplishments at one time. Now I looked at my path and I wanted something different. I was on the fence. Did I want to endure what I thought would be many years of pain and suffering to rebuild my life?

I thought that it would take me twenty years to dig out of this hole that I was in. I was worried about the people who I was selling drugs for and how they would react to my sobriety. I was sick to my stomach when I thought about the drugs that I had at my house and the money that I still needed to collect and pay up. I felt trapped. I knew one thing for sure, if I returned to drug use, I knew that I would die either by suicide or by overdose.

One day in group Otis looked at me and said, "Tyler, I think you should be an addiction counselor. I believe in you and I think you would be able to help lots of people." I thought he was crazy for even thinking about something so silly, but I listened. Otis always built people up, but I thought he was just blowing smoke up my ass. I thought it was a crazy idea but I started to think about it and about my current position as a groundskeeper. I knew that I didn't want to do it for the rest of my life. Maybe Otis is on to something. The seed was planted and he kept watering it daily with positivity and hope. My days at the treatment center were getting close to completion and reality was slowly sinking in.

CHAPTER 57

My Soulmate

During a normal day of treatment after my lunch break I was walking back to the residential unit. Out of the corner of my eye I saw this blonde angel. She instantly caught my eye with her beautiful white porcelain skin, her light blonde hair, and her blue eyes that I could see from across the hallway. I froze up and didn't say a word. I just watched her walk by. I went into the lunchroom and sat down by Jeff at one of the booths. Jeff was in treatment trying to get his wife and kids back. He struggled with porn and alcohol. I liked this guy. Jeff and I talked quite a bit, so I told him about this beautiful girl who I just saw.

Jeff said, "Ask her out, man!"

"You're crazy. She'll never want a guy like me."

"You're going to ask her out, Tyler and I guarantee you will marry her."

"Shut up, dude. I can't ask her out."

"You will and it will be great."

We moved on from talking about the hot blonde and talked about relationships, mostly failed relationships. He was just coming out of a failed relationship and it was not looking good to even see his kids in the future unless he got his life together.

I was completely losing everything in my life and I had no clue what the future had in store for me, but we talked for a while and learned a lot about each other.

That evening the whole group jumped on the druggie buggy and we went to a community support group that we had not been to before. We walked through the door of the church and went up a flight of steps and then through another door. I could smell coffee and hear voices coming from the room. Once through the door, my eyes glanced to the left and sitting on the couch was the blonde-haired, blue-eyed angel that I had seen walking down the hallway earlier that day. I instantly looked away in fear of her catching me looking at her. I sat down in the back of the church on some folding chairs. She was in my line of sight. She looked up at me and smiled.

Another man came in and sat down on the couch right next to her. He handed her a coffee and scooted up close to her. I thought, "She has a boyfriend." Jeff sat in the row of chairs behind me. He leaned over and said, "Is that her?"

"Yes, it's her."

"Go talk to her now."

"I am not going to go talk to her. She has a boyfriend."

"Screw that punk. He looks like a pile of shit. Kick his ass, Ty. Take her and marry her. You have to do something, man."

We both laughed about what Jeff was saying. It was funny and Jeff was right. The guy next to her was a punk who looked like he would have crawled up her ass just to be closer to her. She looked uncomfortable sitting next to him, but I told Jeff that I wasn't going to waste my time on a girl who is in a relationship.

During the meeting we all went around and said our names, our identities, and why we were at this meeting.

I said, "Hi, I'm Tyler and I am a recovering addict." Everyone in the room followed suit. Once it was blonde's turn, she said, "Hi guys, I'm Amber and I am an alcoholic."

Jeff leaned over and said, "Tyler and Amber Auck, has a nice ring to it. Ty, just go drag her boyfriend off the couch and kick him in the teeth!"

I looked back at him and told him to shut up. Amber would look up at me throughout the meeting and smile. The guy next to her would look up at me and glare because he knew that she looked up at me and smiled. It felt like a big old bundle of confusion. The meeting ended, we all stood around in a circle, held hands and said the Lord's Prayer. I kept looking up at Amber and awkwardly looking away when her man friend would look at me. We all separated from the circle and the View group got in the druggie buggy and went back to the treatment center.

Jeff said, "So Ty, now you know her name. You two would make a great couple and I think that you need to go back to that meeting and you need to sit by her."

"Jeff, I am here to get better and I don't want a damn fight over a girl!"

"Just go sit down where her boyfriend sits and take his place. Ty, you have balls of steel. Take his place. He doesn't deserve her and they sure didn't look happy together."

"Just shut up, Jeff! I am going to bed. Good night."

"Good night, Tyler and Amber."

I laid in my room that night and thought about Amber. I decided to take care of myself and not get into a relationship at this time.

Thursday evening rolled around and we went to another community support group at a different church. Amber was there, but this time she was sitting with a female. The guy who she was with at the prior meeting was sitting at a different table. I sat down across the table from her trying not to make it obvious that I was checking her out. Once the meeting was over, we all congregated out in the hallway of the church, socializing with one another, waiting for the druggie buggy to pick us up.

While I was waiting, I noticed that her man friend kept coming up to her. She would kind of blow him off and walk away from him. I sensed that something was up and it didn't look good for him. He kept trying to creep on her and she didn't like it one bit. The druggie buggy pulled up and we all parted ways. Once back at the center I went straight to my room and laid down for the night. I wondered if there was actually a possibility of maybe going on a date with her.

During the next week I spent a lot of time with Oscar. He was pulling double shifts at the View. I was starting to get a little stir crazy due to being in treatment, so Oscar started taking me to the mall for walks. I told Oscar about the blonde girl that I had eyes for. Little did I know that Oscar knew who she was. Oscar started coming up with a plan of his own. While we were walking around the mall Oscar said, "Let's get a pretzel from Auntie Anne's."

We walked down the mall towards the pretzel shop. As we got closer, I could see the workers' heads sticking out of the pretzel shop that was located in the middle of the mall. Once we got closer, I looked at Oscar and he had a big smile on his face. I looked at the workers in the pretzel shop and there was Amber. We walked up to the shop. She turned around from rolling pretzels and we made eye contact. She smiled at me and said hello. She took our orders and served us our pretzels. I ordered a garlic pretzel with spicy dipping cheese sauce. Oscar ordered a regular pretzel with the sweet glaze dipping sauce. She didn't charge us for our order. I couldn't help but notice her hard work ethic. She didn't mess around when she was putting our orders together. Hell of a work ethic, and I liked it.

Standing there looking at her I visualized holding her hand and what she would look like in my arms. She was so hot that I couldn't help myself. I was excited that I got to see her. I was nervous so I didn't say much at all. We said goodbye and walked down the mall eating our pretzels. I looked back and I could see her head sticking up over the wall looking at me. I waved and she waved back and smiled. Let's just say Oscar and I walked the mall quite a few times during that week. I was excited to see her when we would walk by the pretzel shop. We would smile at each other and wave. Oscar was excited because he was working his magic. He always knew how to make me smile and now he was laying the groundwork for my love life and I didn't even know it at the time.

CHAPTER 58

Getting Closer

Monday evening meeting time came around again so we all decided to go to the same church that we had been to the previous Monday. I was excited to see Amber again if she was going to be there. I was full of anticipation in hopes that the guy who had sat by her wasn't going to be there. The van pulled up in front of the church and we all jumped out and ran inside because it was snowing and cold. I ran up the flight of steps, went through the door and saw Amber satting in the same place on the couch as the week before. The seat next to her was open so I stopped right in front of her and said," Hi! Is anyone one sitting there?"

"No. Please have a seat."

I sat down next to her. Jeff walked by and smiled at me. He even pumped his fist a little bit in excitement.

"Hi, I'm Tyler."

I stuck my hand out to shake hers. She grabbed my hand and said, "I'm Amber. It's nice to meet you."

I could feel her grip and it was a hell of a grip. She squeezed my hand like she was trying to break it, but I didn't care. Her blue eyes were beautiful and her skin was perfect. She smelled really good as well. We sat on the couch and talked. I made sure that I kept my distance just in case that guy came in and wanted his spot back. I wasn't going to give it to him, but I also was not going to fight his dumb ass if Amber was his girlfriend. We continued to talk about treatment and how far along each of us has been in our journey of sobriety. She grabbed her purse off the floor and pulled it up on her lap. She opened it up and pulled out a pack of breath mints.

"Would you like a mint?"

"Why, does my breath stink? Do I need a breath mint?"

"No, your breath doesn't stink. My dad taught me that if I pull something out in front of people that I should offer to share, so I am offering you a breath mint."

We both giggled and I took it and popped it into my mouth. I crunched it instantly. She looked at me, handed me another one and I did the same thing. I really wanted to ask her for more, but it was too early in our relationship to be eating all of her mints. I made eye contact with Jeff. He was smiling from ear to ear as he watched us interact. After the meeting was over, we all stood up. I held her hand as we said the closing prayer. My feet and my toes wiggled all out of control inside of my shoes. I could see her looking down at them giggling. She had the most beautiful smile and just touching her hand sent goose bumps down my body. We said our goodbyes and parted ways.

Once we returned to the treatment facility, Jeff came up to me and said, "Good job, buddy. This is just the start to your new life. Tyler and Amber Auck. Awesome!"

"You're funny, man. I am grateful that I have met you, buddy."

"You two are going to be an item. I just know it. Did you get her number?"

"No."

"Get her number next time."

"Okay, I will if that other guy isn't around."

"She doesn't like him. I can tell."

"You can't tell shit."

"I can tell you two are going to be together forever. You better get going and marry her."

"Slow down now and stop getting carried away. She wouldn't marry me."

I knew it would be a whole week before I would get to see her again, and it would be on Valentine's Day. I hated Valentine's Day at this point in my life because my heart was broken and the whole world looked like they were having a good old time being in love. I was hoping that when I walked into the room at the church on Monday evening that I would see Amber's beautiful smile. We left the View and cruised in the druggie buggy to the church. We all jumped out as a group and ran inside, up the steps and as I rounded the corner and went through the door there she sat, but this time she was on the other side of the couch. I sat down on the other end of the same couch. I looked over at her and smiled and said, "Hello, Amber."

"Hi! Are you scared to sit by me?"

"No. I just didn't know if the seat next to you was taken."

She slid on over to the middle spot right next me. She was handing out little cups of candy with suckers and chocolates for Valentine's Day. She looked like she was in a panic when she had one cup left. She handed me the cup and said, "Happy Valentine's Day, Tyler!"

"Happy Valentine's Day, Amber. Thank you for the candy."

"You're welcome."

She had the biggest smile on her face and so did I. I felt alive and connected to something beautiful. It was scary at the same time because I had so many demons that were still inside of me trying to stick their nastiness into my life. There was a heart shaped sucker popping up out of that cup. I needed it so bad. I pulled it out of the cup, unwrapped it, shoved it into my mouth and crunched it. I crunched it until it was gone. I chomped the sucker in less than four seconds. She looked at me with her big blue eyes. The look on her face was a look of concern mixed with "What the hell did you just do?" Then her look changed to a look of excitement. A look of, "Oh, my God! I need me some of that 'messedupness'" crossed her face.

"Tyler, I have never seen anyone eat a sucker like that in my entire life."

I smiled at her as I polished off all of the candy that was left in the little cup and there I sat with my little cup in my hand and this beautiful girl sitting next to me smiling. It felt like I had broken the ice, or should I say, crushed it. This was a turning point in our conversation. I probably shouldn't have devoured the candy like I did, but I couldn't help myself and it worked out because she liked watching me devour it like a rabid animal. She asked me when I would be done with inpatient treatment. I told her that my last day was the next day, February 15. Forty-two days in treatment. She was shocked that I had been in treatment for so long. I told her that they had tricked me with promises of a twenty-eight-day program and then switched it to a forty-two-day program. We giggled together. Bonus! Now she thinks I am crazy and funny.

I asked her what she was doing for Valentine's Day and she said that she was going to spend it with her girls. She told me a little bit about her kiddos and that she is currently living with her dad. I told her that I would be moving in with my mom when I was released from treatment. A match made in heaven. Two grown ass adults living with our parents. She wished me luck. The meeting ended and we parted ways in what I thought would be the last time that I would see her. I wasn't able to get up enough strength to ask her for her number. We left the meeting in the druggie buggy and went back to the View. During the drive I felt a tap on my shoulder from Jeff.

"Did you get her number?"

"No, I didn't. Slow down man, leave me alone. I don't think this is going to work. She doesn't like me like that."

"How can you even say that, dude? I can see the way she looks at you. She likes you and you need to marry her to make all of those dreams that you tell me about come true."

"Screw off, man. That's not going to work out for me. Nothing ever works out for me."

"Don't be a pussy and go after her, Tyler. You have to listen to me.

Maybe Jeff was right. Was I missing an opportunity? I thought Jeff was full of shit, but with all of his persistence I was starting to believe him even if I acted like I didn't.

CHAPTER 59

Lots To Face Once I Am Out

It bothered me that I was building these new relationships when I still had part of my life that I was not able to tell anyone about. It felt like a weight that was dragging me to the depths of hell. My mind was consumed with these deceptions and I was plagued daily with overwhelming thoughts of despair. I was determined to find a way out. On one hand I was on a pink cloud and everything was beautiful and achievable and on the other hand I was spinning out of control. I kept leaning on the people who supported me and who had my best interest in mind. I was surrounded by people who had my back. I was still in daily contact with Scott and Marvis. My little brothers were supporting me along with my mom. I was very grateful for all of their love and support. I had a team and I needed to continue to utilize them if there was any chance in hell of being able to remain sober.

The final stretch of my residential stay was filled with medical troubles. My kidneys were giving me hell and so was my liver.

I was pissing blood daily and in lots of pain. Judy started me on an anti-depressant and I didn't like the way it made me feel so we tried another one and this one made me have constant thoughts of committing suicide. I had to stop taking these meds all together. My THC levels were finally dropping on a regular basis, but they were still off the charts. I was worried about any medical issues due to having to go to the doctor's office because they were my drug dealers for many years.

I was still meeting with Nurse Judy on a regular basis to get my medical stuff straightened out. Judy asked me one day if I had any upcoming appointments that I needed to attend. I told her that I made a dermatology appointment to get a spot on my lower lip checked out about a year ago. Judy had me call up to the clinic and check to see when my appointment was. The clinic told me it was the following day at 2:30 p.m. I couldn't believe that It was the following day. It was like a year's wait to get into seeing this dermatologist so if I wouldn't have called, I would have had to wait another year before I could get in.

Oscar and I jumped into the druggie buggy the next day and went to my appointment. The dermatologist looked me over and told me that I have a fast-moving squamous cell cancer on my bottom lip. I was rescheduled for a thirty day follow up to come up with a plan to have it cut out. I was scared when I heard this news, but Oscar talked with me and helped me find gratitude in my situation. He talked with me about the blessings that are happening in front of me and that if I wouldn't have been in treatment, I would have missed the appointment and with this kind of cancer I would have been in trouble. It is crazy to think how this is all working out because I continue to do what I am supposed to do on a daily basis. I can't believe that I didn't like this Oscar guy in the past. We were becoming really close and he was going the extra mile for me and it was making a difference in my recovery.

On a positive note, I was able to graduate from Beginning Experience and I now had a new understanding of who I was as a person and what I needed in a relationship. My living situation was still up in the air. My mom said that I could stay in her spare bedroom at her house in town. I knew that I couldn't go back out to the rock house and continue to isolate and be alone. So many things were up in the air. I was scared and broken, but I continued to grind it out daily trying to find the good in each day.

CHAPTER 60

Now I Have To Face It All

I finished out my time at the View and left after the group on February 15, 2011. Forty-two days after I first decided to make a change in my life. I felt stronger than when I had gone in and now I had a whole new support system in place that would be my strength when I was weak. I felt pretty damn good about my sobriety. I worked my ass off and put in the time and effort. Once I walked out of the View that day, I felt a new kind of freedom. I actually felt like I had a chance at happiness again.

I had a great plan to stay in touch with Oscar, attend community support groups on a regular basis, and stay in daily contact with Scott and Marvis, but I knew that I needed to take care of my last drug dealings once I left.

The reality of my situation overwhelmed me, and I couldn't wait to get this done and over with so I didn't have anything to hide any longer. The deceit was killing me, and what if I get busted now that I had decided to remain sober. That would be my luck. But, really it has nothing to do with luck, it has everything to do with my choices. It was an emotional day to say the least. I said my goodbyes to my group members and grabbed my black garbage bag with all of my belongings and walked out the door to Scott's vehicle which was outside waiting.

Scott gave me a ride to my mom's house where my Jeep was parked. He offered to go with me out to the rock house to get the rest of my belongings just in case I was triggered to use. But, I didn't want anyone going out there because of the drugs that I was hiding. I needed to make sure everything was still all there. Once at my mom's house I was greeted by Keetah. She missed me so bad. I promised her that I was going to be a good dad from here on out.

I talked with my mom for a bit before I left and went out to get my stuff from the rock house. I parked in the driveway and prepared to walk in. I was hoping that I didn't leave any drugs laying around because I thought that I would do them. It sounds crazy right? I had pounds of pot and kilos of coke and I won't touch those, but if I would have left a meth pipe on the bed I would have been off and running again. It was different because the bigger quantities were always off limits and I didn't dare open them because there would have been hell to pay. I finally found enough nerve to walk in and access what was left of the wreck of life that I left over forty days ago.

I went down the spiral staircase and back through the utility room. My heart was racing as I reached for the light string and pulled it. All the duffle bags were there. I felt a relief and a sickness in my stomach. I pulled the track phone out of the duffle bag and made the calls that I needed to make to reassure Booker, The Boss, and Butcher that I was back and I would be taking care of business soon. They were all happy that I was out. Little did they know this would be the last time I would be working for them. But, I couldn't break it to them quite yet.

I called my dealers and set up times over the following two weeks to make the drops. I played my part to a tee and followed through with my last drug deals, collected the money, and sent it off. I felt relieved. Things were back in full swing for me. I was back to work full time at the Capitol and working my recovery program daily. I was attending aftercare one time per week at the Heartview Foundation for added support. After all of the treatments that I had completed in the past I never followed through with the aftercare piece. But, this time if I was going to have success, I needed to do what the professionals say.

Get this, I even asked my aftercare counselor to be randomly drug tested to hold me accountable. I still had no problem with letting myself down but having to look into the eyes of the people who believed in me so much and tell them I used wasn't an option. I couldn't bring myself to do that. I was getting drug tested one to two times per week. I tested positive for THC for four months. I remember the day that my pee was finally clean. I was so happy to be completely clean from all substances. The day that I squirted all the THC oil in my mouth, I had no clue what a crappy choice that was and I had no clue that it would haunt me for four months.

I started this forty-day journey completely broken. I continued to heal as each day passed. I was finally able to get some medical issues under control. I started to look at myself in the mirror and like who I saw looking back at me. I had a new network of people who loved me and supported me. I found the fight that I had inside of me once again and started using it. I started thinking about relationships and the seed that was planted to possibly go back to school and start a new career. This is one journey that I am glad that I agreed to go on, thanks to Scott. Pain was a beautiful thing when it motivated me to make a positive change before I died.

CHAPTER 61

Unexpected Encounter

The following Monday I met with a friend for dinner at Texas Roadhouse. We sat down at the table and I was a little nervous because of all the drinking that was happening all around me by people in the restaurant. It was triggering me to get high. I was spinning bad. This was way too early in my sobriety to be putting myself in this social situation. My friend ordered a beer. I watched the waitress bring the Corona over to our table and set it down in front of my friend.

My brain started to spin out of control. I traced the beer's shape over and over again in my mind until I could taste it. I knew this would mess everything up and I needed to be strong. I look around the restaurant, scanning each table, looking at the drinks that people were drinking. I was mesmerized by the booze all around me. I could taste it and smell it. I looked over and there was my ex-wife and her new family. Shit. I instantly felt my anxiety rise. I could see the kids that she had after the separation. I kept looking over at her and the kids.

I looked at their faces to see if there was any resemblance to me even though it wasn't possible that they were mine. I was just torturing myself. I wanted out so bad. I wanted to run and go numb the pain. This was way too much to handle. I fought back the tears while we finished our meal. I was in a full-blown anxiety attack. My skin was crawling, the sweat was pouring off my face. This was too much to handle for me. I felt like I was drowning and someone was throwing rocks at me when I would come to the surface to catch my breath.

This was the first time that I had seen my ex-wife and her new family. They were sitting at the table right on the other side of the wall. I could see the kids popping their heads up while they were playing. My heart felt like it was ripping apart inside my chest. The thoughts of all the years we had spent trying to have babies raced through my mind. I could feel myself slipping into a dark place. I wanted to order the whole bar and wreck everything that I had worked for. The cravings for alcohol were intense. My thirst to make this pain go away was just an order away.

I finished up eating my meal with my friend and I told him I needed to leave. I wanted to run. I wanted to get high. I needed to get to a meeting. I looked at the clock and sure enough I had time to get to the meeting, just a little bit late. It didn't matter if I was late. I was in full blown crisis. I was crying uncontrollably and shaking from the emotional pain. All the dreams that I once had were shattered all over again. It felt like the day when Addison left me. I went running into that meeting and sat down. The tears were rolling down my cheeks. Everyone in the room stopped what they were doing and asked me if I was okay. I reassured them now that I was at a meeting I was going to live. It was true because if I decided to go get high or drink it would have been a death wish for me. I don't think that I could have numbed this pain except with a meeting and being around people who cared.

I looked across the room and Amber was sitting on the couch. We made eye contact, but I looked away. I was embarrassed that I couldn't hold it together. I was mad at myself for still allowing this old pain to hurt me so bad. It came around to my turn to talk and I told everyone what had just happened, how bad it knocked me off my feet, and how bad I wanted to go get drunk and high. I left my pain in that meeting that day. I started to calm down. Amber was looking at me across the room with a concerned look in her eyes. I listened to everyone else share stories of their broken hearts and the changes they made in their lives to fight another day. Once the meeting was over people were coming up to me to provide me comfort with hugs and kind words. They were giving me their numbers and telling me to call them if I needed anything.

Amber walked over to me and gave me a big hug. She stood in front of me and wrote down her phone number on a piece of paper and handed it to me. She grabbed my hands and held them and told me to please call her if I needed anything. She told me that she was there for me no matter what. I thanked her as I stuffed the piece of paper with her phone number on it into my pocket. I was consumed by my feelings and of self-pity. I was exhausted. I left the meeting that day, went home, laid in bed, and cried myself to sleep.

CHAPTER 62

The Phone Number

The next morning when I woke up, I checked my pants pockets for any cash that I had and found the piece of paper with Amber's phone number on it. I instantly felt embarrassed that I was a blubbering mess crying about my ex-wife in front of her last night. I thought about texting her to let her know that I was okay and to thank her for being so kind to me but it was 5:20 a.m., way too early to be texting anyone. I got ready for work and went into the shop. I sat in my work chair and put her phone number into my contacts. I was thinking about what I would text her and felt anxious. I thought of a thousand different text messages that I could send.

It was 7:30 a.m. I thought what the hell, I hoped she was awake. I crafted up a nice message thanking her for all of her support and caring so much about me to give me her phone number for extra support. I let her know that I went home after the meeting and I stayed there and took care of myself. I had a photo that I took a few days prior of a beautiful red hibiscus that was in full bloom at the veterinarian clinic when I had Keetah in for her annual visit. I attached the flower to my text message and read over what I had written, making sure I didn't sound stupid. I wasn't sure if I should send the message with the flower attached. Was this too much? Will it push her away? I pressed send. I folded up my flip phone and stuck it into my pocket. I was worried that it might be too early and that the flower picture was over the top. I was grateful for her support and what I put in the text message was from my heart.

I was on the edge, about to jump the night before and she gave me strength to fight another day. My phone vibrated in my pocket five minutes after I pressed send. I was scared to pull my phone out of my pocket and look, fearing the worst. I finally got enough nerve to pull it out and take a peek. It was Amber. She thanked me for the beautiful flower and told me that it made her day. She was glad that I was okay and said how worried she was about me. She told me that I could call her or text anytime for support.

I thanked her, let her know that I was here for her as well, and that she could reach out anytime she wanted. I was relieved that she liked the flower and the text message. I was excited that I had her number and that it was okay if I talked to her. I liked this girl, but I wasn't quite sure how to make a move since I had never pursued a relationship sober. This was uncharted territory, but I was ready to take the next step in my life. We texted each other over the next few days getting to know each other. She told me she had two little girls who were nine and ten years old. She was living with her dad after a break-up and finishing alcohol treatment. She had been sober since July 15th. We set up a time to meet in person at Denny's restaurant on February 27th. Things were going well, and I was getting to know Amber. I was excited for our date.

CHAPTER 63

First Date

Sunday February 27th was a day that was going to change my life forever. I talked with Amber throughout the day. We were set to meet at Denny's restaurant at 7:00 p.m. I got ready and showed up early. I played the claw game and won a stuffed puppy. I guess tonight was going to be my lucky night. I waited in the lobby area until Amber arrived. She walked in, gave me a hug, and I gave her the puppy that I had won. She smiled and thanked me. We were seated at a booth. I looked across the table at her beautiful smile and her blue eyes that melted my heart.

We each placed our order. Amber ordered a garden salad with ranch, a bowl of chicken noodle soup, and a coke. I ordered a bowl of chicken noodle soup, a hamburger, and a diet coke. Everything was wonderful. I felt safe enough with her to tell her about all of the trouble that I had been in over my lifetime and she told me about all of her struggles and a lot about her kids. As she was eating her soup, she started to pluck the chicken chunks out of her soup and put them on her napkin. I watched her pluck each piece of chicken out of her bowl, wondering why she ordered chicken noodle soup if she wasn't going to eat the chicken. She told me she didn't like the processed chicken.

This was definitely odd, but who was I to judge. I grabbed the pepper shaker and twisted the top off so it would come out faster. I poured pepper all over my food until it was black. She looked at me and said, "Do you need any more pepper?" We laughed about each of our quirks. She gave me crap about my pepper problem and I gave her ribbing about the chunks of chicken on her napkin. Everything was working out well and our conversation was flowing along nicely until she told me all about her past relationships. She said that most of them had failed miserably and I told her about my failed relationships as well. I asked her what her last name was and when she told me I was shocked. I asked her if she was related to Darrell and she said yes that is her ex-husband. I know Darrell. I have known Darrel my whole life. Actually, he was trying to date my ex-wife when I first started dating her. My heart sank into my stomach. I looked at Amber a little bit different after finding this out. Damn, I liked this girl, but I was a bit thrown off. If my heart wasn't already in her grasp, I would have gotten up, walked away from that table and left just because she was once married to this guy. But, I couldn't walk away. Something drew me to this girl and made me want to run away all at the same time.

Amber told me all about her kids and her family. She talked about her future employment dreams. She told me that her dream would be to work at parole and probation or to be a cop. My ears perked up when she told me this. Never in a million years had I thought that I could possibly be dating a cop one day in the future. I panicked inside after she told me this, not because of her, but because of the situation that I had going on in my life with trying to tie up the loose ends with The Boss, Butcher, and Booker. One good thing was that she wasn't a cop. Well, two good things, she was also divorced from Darrell. Win, win, for me. We made it through our first date with a few minor red flags but I wasn't going to let a couple little technicalities slow this feeling that I had inside me. Now we were bonded. We even had a stuffed puppy together.

We made it through a shocking relationship revelation and we both weren't afraid to show our wild food quirks. We finished eating, went to a community support group at the church, and sat by each other on the couch. The topic that evening was gratitude. How fitting because I was grateful that I was able to go on a date sober and I survived. I went to my mom's house that evening after the meeting and laid in my bed full of excitement and fear.

I knew in my heart that I wanted Amber as my girlfriend and we were both grown ass adults that lived with our parents. A match made in heaven. I struggled that evening to get any sleep. Then my happy feelings turned to full blown OCD. My brain was forecasting every possible scenario of my future and all of the things that could mess this up. When I was able to finally fall asleep, something was triggered inside of me. Maybe it was my fear of dating sober or that Amber was married to the guy that was after my ex-wife years ago or that she wanted to be a cop and I was still technically a drug dealer even if I was on my way out of the business.

Actually, it was none of these things; it was all the years of trauma that I had gone through. I woke up the next morning after my lovely date curled up on the floor in the closet. I was covered in sweat and had rug burns on the side of my face from thrashing around on the carpet during my PTSD episode. This is not the way that I wanted my morning after my date to start. I wasn't quite ready to have anyone see this side of me. Once I got sober, everything started to get real.

CHAPTER 64

Will You Be My Girlfriend?

We set up another date after a week or so of seeing each other at meetings and talking on the phone and texting. I was really falling for this girl. I was having her come over to my mom's house so we could spend time together. Don't worry, my mom was gone. We spent the night talking and bouncing a ball back and forth playing catch. She told me that she told her sister where she was going, just in case I was a serial killer or something. Perfect, she is on to me. I am going to play catch with her then bonk her over the head with a knick-knack, put her in my mom's room, and feed her pears and gouda for the rest of her life.

I had plans, but none that involved pears and a closet. We were standing in my mom's kitchen and the lighting was dimmed low. Amber was leaning against the counter. I walked over to her and stood really close to her. I looked at her beauty in the light and my heart melted. I could no longer hold back. I went in for a kiss. My arms were wrapped around her body. I could feel her trembling as our lips touched.

After our kiss, I held her hands with mine and looked her in the eyes and asked her, "Will you be my girlfriend?"

She giggled and she said, "Yes, I would love to be your girlfriend."

We kissed some more before I walked her out to her car while holding her hand. I held her car door open and gave her a kiss goodnight before shutting her door. I blew her a kiss as I went into the garage and shut the door. I looked out the garage door window and watched her drive away. I was on top of the world. I couldn't believe she said yes. Jeff from treatment was on to something when he told me that we would be dating and he was right. The gravity of the situation was earth-moving. I kissed a girl sober for the first time in my life and it was amazing, even if it took me thirty-six years to do it.

I could feel my confidence come back into my body. Life was great. She texted me when she got to her dad's house to let me know she made it home safe. We sent nice text messages while we laid in separate beds miles apart until we both fell asleep. After this moment in time that we shared, our lives were kicked into high gear. Well, let's just say that I did the shifting and everyone else just hung on.

CHAPTER 65

Dream To Disagree

Amber and I were falling in love more and more each day. We were working on our recovery program together and started to have dreams of our own. In a few short months we were talking about marriage someday and a move out of our parents' houses. This was a big one for us because we needed our own space. Our love grew along with our love for flowers. After sending Amber that red hibiscus, I started to send her a different flower picture every day to share my other love with my Girly.

We spent a lot of time cooking at my mom's house dreaming of one day having our own kitchen to build these memories in. One day we needed some supplies from the grocery store so we decided to take a walk. It was a beautiful, sunny, windless, May day. We walked through the different business and housing developments to get to the grocery store that was about a mile away from my mom's house. Along the way, we looked at all the flowers blooming in people's yards and local businesses. Everything was going well until we came to the four-lane highway that runs out of town. The crosswalk was down the road three or four blocks. There wasn't a car in sight. Amber looked at me and said, "We need to go down to the crosswalk to cross." I looked at the grocery store that was straight in front of us. We only needed to cross the four lanes to get there.

That was our first disagreement. I told her that I was crossing here and she started walking towards the cross walk down the road. I stood there in disbelief that she wouldn't cross the road without a crosswalk. I guess the cop, rule follower, took over and, hell, I was proud that I was just jaywalking. Our worlds lined up, but they were miles apart. I walked out into the median that separated the four lanes and watched her walking. I looked around and honestly, I could have crawled across the highway and not gotten hit by a car. I crossed the road and sat on the curb next to the grocery store. I could see Amber standing down at the crosswalk, waiting to cross. She crossed the street once she was given the walk signal. As she was walking up the sidewalk towards me, I could see a look on her face that I had never seen before. I could see she was pissed that I jaywalked. I was a little taken back that she was so uptight that she couldn't jaywalk, but I just kept my mouth shut.

She walked up to me and said, "I can't believe you did that."

"Honestly, Amber, I can't believe that you didn't."

Awkward silence.

Our trip through the grocery store was a quiet one. Not much talking. I wasn't used to a girl who followed the rules to this degree. All the girls that I knew would have snorted a line of coke off the middle of the road if I asked them to. This was definitely a switch, but I liked it. We survived our first disagreement and learned a lot about each other that morning. I learned that I should follow the rules a little bit more and Amber learned that it's okay to jaywalk on a Sunday morning when there are only two cars in sight.

CHAPTER 66

She Has My Back

Amber's and my support for each other was strong and we definitely had each other's backs. I was faced with dealing with the cancer that I had on my lip from smoking pot. I was scheduled to have parts of my lip cut off. Amber wanted to be part of it and support me through this difficult and scary procedure. I wasn't sure how I was going to have a surgery without pain meds. Amber and I came up with a plan to avoid pain meds and she agreed to hold me accountable.

Amber picked me up that morning and took me to the doctor's office for the procedure. During the admittance process the nurse went over my emergency contacts. Addison was still my emergency contact for everything because I didn't think to call and change it. I had them change it to Amber. Amber knew that I was scared and nervous, so she sat close to me and held my hand.

I felt safe with her by my side. I was awake through the procedure and Amber was able to stay in the room and watch. She was excited about this. She is kind of morbid like that. The look on Amber's face as the doctor was cutting pieces off my lip was making me nervous. I was so scared that I was going to look deformed. The doctor stitched me up and handed me a mirror to look at his handiwork. My whole bottom lip was covered in stitches. The doctor talked to Amber and me about wound care and Amber agreed to help me through the day. She had my back and it made me feel good. No narcotic pain meds were given.

We left the doctor's office that day and went to my mom's house. I rested on the couch with Amber by my side. This girl was amazing. She took great care of me and helped me through the couple hours of excruciating pain after the numbing shots wore off. I loved this girl with all of my heart, and I was grateful for all of her support and love. I wasn't able to kiss her on the lips for some time, so she kissed me on my cheeks. We made it through our first big life event together and the cancer was gone.

CHAPTER 67

Hang On, Girl

Life was changing fast. Our relationship was beautiful and painful all at the same time. Amber and I were opposites when it came to everything, but our commitment to one another was strong and we worked hard at building our lives together. I still had doom hanging over my head with the drug world still knocking at my door, but I was choosing not to open it. I was bound and determined to get our lives going on the right track so I talked with Amber and we went out and got an apartment together. Well, I wasn't supposed to be in the apartment because I was now a full-time college student working towards my new dream and they didn't allow college students due to it being an income-based apartment. This time we were breaking the rules together. I had to hide my clothes on the back side of the closet when the apartment management would do their routine inspections.

We finally had our dream of having a kitchen to cook in together. Amber started her new career at parole and probation as administration staff. She started at the bottom to get her feet in the door and now she was well on her way to doing what she always had dreamed of doing. I listened to Otis, my addiction counselor, and was taking the steps to be an addiction counselor myself. Amber and I talked about marriage and Amber's wishes were to wait a year before I would ask her to marry me. I couldn't do that so I popped the question ten months into our relationship. I called her dad and set up a meeting to ask his permission to marry her and he hesitantly said yes. I went and bought one of the rings that she had picked out. This ring was beautiful. It had flowers on it and a beautiful diamond that lit up my heart when it sparkled in the sunlight.

I thought of all the crazy ways to propose but decided to go with simple. I went to my favorite flower shop and bought a dozen red roses because they screamed love. I went to our apartment and cleaned the place really well, so it was perfect. I placed the roses on the table so when she walked in the door, they would be the first thing that she would see. I had the ring ready to go in my pocket. Amber came home and walked through the door. She made eye contact with me and instantly knew what I was doing. I told her how much I loved her and that I was going to spend the rest of my life with her and the girls.

She looked at me and said, "What do you have for me?"

I got down on one knee and asked her to marry me. She said yes. I got up from my knee and we held each other crying tears of gratitude and joy. That crazy Jeff guy from treatment was right about what he saw for our future.

'Tyler and Amber Auck has a nice ring to it.'

We were working towards our goals together. We were crushing it and staying sober all at the same time. We had many struggles, but we powered through them with grace and teamwork. We talked about adding to our family. I now had an instant family with Amber's girls but I wanted to experience what it was like to have a baby of my own. We even picked out a name for our little boy. We wanted a little Charlie so bad. I was falling in love with Amber more and more each day. I finally had a relationship that I had always dreamed of. Our parenting styles were different when it came to Amber's girls, but we managed to do our best with the cards that we were dealt.

Our new life was crazy beautiful. I am sure people thought that we were crazy about how fast our lives were coming together and the workload each of us was taking on, but we didn't care because we were crazy in love and there was no holding us back. This was meant to be and we both deserved something different in our lives than the train wrecks of our pasts. I believed in Amber and pushed her to be a stronger person who could finally love herself unconditionally. She believed in all of my crazy dreams, insane workload, and drive. Everything was falling into place.

CHAPTER 68

Home Sweet Home

Please put me in a house with people who have guns and want to hurt me. Help me out of this messed up feeling of safety and normalcy. I would have given anything to go back to the uneasy feeling of my past life. The feeling that everything was on fire all around me. The feeling that things will never get better. I was used to that life. I understood that life. I could control that life and thrive. Now I was sitting in an apartment with my wonderful girlfriend, Amber, and her two daughters. Talk about an uneasy feeling. I was newly sober and having to deal with the normal things in life. Well, more normal than I was used to anyway. Come to find out that normal is only a setting on a washing machine. We all have issues in one way or another. This normal life was very difficult to deal with and understand. I had never dealt with any of these normal things in my life sober.

The chicken noodle soup was cooking on the stove, the sun shining through the third-floor patio window of the apartment. Our home was clean and put together nicely. I was sitting on the leather couch and my brain was going in a million different directions. How could such a beautiful thing feel so messed up? I was not sure, but I was full of anxiety and fear. I wasn't quite sure how to deal with life sober. I would think back to that day when I was trapped in the outhouse being tortured. I remembered the hopelessness of struggling with my addictions and the pain I was experiencing in the chaos that was engulfing my life. During the hard times of my life, I felt more comfortable in that outhouse being tortured than I did in that apartment that summer. I had no clue how to deal with being sober and going through the normal things in our new life. I felt more comfortable in a room full of people with guns wondering if someone was going to start shooting, than me sitting on that couch feeling the sun's rays on my face with the smell of chicken noodle soup lofting through the room.

Life can be really difficult, and sometimes the crazier stuff that I went through, the more comfortable I became in that insanity. Every dream that I had ever dreamt was in motion of coming true. I struggled to cope with the feelings of having a dream that was coming true and uncertainty ran through my veins. I was waiting for the next ball to drop because I usually dropped it. I went through a lifetime of crisis after crisis, and now when I had so much to lose, the next crisis scared me to death, but I craved it all at the same time. Never in my life had I been afraid of a crisis and never passed one up. I felt comfortable in brokenness.

My true test was now to find peace within peace. Silence killed me. The voices in my head would overwhelm my thoughts with negative feelings and horrible self-talk. Finding peace in lying next to a dumpster dying from an overdose was no more. The only comfort that I enjoyed in silence was when I was punched in the head or hit with a baseball bat. Physical pain has always been very comforting to me. I craved it. I loved it. I sought it out. The feeling of punching a cement wall, feeling my skin split open on my knuckles, and then watching the blood rushing out as my bones snapped. I found great comfort when I was a child and my father pinned me against the refrigerator, with his big hands wrapped around my throat with my feet off the ground while calling me names.

The silence that I found most comforting was when the crisis was almost over, and everything was broken, when the people whom I loved the most were hurt. Once the adrenaline dump happened, there was peace. When it got so screwed up that I couldn't even comprehend what just happened, peace settled into my soul. There were so many things in my life that I couldn't comprehend. Taking things to the edge of death was always a place that I enjoyed.

I was constantly looking over my shoulder, wondering when the balls were going to drop. All these things were easier to deal with and felt more comforting than sitting in that apartment with the most beautiful gifts that a man could ever dream of. I knew how to mess it all up and that option was on the table. That was easy to do, and I had no problem doing it. The difficult part of this new life was keeping it all together without sabotaging and blowing it all to pieces.

I looked back on that summer in that apartment building and it was one of the scariest times in my entire life. Building a life that I truly wanted was scary and it hurt for a little while. Will I screw it up? Will I hurt the people who I love more than anyone in my entire life? Going through this life trying to be normal had been beautiful, gratifying, and rewarding. I was getting a thousand chances to make it right. But, I don't think that I will get a thousand and one chances. I am blessed that I found the strength to sit through my uneasiness in that apartment building, until I believed that I deserved everything in front of me and more.

I started to believe that the love that I was receiving was not going to go away. The sobriety that I was building was getting stronger not weaker. Trying to figure out how to be a stepdad to two young girls was hard. I did the best that I could. Amber says that I knocked it out of the park. I still don't see it. How can I go from a crazy, messed up life to a life that is worth living? I am blessed for that time in that apartment building even though it was on the third floor. Don't ever get an apartment on the third floor without an elevator. Not recommended, but I would do it all over again.

The summer of 2012 was a whirlwind of craziness. We were coming to the end of our lease on the apartment and now we started looking at the possibility of owning our own home together. Sure, why not stack some more stuff onto our plates that were overloaded already? We were pushing ourselves to the breaking point. I was always waiting for something to happen that would strip it all away like it had throughout my whole life. Impending doom is what it felt like sometimes, but I had to power on. I loved Amber and I was willing to work through anything that life threw at us. I was going to school full time, working a full time job, working a side job, going to therapy, raising a new family, loving my Amber with all of my heart, working a recovery program, moving, taking care of a new home, looking for ways to completely separate from the black market, vacationing to South Dakota, all while planning our wedding.

We were struggling to parent the girls together.

This was one of the hardest things that I had ever done in my life. Instant family and raising two girls with no parenting skills was tough. It was hard because no matter what I did, I couldn't win. I was being blamed by almost everyone for issues that these girls were going through before I was in their lives. I was getting all of the heat after giving all of myself with not much reward. I was tired of being walked on by everyone in my life.

It was a difficult transition but there were silver linings to the dark clouds that circled my head. One of the things that kept me going was Amber's little girl Tess. Tess and I worked on building a stronger relationship. Tess was the oldest. Tess is the sweetest most soft spoken little girl whom I had ever met. Her heart is made out of gold. I hit it off with her instantly. Maybe because she needed me as much as I needed her. Tess's dad had never been in the picture. Let's just say the sperm donor didn't participate in the raising of his daughter.

I started to second guess everything. Staying sober was still very difficult and I struggled with it daily during this time. Our relationship was no longer a bed of roses, we were now feeling the thorns. I guess that's what happens when a new relationship grows so quickly during a time of crisis. Just a year into it we had accomplished so much together that we didn't take time to look at the process of healing as a couple. I was seeing a psychologist one to three times per week trying to survive this new life that I had chosen. I continued to work on myself and tried to bring what I had learned back to Amber, but she wasn't ready to make these kinds of changes.

We all change at different speeds. I just chose to kick it in high gear. I had wasted enough of my life on pain and misery. Don't get me wrong, I was all in on this relationship, but it was hard and a lot of times I felt alone. I knew all of the pain and trauma Amber had gone through in her life and I was going to do everything in my power to not let her sit in her crap any longer, even if it meant that she would dig in her heels, kicking and screaming. She definitely did that, and she rebelled against me for some time, falling back on some of her old drinking ways, even though she was still staying sober. Our life was great for two months, then it would break and fall apart. This was a cycle that would continue for many years to come.

CHAPTER 69

Separation From The Black Market

Over the last year, I was being pressured by The Boss and Booker to get back to work. I kept making up bullshit stories to keep them at bay. I told them that one of my dealers was being watched. I reiterated my lie from before and told them after the storage unit was robbed the cops were involved and now everyone is being looked at. This worked for a while.

During this time of my sobriety I was moving forward in a positive healthy direction. I had wonderful people involved in my life. I started school and had a new family that I was caring for. I knew that I was not going back into my old life, no matter the cost. Booker's friendship was starting to dissipate. I always cared greatly for this man, but I knew that I could not continue on with him. The excuses were running out, this needs to stop, now! My girlfriend was working at the probation office and I needed to stop the minimal contact that I was having with the dark side, but I was scared.

The wheels were turning, a brilliant plan of an exit strategy to get out of the black market was forming in my mind. I was gambling everything including my life, but I knew I had to do something.

Over the years I started to understand how The Boss and Booker clicked. I knew their likes and dislikes with their dealers. One of their deal breakers was someone who used drugs by IV. They always thought that if you were an IV user, you were no longer reliable. I sat in the basement of my house all alone coming up with a plan. My plan was to send a text message to Booker on my disposable phone to blow this fucking shit out of the water for good. My text message went like this.

"Hey buddy, I have to tell you something. I have been using heroin over the last month. This shit is getting crazy and out of control and the cops are watching me. I am sick and tired of your guys' shit. You do nothing for me, and I don't give a fuck if you mothefuckers send your boys to kill me. Bring it, motherfuckers! I am willing to take whatever you have, so shove it up your ass. I'm overdosing again, fuckers, and I'm dying. People are after me so come after me, go ahead. You were my friend until you started to fuck me over. The Boss did this too by not paying what he said he was going to pay me. I did everything for you and I was a good little boy. Now I'm out, so send The Boss up to fight me. I have my gun in my hands at all times ready for whatever you want to do to me. My fucking veins in my arms are exploding. I can't even find a place to stick this needle anymore. All the money's gone. I used it to buy heroin because I banged it up my arm over the last two weeks. I love you and I hope that you know that. Stay away from me, motherfuckers."

I made sure to spell everything wrong to make this believable and show that I was really high. I pressed send. I received some text messages back from Booker asking me what the fuck was going on. My phone instantly rang and it was Booker. I answered the phone and immediately hung it up, he called back, I hung up again. I blocked his number. What did I just do? I was shitting my pants. What's going to happen now?

I destroyed the phone once and for all. Now it was the waiting game to see if I was going to pay the consequences for what I had done. I was paranoid for some time, but I was hoping that they were just going to leave me alone. I was leaving them alone. I think they were just as afraid of me as I was afraid of them. I was more afraid of The Boss than Booker. Booker was my friend and there was a bond that we had that I hope carried onto the next life if there is one. If there was going to be repercussions from what I had done it would have been directed by The Boss or Butcher.

That following winter I was moving snow in a skid steer in the Governor's driveway. I watched a man park a car on 4th Street. He got out of his car and walked into the yard up to the skid steer that I was in. He stood about twenty feet away. He had a face mask on so I couldn't see his face or mouth. Only his eyes were visible. We were looking right at each other. My senses were on high alert. I was ready to use the skid steer as a weapon if I needed to. He pulled a camera out of his pocket and took a picture of me. He then pointed his finger at me and shook his head. I knew that this was something that The Boss had orchestrated. It was a threat towards my life. See how easy we can walk up on you and press a button or pull a trigger. Threat taken. I got it. This really scared me up for some time. I was on high alert at my home for my family's sake. Nothing ever came of this threat. Over the next eight years, I would often think that it sure would suck if they got busted and thought that I was the one that snitched.

"What if someone robbed them? They would think it was me." No matter how bad they had done me wrong, I would have never snitched on anyone. Sometimes things can get cloudy and people can assume.

I worried after this, what would happen if the feds came and kicked in my door and took me down. I have a new life now. This can't happen. Yes, it can and it happens to people all the time. I was always told that the statute of limitations is seven years on a federal drug charge. I still have that little doubt in my mind that this could all end very badly. I did what I did and I deserved the consequences if they ever presented themselves. I still look over my shoulder thinking the worst. I still think of my friend Booker and our friendship. Having to walk away from my buddy was very difficult for me. I have shed many tears thinking about my friend over the years hoping that he is okay. I wish that I could tell him that I miss him.

The drug business always gets cloudy. I took the best way out that I could think of at the time. My heart still hurts when I think of losing such a friend. I miss you buddy. But, I don't miss that life, because I knew if I was still in it, I would have been arrested or six feet under by now. Growing up I always witnessed drug dealers who had the world by the balls. They had everything, Corvettes, Porsches, big jacked up trucks, custom built Harleys, and lots of beautiful women, and don't forget the tons of cash. As life goes by and you see them later on in life, it all gets torn away because addiction is involved. It never lasts. Addiction kills and it takes away everything that we love and dream of. Material things do not really mean shit to me today. The things that mean the most to me today are the ones who I love. I am glad I got out. I feel blessed that I was given another chance at a nice life, a life that I have always dreamed of and the one that I never thought would come true.

CHAPTER 70

Wedding Bells Go Pop

We decided to get married at the state Capitol grounds to keep it nice and simple. Amber had her judge friend officiate our wedding with all of our friends and family attending. The day was coming up quickly. We had picked September 1, 2012. I prepared the beautiful spot in the tree grove on the grounds while I was at work. I mowed the spot and picked up all of the sticks preparing for a beautiful day and moment. This was Amber's and my second wedding, so we wanted to do this right. We got ready for our special day. Nothing fancy since we just moved into a new home, but it was going to be perfect. We drove to the grounds together as a new family.

Tess was super excited. When we arrived at the grounds, we placed balloons where the ceremony was going to happen, but the wind blew them over hitting the ground and popping them instantly. Just a minor mishap, let's move on. Amber and I held each other's hand and greeted everyone when they arrived. I looked at my beautiful soon-to-be wife and I was full of gratitude and love. She was so beautiful on this wonderful day.

Our family members showed up with big smiles on their faces. This always caused large amounts of stress because families have their way of raining on my parade. A group of people who were all dressed up walked over to where we were standing. I guess there was another wedding happening at the same time on the grounds that day. We let them know that they were in the wrong spot. We all laughed, and they walked away in search of the other wedding.

I was excited to marry my beautiful girly. I was going to do my best to make it nice for Amber and the girls.

I bought the girls flowers with a card telling them how grateful I was to be in their lives, that I would do my best at being a stepdad, and how important they were to me. Tess was happy, and thanked me. The judge showed up and the ceremony started. I was blessed with a beautiful wife and new family. I remember looking at Amber smiling at me and looking into my eyes. I knew in my heart that we would be together for the rest of our lives.

I was able to kiss my bride. Amber and Tyler Auck, sure does have a nice ring to it. My heart was full as I held my new wife with so many dreams ahead of us. We had the reception at our home and it went well. This day was beautiful and awkward all at the same time. That's life, nothing is perfect and if it looks perfect, I always wonder what people are hiding. Amber's guest list consisted of half of the parole and probation department. This was a change for me, seeing quite a few probation officers that just two years prior were going into a house and confiscating the drugs that people were selling for me.

Now they were at our home to support this relationship and cheer us on. Never in a million years would I have thought that on my wedding day there would be cops sitting in my backyard. This was definitely a new kind of gathering than in the past. The last gathering I was at consisted of drug dealers and a couple of bank robbers. Sobriety is beautiful and our life was just getting started.

CHAPTER 71

Keep Watering The Grass So It Stays Green

Years of building this relationship was the hardest thing we have ever done along with getting sober. Let's be real, there were a lot of hard things that we had gone through and will continue to go through in our lives. That's what a relationship is, working your tail off to have something special, something that will last. The grass is always greener on the other side of the fence, but once you hop it, piss on it and don't water it, it will soon turn brown just like the side that you left because you are still there. I know this from experience. I have killed a lot of grass over my lifetime. Now, I need to just stay put and water the heck out of our grass to keep it healthy. We need to continue to let our guards down and expose all of our insecurities. The honeymoon phase is over and now the hard work starts.

The hardest part for me is trusting completely. I struggled with being disrespected by other men in our relationship, especially if it was right in front of my face. Let's just say there have been some stupid text messages from guys with eyes for my wife that have come in late at night that don't line up with a healthy relationship. Actually, these messages didn't line up with me holding it together and not going to jail for knocking down a door and pounding someone's head in with my fists. I didn't need another aggravated assault on my record so I chose to communicate with my wife and encouraged her to set some healthy limits and boundaries so this bar room play would stop. Roses are beautiful, but then there are the thorns. Amber came around once I was able to show her what it felt like. It's hard to walk in other people's shoes so sometimes you need to sneak in the back door and slip them onto their feet, so they know what it's like.

I did what I have always done in relationships and that was to show my pain in the most appropriate way possible, so it was understood. I reached out to a girl from college, told this girl about the text messages, made some shit up about what was really happening, provoked some dirty jokes and made her feel that it was okay to text me intimate things late at night just like the things that were making my wife's phone go off. My shoes were a little big on Amber, but she was able to see and feel what it was like to have the person who she loved with all of her heart and soul get a message from another girl that was inappropriate. She didn't like it and it made her sad. It really hurt her but where there is pain, there is change.

We continue to work a program of recovery and it all doesn't happen at once. I know that Amber would have never cheated on me, but it wasn't a good thing for our relationship. Things needed to break before they would get better. I was in the wrong, because I should have never manipulated the relationship like this with another girl. But, that's how I understand things is by reality therapy. I felt like I needed to do this or else I was going to ask for a divorce.

Amber got the picture and made the changes in her life so they lined up with our dreams of a life of happiness. She didn't do it for me, she did it for the respect of herself as a woman and maybe some fear that I might reach back into my bags of tricks and smack someone. They definitely would have deserved it. Once again, the leopard still has his spots and claws. He just chooses not to use them to hunt for fun or revenge. Love is painful and cruel at times. I am not here to paint a picture that is not true. Love has been hard way more than it has been good, but the beauty in the good outweighs all of the bad. All of the pain is worth it.

Communication is key to a healthy relationship. That's what they say anyway. I am a communicator. I will talk through issues for days. Amber isn't or wasn't a communicator. Amber had a steel wall that can slam shut for days. When our love was new it was easy to talk about life and dreams. But, once the new wore off and it was time to roll up our sleeves and put the work in, communication was next to impossible with us. Looking back on that day of the jaywalking incident, I could see the steel wall shut down around Amber and the lack of communication. The wall that day had beautiful flowers planted all around it and I wasn't able to see it because I was blinded by love. The steel wall became cold and lonely over the years.

I wasn't quite sure what to do with it. I just decided to love my wife and give her space until she was ready to talk. Sometimes this took days. I struggled at first trying to bust down the wall, but this just made it worse. I could talk myself into a hole really quickly. I also sucked at communicating because I would just talk and talk and not really try to listen or feel things out. I have always been good at talking myself out of things. When I would get in trouble, I would talk and try to spin it in my favor. This didn't work in our relationship. We were two really messed up people with good intentions and a dream to make this relationship work at all costs.

Amber's steel wall was constructed by pain and trauma over her life. Her wall kept her safe. I was able to stop banging my head off her wall and step back and look at more creative ways to stop it from slamming shut. Love and understanding made us come together as a couple and accept each other for who we were. I snuck into Amber's space and jammed my big ass feet into her shoes and walked for a while to get a good understanding of what she went through and what she continues to fight through today. I encourage everyone to try and walk in someone else's shoes.

Today, we are respectful of each other and willing to talk things out and let them sit and cool off. I no longer talk myself into a hole. I walk away or just shut up and listen. Amber's steel wall is now conditioned with love, respect, and safety. Now, it doesn't slam shut for days. Today, our communication style is built to fit our traumas of our past. Our communication isn't perfect, but it's not painful or scary anymore. It has been built from the ground up to work for us. They are right when they say communication is key to a healthy and happy relationship.

CHAPTER 72

For My Little Girl

Raising someone else's kids isn't easy. I have had a lot of big, mean, grown men throughout my life who have tried to break me. I tell you what, they don't hold a candle to getting into a relationship with someone who has two little girls. Let's just say we all needed therapy. My relationship with one of the girls failed miserably because I sucked at being rejected and didn't know how to live with someone who disliked me.

Tess is the oldest. She is the one that needed me because she was rejected and felt alone. I was able to give her what she has always needed and that was unconditional love and to walk next to her to build trust. Tess was open to receiving my love. I was stuck between a rock and a hard place. I have always tried to treat both girls the same way, but this was impossible when the treatment wasn't received the same way. I tried my best, but honestly it broke me in half. This piece of the story is very difficult for me to write because I am still trying to do the right thing.

I had lots of blame placed onto me because I wasn't able to cater to both kids. Everyone always focused on my failures as a stepparent and never really gave me any kind of recognition for the things that I was doing well or the sacrifices that were made. I wasn't asking for an award or anything. I was just asking for people to stop throwing rocks at me when I was doing my best to tread water. I refused to have people throw rocks at me and tell me they love me at the same time. I love both of these girls the same, but it looks way different. Not by my choice. I would give anything to change this, but I can't. I have tried. I had to walk away from some fights. And that broke my heart. I had to cut my losses and step away from some of the pain, not because I was running, but because I had to in order to stay sober and sane.

Tess let me in and accepted me for who I was and the person that I was trying to be. Tess also went through lots of pain and rejection over her lifetime. We were a match made in heaven.

One day, Tess and I were driving back to our house where she stayed part time and she leaned over, hugged my shoulder, and started to cry hysterically.

She looked at me and said, "Dad, please don't ever make me go back to Darrell's house. Please, Dad!"

I comforted Tess and reassured her that she will never return to that house ever again. I let her know that I had her back no matter what.

Tess told me one day that, "I just need you to keep being my dad and stay in my life every single day."

She was right. I did do it every single day and I will continue to do it for the rest of her life. Tess allowed me to be her Dad and I was willing. My heart was full even with the backlash.

Amber and I found out that we were going to be having a baby together. We were on top of the world ecstatic. October was our expected date. We were making our dreams come true, but there was one thing that I needed to do first and that was ask Tess if I could adopt her and make it official. I talked with Tess that evening.

"Tessers, I need to talk with you about something really important."

"Okay, Dad."

"I love you with all of my heart and soul and I want you to know that and I don't want you to ever forget that."

"I love you too, Dad."

"I was wondering if it would be okay to adopt you and make it official. I am your dad no matter what, but it would be special for me to adopt you."

"Can I keep my last name? I want to keep my last name."

"Yes, you can keep your last name. The last name thing doesn't matter to me and I know how much it means to you."

"I love you so much, Dad and yes, it would be an honor for me if you adopted me!"

"Thank you, kiddo. I love you so much and I'm so excited."

"Dad?"

"Yes?"

"When you and mom have the baby, are you going to treat it differently than you treat me?"

"Well, yes, because it will be a baby, but my love will be the same. I will love the baby as much as I love you, Tessers."

She smiled at me, gave me a big hug, and we cried tears of joy. I was excited and Amber was happy that Tess allowed me into her life.

This adoption was far from an easy feat. I hired an attorney and had to jump through a bunch of hoops. The attorney was having a hard time finding Tess's sperm donor. My persistence and some skills that I had learned from my days in the black market came in handy. I found Tess's sperm donor in thirty-five minutes. I had him on the phone in forty minutes. My attorney asked me if I wanted a job. I told her no, but how about a discount. We laughed. The sperm donor wasn't very cooperative. He called Amber a bunch of names so I threatened to come to Montana that evening to assist him in shutting his mouth and taking the things back that he said about my wife, whom he abandoned years earlier. He shut up really quick. Once again, the leopard still has its spots. I just chose to use them for good, but I still have claws and I have never forgotten how to sneak around in the dark.

Sperm Donor just wanted this to all go away, so he decided to sign over his parental rights just as long as no one in his family found out. Turns out, he hadn't told anyone and after all of these years his wife and kids would probably look at him a little bit differently if they knew. He signed the paperwork and now we waited for the court date to make this official. I wanted to get this done before the baby was born, but it wasn't looking like it was going to happen.

CHAPTER 73

Nine Months

The nine months leading up to the birth of our baby, my first biological child, was pedal to the metal. I was going to school full time, busting my butt working two jobs, and still making time for my wife and kids. My favorite time of day became 3:30 a.m. I figured if I sacrificed sleep then I wouldn't have to sacrifice time away from the people who meant the most to me. It was like I had this secret separate life because no one was able to see all of the work that I was doing behind the scenes. Just like now. I am writing this book. It's 3:45 a.m. and my beautiful wife is sleeping upstairs, and our little person is in a bed full of stuffed animals covered with soft blankets.

I bet you thought that I was going to spoil the story with the gender of our child. Five years old, that's all I am going to leak out now. Anyway, back to the story. I was getting stuff done. During our vacation to Omaha, Nebraska, I was at my heaviest weight. I traded drug addiction for a bad case of food addiction. Food was the same for me as drugs because I was using food to hide my feelings and disappear into pints of Häagen Dazs. My aunt sent us a family picture in the mail and Amber put it in a picture frame on the end table in the living room.

I was sitting on the couch one day when I looked over at the picture and looked at myself. I was disgusted. I struggled with body dysmorphia my whole life, but this was different. This time I felt sick to my stomach and motivated, so I joined Weight Watchers. We both knew I needed to do something, and I did. I wanted to be healthy when our baby was born and when I adopted Tess. I was scared that I was going to die from a heart attack if I didn't make the changes. I finally found enough strength to go to my first Weight Watchers meeting right after my home community support group. I weighed in at three hundred and thirty-six pounds. I was disgusted with myself, so after the meeting I went to the grocery store and got Amber and I each a pint of Häagen Dazs ice cream.

I got vanilla and Amber got her usual chocolate. We sat on the couch and ate it together. I was supporting my wife in her pregnancy by looking pregnant myself. This was the end for me. I kicked it into high gear and started losing weight. This was easy for me because I also have an eating disorder. Hell, give me a cookie because I will throw it up when no one is looking. This is something that I hid from Amber. I hid it from myself all these years. Some things take time to address and this wasn't the time. This gave me insight to the problem that I have with food. My metabolism was jacked up from the twenty some years of drug addiction. The weight was coming off so fast that some of the coaches at Weight Watcher were getting a little concerned, but I reassured them that it was all hard work.

I wasn't lying, I was working my butt off literally, but I wasn't going to tell them that I was starving myself as well. I was eating eight pounds of carrots per week, salads at every meal with a small chunk of chicken. I started paying at the pump at gas stations to avoid the smorgasbord of goodies that I didn't have the strength to pass up. I loved the feeling of starvation and it was working. Amber was getting bigger and I was shrinking. I had lost one hundred pounds at about month eight. People had been noticing the big change and asking me how I was doing it. I went to my home group for substance abuse support and they asked me, so I told them it was Weight Watchers.

I had one guy say, "So you go hang around with all of those fat people?"

Some people were so judgmental and it pissed me off. I went to a Weight Watchers meeting and the coach asked me if I would tell my group a little bit about my journey, so I did. I told the group that I am a recovering drug addict and that I gave up meth and switched to food. The look on the group's faces was horrifying. Some of these people with eating addictions were judging me because of my past addictions. I was blown away. I was thankful that I have a problem with most things in my life because I have a good understanding that an addiction is an addiction. It doesn't matter what the addiction is because my addictions all have the same traits in common. Each of my addictions were painted on the same canvas just with different brushes.

I lost one hundred and twenty-one pounds over eight months. This was crazy. I was now just sick in a different way. I was shooting for a healthier me, but I wasn't hitting the mark. I looked sick. I couldn't hold my lowest weight because I couldn't starve myself any longer. My body was failing. My last weigh in was intense. I had a hard time standing because I hadn't eaten in two days and I was taking ex-lax pills to cleanse all the liquids out of my body. Amber had some clue what was going on with me because of the weight loss, but I had so many secrets that I wasn't ready to share until now. I was fighting a fight that only I could see all while being the best husband and step dad that I could be.

CHAPTER 74

Enjoying The Expected

Being there for Amber when she was pregnant was the most amazing gift that I could have ever asked for. I took care of my beautiful wife and rode all the roller coasters of craziness with her. We would lay in bed at night and talk to our little Noodle that was growing inside of her. This was what we called our baby, our little Noodle. We were both so happy and excited for the birth of our baby. I would play music and put a little bit of AC/DC "Back in Black" up against Amber's belly so Noodle could rock out. I would kiss her tummy every night telling our little Noodle how love was flowing through me and that I was going to be the best daddy in the world. I would whisper beautiful words about Amber and how amazing she is and how lucky Noodle was to have her as her mommy. I was the messenger of beautiful conversations.

I took good care of Amber and made sure she had everything she needed and then some. Our dreams were coming true all around us. I attended every appointment with her. We were both taking it all in and loving every moment and the whole process. Gratitude was flowing out of us and it was breathtaking. She was enjoying my excitement and enthusiasm. We decided not to find out the gender of our Noodle. We wanted it to be a surprise. This was difficult for me because I needed to have everything in order and done before it needed to be done. The last month of our pregnancy, I worked ahead on all my online classes. I completed fifteen credits in three weeks. This was all normal for me. I am a grinder and my persistence will probably kill me someday. Everything was falling into place.

It was getting close. We had a date to go in and get induced, October 15, 2014. We were both on top of the world. Amber was ready to get this little Noodle out of her. We were preparing to meet our baby and we couldn't wait. We were told to show up a little bit after midnight. We tried to get some rest the night before, but the excitement and anticipation was too much to handle. When we left the house, we talked about the next time we came home we would have our baby with us. I had everything we needed packed into a duffle bag, including Amber's pillow.

While we drove through town everything felt like it was in slow motion. I made sure to take it all in. The moon was a little over half full. The temperature was at thirty-eight degrees. The streetlights were surreal and kind of spooky as we pulled up to the hospital. We walked across the parking lot. I had the duffle bag over my shoulder as I held Amber's hand. The dried-up leaves would occasionally crunch under our feet. Once we were checked in and shown to our room, we were both amazed at the nice room they gave us. She was checked over by a nurse. We were told that we had some time to wait so she laid on the bed to rest while I sat in a chair next to her.

Amber fell asleep for a little bit. I sat there looking at my beautiful wife with gratitude and tears of joy running down my cheeks. I was blessed beyond belief. This didn't seem real. I was nervous so I started tracing everything in the room to soothe my mind. This was the calm before the storm. The nurse came in and woke her up. We were getting ready. The doctor was on the way.

The lights came on and the surreal feeling turned to adrenaline. They were giving Amber a spinal tap while she was moaning from the pain. It went from zero to one hundred in two seconds. My wife's legs were up in the stirrups. The nurse was working on her, telling her to breathe. I held her hand when the nurse told her to push a few times. I was helping Amber with the breathing techniques that we had learned in Lamaze class. I thought we were just practicing because the doctor wasn't there yet, until the water broke. It hit me like a ton of bricks that this wasn't just practice anymore. I held her hand and kissed her forehead as I calmly expressed my motivation for her to stay strong. The doctor came into the room and she was ready.

She said, "Let's do this. Are you ready to be a dad?"

"Yes, yes, I am!"

"Alright, Amber you have been through this before so you got this."

I stood there holding Amber's hand. It was like an out of body experience. I was full of gratitude, excitement, and fear. I could hardly talk. She did amazing.

The doc yelled, "Here it comes! Look Dad, look!"

I looked at it and it definitely wasn't a noodle. Everything looked confusing down there. All I could see was a head and hair until the baby finally came out. I watched our baby get held up in the air in front of us before getting handed to a nurse.

I could see a little Noodle going across the room as the doc said, "Congratulations, it's a boy!"

I still had a grasp on Amber's hand. Our little boy. Our little Charlie Tyler Auck was taken over to a table with some lights. I wasn't sure what to do. I wanted to run over to Charlie and I wanted to hold Amber's hand and continue to celebrate with her.

The doctor said, "Get over there, Dad, and see your little boy."

I let go of Amber's hand and went over to the table where Charlie was lying and the nurses were cleaning him up. I was able to cut the cord. I grabbed his little hand, told him that I loved him, and that I was his daddy. I promised him that I was going to be the best daddy in the whole world. He was amazing and beautiful. I felt like the luckiest man on the face of this earth. Amber and I held Charlie and cried together.

This was the best experience of my life. He was healthy and we were happy. The day that we brought Charlie home was amazing. I remember looking at his little feet and the tiny socks in between my fingers. I was wondering how I was going to get something so small on his little feetsies. I did it and I did it well. Life was amazing. I was able to take about a month off work to stay with Charlie. I would just sit and hold him and watch him sleep. I have never been able to sit that long, but I did, and it didn't even phase me. Our blessings came true. We were parents to a little boy.

In November, I was blessed with the gift of adopting my beautiful daughter. My heart was full and I was enjoying every precious moment. The day that I adopted Tess was as beautiful as the day Charlie was born. This girl had my heart from the beginning and she loved me as her dad. Tess is my daughter due to dreams that didn't come true in my life. but, in reality, I was just dreaming the wrong dreams. All my dreams came true that day that we walked out of the courtroom and Tess Karen Griffin was officially my daughter.

CHAPTER 75

Flowers

Flowers have saved my life. I stopped sticking a gun in my mouth. I put the gun down and picked up flowers and found more strength than I ever knew existed. I found spirituality in petunias, peonies, and roses. The wave of love from my flower obsession had been spreading through different circles of people in my life. I have caused a chain reaction within my family and friends that is beautiful. My kiddos are little flower addicts. My wife gets the brunt of my obsession and it has changed her and now beautiful flowers fill her soul. If I look at the impact that flowers have had over my lifetime it is profound and nothing short of a miracle.

Flowers have always had a positive impact on my life, even when the storms raged, even before I realized the part they would play in my life to help me survive. The traumatic events that I have had in my life usually were altered by nature in a positive way. I feel that God has given me a gift of creativity, so I was able to use the flowers and plants around me to survive. God didn't save me, but he gave me the tools which helped me make it through the most difficult times in my life that I am grateful for today.

Growing up as a kid I always remembered taking the time to smell the flowers. My mom always loved flowers and she would always point them out to me. She helped me find the beauty in the little things in life. Mom would put fresh lilacs on our table even though my dad would bitch and complain; but one time I watched him smelling the lilacs on our table and it sure looked like he was enjoying himself. My mom also was blessed with the gift from God of creativity.

As kids, we would spend hours at a raspberry bush picking it clean and looking at their flowers in their backyards. I remember sneaking into people's backyards just to look at the beautiful flowers growing in their yards. Flowers meant something to me as a kid, but I honestly didn't understand the impact that they would have on me over my lifetime. Flowers would always take me to a magical place, away from all of the things that I wanted to separate from. Being around flowers made me feel free. When I was a kid, I would always dream about going to the mountains, finding a big meadow full of wildflowers, and then spending the rest of my life there. I figured everything would be ok if I was surrounded by flowers. These dreams that I had as a kid were preparing me for the miracles that would happen years down the road.

I used to draw flowers on my notebooks when I was a kid, but I made damn sure to draw the flowers on the inside of the notebook so no one else could see them. I was taught that boys are supposed to be tough and if you had anything with flowers on it you were a little pussy, queer bitch and I would have probably got my butt kicked by some dick head. I hid this part of my life and stuffed it way down deep into my mind for safe keeping. The only person who made me feel safe enough to say it out loud that flowers are beautiful was when I was with my mom. She always made it a safe living place for my obsession with flowers. Shit, she even bought me girl shoes up until sixth grade because

I liked the pastel colors and they reminded me of flowers. See why she is my angel.

If I look deep inside and explore the traumatic times in my life where I was hanging onto life or death by a thread, there were always flowers or nature involved in some way. Whether it was a suicide attempt or an overdose, I always was distracted by flowers. Why was it that after one of the times I tried to hang myself from a tree, I hit the ground and untied the extension cord from my neck I ended up looking at the beautiful ornamental grasses swaying in the flower beds? Their beautiful movements and sounds from swaying back and forth soothed me enough during the storm that raged inside of me to not climb the tree for a third attempt.

Why, when I was watching a man get beaten on the ground when I was a kid, did I watch the grass swaying in the wind? Why, when I put my head in the bucket of chlorine on that dirty shop floor and then I awoke, alive, the first thing that I noticed was the vase of flowers that my aunt had bought for her desk? Why would I stop doing the things that I was doing in my active addiction and put my gun down and start smelling flowers? I will tell you why and that reason was God. He or she was next to me the whole time making sure that I was okay, even when I didn't want to be okay! I have always loved the footsteps in the sand saying about the whole God thing, but my God thing didn't have sand. My God thing had flowers!

Once I took a picture of every single flower on the Capitol grounds. I would venture out to people's yards, churches, banks and anywhere else that I could get a beautiful picture of a flower. I knew where all the free flower pictures were throughout our community. I send different flower pictures to many different people. Not because I loved them in a romantic way, but because I wanted to share the beauty that I was experiencing. I send flower pictures to my kids, family members, and anyone else who I have in my contacts. I always make sure to let them know that this is a friend flower. I didn't ever want to make anyone upset over something so beautiful. I have sent out thousands and thousands of different flower pictures over the years to many different people.

At first when I started this, I would get a thank you back. Then some things started to change from the people that I was sending these nice messages of gratitude with a flower picture attached. I would let people know how grateful I was to have them in my life and that I just wanted them to have a beautiful day. My simple text messages of gratitude were having a positive impact on not only my life, but other people's as well. I started getting messages back from people letting me know that this simple message and this beautiful flower picture changed their day and lots of times people would say, "How did you know that I needed this today?"

I didn't know, but I knew that we all go through things in life and some of the most beautiful gifts come at the times in our lives when we least expect it. After a while I started getting flower pictures back from people. I have friends who have sent me flower pictures from all over the world. I have been working through making lifelong amends and flowers have helped this process.

In the wintertime I spend a lot of time at flower shops and grocery stores to build up my stash of flower pictures. These are great sources for beautiful flowers during our long cold winters. I have had people come up to me at the grocery store and ask me why I am taking pictures of flowers. I let them know that I send out flower pictures to people in my life to show that I care about them and that I would like them to have a nice day. I have been telling people about my flower routine for years. My wife, Amber, and my daughter, Tess, started taking pictures of flowers, sending them out to me, and to many different people. In fact, Amber sends out a flower picture to everyone in her office on their birthdays, just to let them know that she wishes them a happy birthday. It's crazy to think that some of the people in her office used to raid the houses of the people that were selling drugs for me and now their days have been made better from a flower picture that I probably have taken. The chief of police has even received flower pictures from me.

I have noticed a trend that flowers have made a big difference in people's lives and it's had a snowball effect. It just keeps getting bigger and stronger. Once we start something so simple it can have a profound impact on people's lives. I hope my love for flowers has made other people take a moment out of their day to see the beauty that is all around them and has encouraged them to slow down and smell the flowers.

I am able to get my wife a bouquet of flowers every year. I get my flowers from Dutch Mill Florists and I get to see my friends who work there. We have talked about so many different things over the years about life, pain, love, and the beauty of flowers. I love it because I walk in there and it is like the red carpet is laid out for me and I feel so special and loved. They allow me to go into the coolers and pick out the flowers that I want for my wife. I love this moment, because not only is my wife getting something that I handpicked, but I get to spend time with some of the most wonderful people on the face of this earth while I am surrounded by flowers.

I feel that if we pass on words of gratitude and love, and attach it to a flower picture, this simple gift will change the world forever. Flowers have allowed me to be a man and to express myself in the most beautiful way that I know possible. I am teaching my kids that it is okay to express how they feel. I teach my little boy, Charlie, that flowers are beautiful and that it is okay to be a man or a boy and love flowers. The other day Charlie whispered in my ear, "Daddy, I need your help."

"Okay, Charlie, what do you need help with?"

"Daddy, I wanna get my friends at daycare flowers for Valentine's Day."

This just melted my heart knowing that he feels safe to talk with his dad about the beauty of flowers. He has a family that is tied together with flowers. Flowers have an impact on our lives weekly. I am blessed with all of the flower pictures that I have gotten over the years from random people. I am grateful that I have been able to make a difference in people's lives by sending something simple and beautiful as a flower. I am the lucky one because not only do I get to get out of myself by giving back, I get to take the time to slow myself down for a moment and take in the beautiful details of life. Flowers have changed me forever and I will continue to send out messages with a flower attached. The simplest gifts are the best.

I struggled over the years with the whole God thing. Between my addiction and the negative people in my life, I pushed God further away each day. Newly into sobriety, I went to almost every church in town seeking something that I thought was missing. I would attend Bible studies with some amazing people, but it got a little strange when they started praying over me. It felt like I had so many people try to save me.

Once again, I couldn't handle the people part of God. I stopped going to church. I explored spirituality. Spirituality is my flower. I always thought that if I must go to a building or get down on my knees to pray to be accepted into heaven, I will pass on the heaven piece. The heaven that I will teach my kids about is a beautiful place that will accept us even if we find our spiritual feeling from a flower or nature. I do not judge anyone who attends organized religion. Don't get me wrong, I have judged organized religion over my life. But, today, I respect the way others do what they need to do to find peace in life.

We all go through situations in our lives and we all lean on God/spirituality at different times in our life. I have some very good friends who are religious people. I love listening to them talking about God because their God seems like a beautiful God. These people tell me about God in the most respectful nonjudgmental ways. Today when I think of God, He or She is kind, loving and accepting. I am grateful for the path that I have been on seeking God. I am grateful for all the ups and downs and the pain that I have experienced because I truly feel that I will be a seeker of a spiritual feeling for the rest of my life. I will always be that guy that gets excited about the mysteries of life and the miracles that happen in front of us every single day.

CHAPTER 76

The Start Of The Amends

One of the steps in sobriety consists of making a list of all the people who I have wronged as a result of my drug use and alcohol use. I sat down and made my list. Wow, the list was long, longer than I had thought when I started. The wrongs were serious wrongs and it was way too much to handle at that time. It was overwhelming. It depressed me. So, I set the list aside for a time when I would be better able to handle it. I "fired" my second sponsor from my home community support group.

I was still wet behind the ears from all the years of drug and alcohol abuse. I really had no clue what to do with my time. I was scrambling to find myself and find something fun to add to my new life.

My wife, brother in-law, sister in-law, and I all took tennis drills. I was super-excited, but nervous. My wife and I went down to Scheels and bought two nine dollar tennis rackets and two cans of balls the night before drills. We were ready to embark on a new journey together. My wife and I had always struggled to do activities together, but this time was going to be different.

The first night of lessons were fast paced. It was the most fun that I had had in a long time. I thought it was going to be easy. It looks easy on TV. Growing up, I hit lots of rocks with old wood tennis rackets, so hitting a tennis ball shouldn't be any different.

The class was full, eight people were taking part in the drills and they were all better than me. I would either hit the back wall, the ceiling, or smash it in the net. I was having so much fun. I was out of shape. My wife spent most of the drills following her brother around, so I was sure that I was embarrassing her and that she wanted to stay away from me. I might have been a little bitter because we did buy matching tennis rackets and we did go as a couple, but it just wasn't our time to play together. We did this as a group for a few different drills and then we even took some private lessons.

Our instructor Brittany was a short little ball of ornery. She cut me down and let me know how crappy I was at tennis. I didn't take her crap for too long, so she stopped being mean to me. I was hooked. I knew in my heart that I found something so beautiful that filled that giant hole that the drugs and alcohol once occupied. No, it wasn't Brittany, silly, it was tennis.

We continued taking lessons until I was the last man standing from our group. I kept on going, I was addicted from the very first ball that I hit and the smell of those beautiful tennis balls when you first crack open a can. The smell is unbelievable. Yes, I sniff balls. Stop laughing and stop picturing me sniffing balls. You are as twisted as I am, and more than just a little sick. Over the next year I continued with drills, cardio-tennis, and intermediate mixed doubles league. For the record, I took last place.

The next season I signed up for tennis drills just like I had done before. They were scheduled in the evening, so I didn't have to miss work or school. That night I went home from work feeling excited that I was able to play some tennis. I grabbed my green, beat up, old mountain bike backpack, and dumped all my bike stuff out of it onto my work bench in the garage. I put my racket, water bottle, and new can of balls inside of it. I arrived at Capital Racquet and Fitness early and sat and watched the others who had court time. That night I watched the people walk in who were signed up for drills.

The drills were six weeks long. It was very awkward and scary, but once we started playing some of the thoughts and the anxiety started to go away. Tennis was my new coping skill and I didn't even know it. We finished up drills that night and I walked over, grabbed my bag, and put my tennis racket in it. I had no clue that I would be getting ready to be introduced to the next step in sobriety and that was to make direct amends to people who I had harmed. This guy from drills walked over to me.

"Hey, there is thirty minutes of free play on the courts after drills, do you want to play?"

"Yes, I would."

We didn't exchange names, we just got right to playing tennis. It was fun playing against him. He was a better player than me, and I tried hard to beat him. It was an intense play for thirty minutes. We were both exhausted when the final ball was hit, and our time was up.

We met at the net and shook hands. He looked me in the eyes.

"Do you remember me?"

"No, I don't."

"You don't?"

"No, I don't recognize you."

He pointed to his face.

"You messed up my face. You made me have seizures for ten years!"

I was standing across the tennis net from him. We were about three feet apart. My mind instantly went into survival mode thinking that a fist would be thrown next and I would have deserved it. I could feel the rush of uncertainty and an overwhelming sickness in my guts. I didn't know who he was and was this really happening?

"You hit me one night, years ago. You don't remember me?" He looked stunned that I didn't remember him.

"Man, I am sorry, I don't remember you. I've hit a lot of people in my life. I've hurt a lot of people."

"My name is Chuck." When he told me his last name, the bell rang and now it was all coming back to me.

I had seen his name on the restraining order and the aggravated assault paperwork. My mind was racing with scenarios of that night when I hit him. This is the guy who went to my mom's work trying to shake her down for $10,000 to pay for his medical bills. The last time that I saw him, he was laying on the street knocked out cold.

This is one of those moments that no community support group or years of sobriety could ever prepare me for. I didn't know how to make this amend. And what was his part in it? He wasn't innocent. He shouldn't have put his hands on me. He tried to take my mom for $10,000. His girlfriend should have shut her mouth and stopped screaming. The justifications came rushing into my mind. It's crazy how in a moment's time I could completely spin it so I didn't have to look at or feel the scary feelings that were churning inside of me. I had put a lot of hard work into my life making things different and making the wrongs right. My heart ached for this guy because of what I had done to him years ago.

We stood there in the middle of the tennis court looking at each other not quite sure of what to do next. I had hurt this guy badly.

"I can't even say sorry to you because sorry is not a word that will work. Sorry isn't good enough for the pain that I have caused you, but I am truly sorry."

I was looking him in the eyes just standing there in awkward silence. No words were coming out, so we just walked towards the door. I made sure to have him walk out in front of me to guard myself from a potential attack. I was sorry for the damage that I caused him in his life.

"Don't worry about it, man, I'm okay now."

He stuck his hand out and shook mine and said, "Well, I better be getting home."

We parted ways and I watched him walk across the parking lot and get into his vehicle. I walked over and got into my Jeep. I was overwhelmed with emotions.

I shut the door on the Jeep and started the vehicle. The tears started running down my cheeks. I was crying uncontrollably; I couldn't catch my breath. You know the kind of cry that shakes your whole body, the ugly cry where snot and spit come out. These emotions were something that I wasn't used to feeling, let alone having to manage.

I left the parking lot of Capital Racket and Fitness aand drove up the street before taking a right towards Century Avenue. I looked over at Captain Jacks Liquorland on my left and had thoughts about getting a bottle to make this all go away. I contemplated getting drunk. But, the thoughts of all the people who cared about me and helped me over the years flooded my brain. I thought about all the people who I would let down. I thought about my family and school. I thought about all the hard work that I have put into my sobriety to get to this point. I couldn't mess this up, so I kept driving.

This had nothing to do with wanting to get drunk. It was about making the feelings go away that I didn't know how to cope with. I cried all the way home feeling bad about what I had done to different people in my life. The images of the others who I had left laying on a street knocked out raced through my mind. I would have never thought that I would run into somebody who I had smacked and hurt. I was feeling sorry for myself and feeling sorry for Chuck. I was a mess. The feelings from seeing Chuck drained me. I actually felt bad for what I had done even after all of the years of glorifying the damage that I had done to my community and all the people. This was too much to handle. I needed to go home, shower, and sleep to make it all go away.

I pulled into the driveway, opened the garage door, and sat there thinking about quitting tennis and never going back. I finally cleared the tears out of my eyes and mustered up enough nerve to go into the house. Once inside the house I was met with a hug from my wife. She looked at me and instantly knew something was wrong.

"Are you okay? What happened babe?"

I told my wife about what had just happened and how stunned I was. I couldn't even process this with her, but I said it out loud anyway. The power of saying your feelings out loud to someone who has your back is life altering. I instantly had some of the weight of the night lifted off my shoulders. This girl is my rock, she is my everything. We stood in the kitchen talking. I told her everything that I was going through. She held me in her arms as tears ran down my face.

"It will all work out babe, I love with all my heart and soul. I am here for you, I have your back."

I woke up the next morning thinking about the next five sessions of tennis drills. I thought about not going back because it was too much to deal with, but I had to. I signed up. I paid the price and now I have to face my past. Over the next week, I did lots of soul searching. I reached out to all of my supporters. I attended community support groups. The going consensus was that I had to face my past and continue playing tennis, and not use alcohol or drugs. I could do that; it was easy when you are open and honest with the people who have your back and who have walked similar paths. I took their advice and stepped up to the plate.

The following week I walked back through the doors of Capital Racket and Fitness Center and participated in drills. This week was different, I wasn't scared of my past and the awkward part was already over. I noticed Chuck was hitting the balls back at me extra hard. I am sure he was working through his own stuff.

The next three sessions went well. The battle axe pushed us extra hard and challenged us to be better than the session prior. The last night of drill, Chuck walked over to me and shook my hand. He stood in front of me with a puzzled look on his face.

"I don't think that you're the Tyler that hit me."

I looked at him and explained that I am, in fact, the guy who did just this.

"I hit you, Chuck. It was me."

He then asked. "Can I see your driver's license? You don't seem like the Tyler that I have heard about over the years. It's hard for me to believe that it's you."

I pulled my wallet out of my backpack and pulled out my driver's license and handed it to him. He looked it over.

"It's you. People have told me about the animal, Tyler Auck, and it's crazy to see you now. You're a nice guy."

I replied, "Chuck, I am glad that our paths have crossed, and I hope we get to play tennis this summer, you're a nice guy too. And I am truly sorry for the pain that I have caused you."

As I was walking out of the building, I thought what a better way to make an amend when sorry doesn't work. That first night I was concentrating on the person who I used to be when I should have thought about the person who I am today. The person who does the next right thing and be the person who faces life challenges with pride and respect.

When I look back at my Colorado experience I think about Skip and his little boys, and hope they are okay. I send Linda my strength. Once Skip moved out, I never spoke to him again. Over the years I thought about that fat man and revenge. I always wondered if the fat man and his crew went to prison for life for the murders and what they had done to that prostitute stabbing her all of those times and throwing her off that train bridge.

Once again, my big heart leads me astray and people continue to hurt and there is nothing that I can do about it.

I finished writing this story and I broke down crying. The tears are falling down onto my keyboard as I am typing. My heart breaks for the people still out there suffering, for the Linda's that are trading their bodies for drugs and for the prostitutes that get thrown away to die. I think of the Skips who stay stuck in their shit because they don't know how to get out and don't think they deserve anything but pain, and the Lukes and the Pats who don't get the love and attention they need and cry themselves to sleep at night and go on to live messed-up lives because they don't know any differently.

Maybe my heart didn't lead me astray. Maybe it was in the right place at the right time for the people who needed it the most. I hope I showed these people all of the love that I knew how to give at that time in my life. I hope I did the best that I could under those circumstances. I still think about shooting the fat man in the back of the head so I guess the old saying goes: can a leopard change his spots? No, I just choose to do things differently than my instincts tell me to do. Every day I have a choice to either lead with my heart and do the next right thing or make a trip out to the fat man's Auto Repair and Used Cars and walk up behind him and shoot him in the back of the head.

My buddy, Scott, would always tell me, "Give it five years Tyler and you will look back on your life and you will never believe how far you have come. You will have a house, kids, a dog, and that beautiful wife that will love you unconditionally. Your dreams will come true."

I didn't believe him but he could see the beautiful things that happened when a person gives sobriety a chance. It was hard for me to understand because I was so miserable so many times in my life and I was not quite sure if I wanted to live or die. I was facing all kinds of hard issues that were coming straight at me but my heart kept peeking out of my chest looking for my soulmate who I had always dreamed of. Today, looking back, Scott was right. I have everything that he told me about and more.

PART VII

Giving Back

The next two chapters are stories of forgiveness and a true friendship that has come from the damage of my past. The paths of two people from opposite sides of the law came together in an unlikely friendship. These stories are very dear to my heart. I am blessed with people who have looked past my crazy life and gave me the opportunity to give back and build something that continues to help people. Sometimes in life, the most beautiful gifts are given that can never be repaid. The only thing that a person can do is pass these gifts on to other people along our journey.

Brenna Gerhardt is the Humanities North Dakota Executive Director (Aka my agent). It's hard for me to put into words the support that this woman and her team have given me, both personally and professionally. Our story of The Cop and The EX Criminal was featured in the Humanities on Second Thought Magazine Fall 2017 issue. This story took off like a rocket along with their supporrt. They provided us with an unlimited supply of copies to hand out at our speaking gigs. Their support has changed my life forever, and I will continue to give back in their honor. It's beautiful when people believe in us!

CHAPTER 77

The Cop (Retd.) By Dan Donlin

In 1988, I began my law enforcement career as a police officer with the Bismarck Police Department. During my career I was involved in making hundreds of arrests. I cannot begin to remember the names of every individual I was involved in arresting; however, during an officer's career some names just stick with you. During my years working on Patrol and as a detective in Investigations, "Tyler Auck" was one of those names forever embedded in my mind. Anytime I heard the name "Tyler Auck," my immediate thoughts were-and I emphasize the term were-burglar, thief, drug user, fighter...criminal, foe!

While I was progressing through a very blessed and successful law enforcement career path, Tyler was progressing down a very wicked path of drug and alcohol abuse as well as frequent criminal activity. Tyler's first arrest was at age ten, his first assault at age fifteen, his first DUI at age sixteen, and his first felony arrest at age seventeen. Ultimately, with our agency alone in a twenty-one year period (ages ten to thirty one), this kid was a suspect in twenty reported cases and was arrested ten times. I would never forget the name "Tyler Auck"! He was definitely headed on the path to prison or death.

Fast forward to 2015; I was serving in my twenty-seventh year of law enforcement and was now the Chief of Police of the Bismarck Police Department. I had not heard or even thought of the name "Tyler Auck" since probably about 1998, or roughly seventeen years.

On September 12, 2015, I attended an early morning event called, "March into the Light." This was a walking event hosted by various entities involved in drug and alcohol addiction/treatment and was a public event to celebrate National Recovery Month. I have a lot of empathy for those struggling with drug and alcohol addiction, and I wanted to show the addiction community that I, and the police, support them in their battle.

I don't remember exactly how, but all of a sudden, out of the darkness of the morning, within the crowd of participants, I heard someone mention the name "Tyler Auck." I had not seen Tyler for a very long time and was very unsure of what Tyler would think if, or when, he found out I was among the people there. Well, we were able to meet face to face.

I saw him pushing a small child in a stroller and we shook hands. A little hesitant as to what to say to him, he immediately apologized to me for all the havoc he created for the police in his past. I told him, "Hey, that's okay, we all make mistakes." He went on to briefly tell me about his recovery and his recent life. All I could think was, "WOW! What a turnaround this guy has made" and I was very happy for him. We participated in the event and parted ways. I wished him good luck.

Since this chance meeting, Tyler and I have become very good friends and partners in educating and working with the community on drug and alcohol addiction issues. I have witnessed

Tyler on statewide addiction issue panels and committees, and he is not afraid to tell his story. I have learned of the personal horror this "kid" has gone through in his lifetime, not including the extreme challenge it is to battle addiction, get sober, and maintain his recovery. If anybody has an excuse to do drugs and alcohol for self-medicinal purposes...to forget the pain...Tyler has it! BUT, Tyler has made the choice to fight the fight and maintain his sobriety in a healthy recovery. He has told me many times, "I just want to right the wrongs I did in my past."

The past, as horrific as it is for Tyler, has made him who he is today; a husband, a father, a family man, a man fighting to stay in healthy sobriety. He is a man working a full-time job, raising a family, and attending college to obtain his degree to become a Licensed Addiction Counselor, and he is now interning as an addiction counselor at one of the top treatment facilities in the Upper Midwest.

Today, Tyler and I will meet for coffee and talk about old times, drugs and alcohol, addiction issues, our families, and what lies ahead in our future. We laugh when he says, "I can't believe I have the police chief's personal cell phone number." He invited my family to his son's birthday party; wow, what an unlikely friendship.

Tyler tells me he looks up to me, but it is I who look up to Tyler. He has gone through more difficulty and struggles in life than I can even dream of, let alone ever actually had to deal with. It is my honor to call Tyler Auck my friend. No one can understand the hell he and others like him have had to go through to make it where he is today. I'm glad he crawled out of hell, screaming and fighting, because this man is making a positive difference. Now when I hear the name, "Tyler Auck," my immediate thoughts are friend, success, integrity, compassionate, helper, credible, forgiver, family man, conqueror...HERO! Tyler, friend, YOU are a positive role model and I couldn't be any more proud of you than I already am!

CHAPTER 78

The Criminal (Retd.)
By Tyler Auck

My life in addiction started out from the time I was born. My family was damaged by the disease of addiction many generations before me, and it will continue for many generations to come. Growing up in a home where addiction ran rampant, l experienced physical abuse, verbal abuse, and pure mental torture as a young child. My young green eyes saw things that no child should ever have to see. My innocence was taken from me one horrible moment at a time. Sometimes, I look at pictures of myself as a child; I look into those innocent eyes and see the pain and feel the fear that still haunts me today.

In 1989, I tried my first drink and it was the most amazing feeling in the entire world. I felt stronger than superman, but in reality, I was so drunk that I couldn't get up off the ground. This simple act of experimentation lit the fire of addiction in my soul and I was instantly a full-blown addict. My disease progressed until it became stronger than life itself. After the alcohol I tried marijuana, followed by pills, cocaine, and methamphetamine.

You name it, and I would do it. I took great pride in my using and my ability to consume more alcohol and drugs than anyone else around me.

Even before my first use, I was involved in some simple assaults, vandalism, and many fights that I was never arrested for. But once chemicals were added to my system, all of the horrible violent behaviors escalated and had a negative impact on my life, my community, and everyone else who happened to get in the way of my addiction.

My path of pain and destruction began early. At the age of fifteen or sixteen, I was raped by an older woman because I was too drunk to defend myself. At sixteen, I received my first DUI and experienced a couple of alcohol and drug related overdoses. By the time I was seventeen, I had already been arrested several times and was well known to law enforcement and the community as a thug and drug user. During this time, my drinking escalated to expert level. I would wake up in the morning already shaking and craving some sort of chemical to ease the demons inside of me. I felt as if my choice to not use was taken away one second at a time. As I fell deeper into my hole of addiction and pain, I became desperate. I started to burglarize businesses as a way to fuel the fire inside of me for adrenaline and the high that I craved. I was slowly dying and each day I tried harder and harder to help death along.

During this time, "Dan Donlin" was a name that I heard often, because he was one of the lead detectives assigned to investigate me. I hated law enforcement because they were hindering my ability to feed my addiction and trying to stop the rampage and chaos that was my life. In a sick and twisted way, I was enjoying it and was secretly proud of the fact that law enforcement couldn't pin anything on me. But soon enough my luck ran out.

By the time I turned eighteen, I was facing several criminal charges, including burglary, assault, and theft of property. They were going to try me as an adult, and I was facing thirty five years in prison. Somehow, I managed to slip by with house arrest and probation. Most would think that this would have been my rock bottom or a wake-up call, but it never even slowed me down.

In 1994, I moved to Boulder, Colorado. I needed a fresh start and get away from Bismarck, Dan Donlin, and all of the people and things that were out to get me. It also helped that I heard there were lots of drugs there too. Once I was established in Colorado, things got worse for me. My addiction picked up right where it left off and the violence and self- induced bad luck continued (for a long time I was convinced that Bismarck PD called ahead and told them about me.) I was broken and out of hope. I ended up with a criminal record in Colorado and was forced to move back to Bismarck with a degree in LSD, marijuana, cocaine, heroin, and drug dealing.

In 2001, I married a girl back in Bismarck and over the next seven years, our lives and relationship spun out of control. During this time, my violent behaviors started to slow, but my disease became increasingly worse. My addiction tricked me into thinking that I had major medical problems and over an eleven year period I had twelve surgeries. In reality, I probably only needed two; the others were just a way to get pain meds. I started to get meds from veterinarian clinics to feed my habit. Methamphetamine was also a huge part of my daily life. I was hospitalized on a regular basis and lied, cheated, and sold drugs to get what I needed. By 2009, our marriage was over and the thoughts of suicide that plagued me early on in life reared their ugly head. I made yet another attempt to take my life by placing a gun in my mouth and pulling the trigger. For some reason, my higher power had other plans in store for me and the gun failed to fire.

During the divorce, I checked myself into treatment, with the hope of saving my marriage. I had been through many treatment centers before and inevitably this one failed as well. I had not yet felt enough pain in order for me to stay sober. Over the next few years, I managed to put together about eleven months of sobriety, but I could not find peace or happiness. I crashed once again and went on a three-week violent, suicidal, meth and opiate induced rampage. Finally, I had had enough and on January 5, 2011, I checked myself into the Heartview Foundation.

Since that cold, miserable, beautiful day, I have remained sober and in recovery with the help of so many wonderful people. In February of 2011, I met the girl of my dreams and we formed a beautiful relationship and married in 2012. We have a home that is filled with recovery. We have two children together and my wife has one child from a previous relationship. It is such a beautiful gift to have a woman that I love so much and to have her back and know that she has mine, even after learning about my past.

My wife is in law enforcement and on several occasions, we have run into my old friends. They ask if that's the "side" I'm on now and my response is yes! Today, I am ethical and law abiding and I support the love of my life and the Thin Blue Line.

Over the next several years, I often thought about my life of destruction and the pain I had caused others. Then, on a cold day in early 2015, I was in a skid steer clearing snow on the south side of the State Capitol when I saw a man walking into the building. My stomach got a sick feeling and my heart raced. My eyes zeroed in on Dan Donlin, the man that, so many years before, I had hated and despised. But this day was different. The hatred was gone, replaced with so much guilt and shame. I wanted to jump out of my machine and run to him, to tell him how sorry I was for all the chaos and damage that I had done to our community and to the Bismarck Police Department, but that particular day I could not fight past the fear and shame and bring myself to do it.

Then, in September of 2015, I was asked to speak at "March into the Light" recovery walk organized by Face It Together. It was dark and cold as my family and I all huddled together around the shelter. In my head, I was rehearsing the few words I had prepared to say to the crowd. Suddenly Dan Donlin, Chief of Police, was introduced as the first speaker. My immediate thought was to run, but I couldn't. I made a commitment to do this and I was going to see it through.

When Dan finished speaking, they called me up front, handed me the microphone and I said, "My name is Tyler Auck and I have been sober since January 5, 2011. Dan used to investigate me. Hi, Dan."

Through the darkness and the fear, I heard a voice say, "Hi Tyler."

I finished speaking and walked through the crowd to shake the hand of the man that I once hated and feared. I was greeted with a big hug and the words "I am proud of you, Tyler." Then, we walked. I pushed my little boy, Charlie, in a stroller and held my wife, Amber's, hand as our daughter, Tess, walked next to us. We took a stand for recovery and the people still out there suffering from the disease of addiction. After the walk, we all stood around and talked to the man that was once one of my biggest enemies.

That morning something very beautiful happened between a cop and an ex-criminal - and from that moment on, we formed a wonderful friendship. We have coffee and talk about life, family, and what we can do as human beings to make a difference in our community. Dan and I joke around sometimes in disbelief that we have each other's personal cell phone numbers. In 2016, Dan and his family came to my little boy's second birthday. The man that once built a criminal case against me is now one of my biggest supporters in life and my recovery. I'm proud that today he calls me "friend".

On May 27, 2017, I sat in front of my computer putting all of these thoughts down on paper as my beautiful family is in the background giggling and full of life. I often say that my life is full of broken gifts. They may have been delivered to me in the ugliest, most horrifying package, but I wouldn't change it for the world.

Today, I am blessed with a beautiful family, great friends, over six years of recovery, and the privilege to intern at the Heartview Foundation to become a Licensed Addiction Counselor and help people just like me and you.

This story is more than just a criminal and a cop. It is about breaking down the barriers our communities face each day. It shows that change is possible, and no matter how far down the hole of addiction and pain we fall, there is hope!

CHAPTER 79

Broken Gifts

I have spent the last eleven years of my life exploring what the broken gifts in my life were all about. I have been given so many broken gifts in my life, from the time that I was born all the way up to this moment. I have never asked for these broken gifts. I remember the first time that I said that I was grateful for being physically, verbally, and mentally abused. I was taken back by my own words. I say this not because these things were great, but I say this because there are beautiful things that have come out of each of these moments of pain.

One beautiful thing about knowing how to hurt people is having the insight to not hurt them. I have always been hypersensitive and this is one of my favorite broken gifts. I am able to see things and feel things in my relationships with my wife and kids before they even become close to hurtful. I often look down upon my hands and wonder why I am not hurting the people who I love the most? Why am I going the opposite direction than I was shown? I truly believe that it's because I look at all of the horrible things that happened over my life as gifts. I look at the beauty in pain and the change that it has invoked inside of my heart to make me a better person.

I was speaking at a treatment center when I told a group of people that I was raped. I had never told anyone in my entire life of this pain. That night, after the anger and confusion passed, I forgave myself and the healing started. I was able to find gratitude in my pain. Let's get this clear: I wasn't grateful for the abuse or the years of trauma that still haunt me to this day, but what I was grateful for is after I say it out loud to a room full of people at a speaking event, I always have a man or a boy come up to me afterwards and tell me that they have been raped and that they have never told anyone until now. This is the broken gift that I speak about. There is something beautiful in sharing our pain and suffering with others because it shows us that we are not alone. We all have broken gifts. They are everywhere once I opened my eyes. The years of therapy didn't hurt either. The more that I share my broken gifts with people the more that I can see how it changes them and it allows them to look at pain differently.

I don't recommend for anyone to get so used to pain that you choose it over peace and serenity. I have found many broken gifts along my journey. I am blessed that I can work through them appropriately. Broken gifts have been the most beautiful discoveries that I have ever had in my life. To find something so beautiful in something so broken. We all have broken gifts. I wrote myself a letter after my first month of sobriety and I promised myself that when I fall down, I will not stay down, I will get back up no matter what the cost and no matter how broken I am at that time. We all experience painful things in life and trudge through difficult times. My advice to you, is to get back up and put one foot in front of the other. Reach out for help. Look yourself in the mirror and tell yourself, "I love you. We got this. We are a community. We are never alone."

I have moments in my life that I cherish with my whole heart. I try to take nothing for granted. When I leave my home, I make sure to kiss my wife and kids and look into their eyes and cherish that moment because It might be the last time that we ever get to see each other.

Flowers are beautiful, but I know that when I have a flower bloom in my backyard that it will only be there for a small moment in time and if I don't cherish it, tell it how grateful that I am for it, and share its beauty through a photo, I will miss the beauty that it's sharing with me. Life is my flower; it is constantly changing and the beauty is only for a moment and that's what makes it so beautiful.

There is lots of pain in having broken gifts, and if I don't use my superhero powers for good, they will destroy me and everyone around me. I have to find the beauty in my pain or I will die. I have been given a gift. It was given to me in a damaged box with some torn up wrapping paper. It was dirty and it stunk. It had a bow that was tied in a knot and the delivery people left it in a hole with snakes and sharp dirty broken glass.

Once I was able to slowly open the gift over the years, once I was able to look past all of the pain and suffering, I was able to find the beauty inside. I wouldn't be the person who I am today if these broken gifts weren't given to me, and I am proud of the person who I have become because of my broken gifts. I am truly blessed that I have the ability to open the gifts that are in front of me before judging them by their appearance or where they are at in their journey on finding out what is inside. Everything that I have been blessed with in my life is because something went wrong somewhere along the way. Pain has to be felt. My pain is no different than your pain. We just use different brushes to create our own individual story. Broken gifts have changed my life forever and I feel blessed that I get to share them with you. There is a reason that I am not dead and I can't wait to keep watching all the miracles in my life unfold before my eyes..

For My Dad

This memoir is dedicated to my dad.

Dad, as I think of sitting in front of this keyboard at 4 a.m. on countless days, I can't help but wonder if you were looking down on me as I typed some of the worst things that you did to me and our family. But, I knew in my heart that if you were alive today you would have believed in me and supported what I am doing by writing this book. I believe you would support my soul intention of helping people, even if it meant revealing some of our deepest darkest secrets.

There is one thing that I know well and that is, change is possible no matter how deep the hole that we are in. I want to thank you for the changes that you did make in your lifetime and I want you to know that they didn't go unnoticed. I think of the pain that you must have carried as you struggled with the disease of addiction and those times that you did unthinkable things to me and then regretted them. I know that you were human even if you struggled to show your true feelings. I have worked through most of my issues that were caused by what you did to me, and I am a better person today after putting this all in the past.

Today, I choose to tell my kids all the good things that you brought to my life because they aren't ready to hear the things that I have written. I look at my little boy and my daughter and I wish that they could have met you because I know in my heart that you would be an amazing grandpa today. I know that you would love my wife with all of your heart and you would have supported her loving me.

Just so you know, I broke all the vicious cycles of abuse and addictions that have plagued us. I even cried when I wrote this. And, dad, do you see who I am today? I am a strong, beautiful man with tears running down my cheeks. I feel your hand on my shoulder supporting me, telling me that it's ok to cry.

I hope this memoir helps people because I grew up watching you and mom helping the people that were discarded and abandoned by society. I am grateful for the lessons that were taught on how to treat people when they are down and out. These lessons come in handy today because I am blessed with the gift of helping the broken people of the world. It is my honor to serve with kindness, gratitude and guidance. I have a saying and that is, Love the people that are the hardest to love.

Dad, I hope you know in your heart that I will never live without the pain that you have put on me but I am stronger because of it. I am able to find the beauty in all the broken gifts that you have given me and the ones that I have created on my own and use them as superhero powers to survive and thrive.

I forgive you and I love you!

ACKNOWLEDGEMENTS

Thank You!

Kurt Peterson, I want to thank you for believing in me and pushing me in the kindest most gentle way and teaching me to write a sentence that makes sense. I was nervous to write this part because I thought, how do I write a thank you that makes sense without your help and how would I ask you for help to write my thank you to you? Anyway, I have been blessed with the gift of knowing the real you and it is inspiring. People come into our lives when we need them the most and I will never forget that night at writing class when I told the group that I have only read two books in my entire life. Everyone in the group was telling me that I needed to start reading if I wanted to write a book. I thought they were all crazy because it took me forty-five years to read two books so reading wasn't going to happen. You sat in silence for a moment looking across the room at me. You told me what a gift it was for me to not be influenced by any writers and you told me to not read anyone's work until I was completed with writing what I needed to write. That was it my friend, and we were off and running. I came home after our first meeting and my wife looked at me and said "How was it?" I told her it was awesome because you are fucked up just like me and she said "I can tell by the smile on your face." This memoir wouldn't have happened without the time that you have given of yourself as a writer and as a friend.

Sue Skalicky, thank you for being so badass and helping me design the cover, edit my memoir and walk with me through the publishing process. This has been a hell of a journey. Thank you for thinking outside of the box and teaching me so much about this process. I entered your writing class, full of self doubt and with the thought that there was not a chance in hell that I would be able to be a writer, a page let alone a whole book, but you lit a fire under my butt that sparkled through my eyes. Your teaching style fits with who I am as a person and I want to thank you for inspiring me and believing in my voice. I can't believe that you thought that my email was TylerSucks@gmail.com but then again my penmanship needs some work. I am blessed beyond belief to call you my friend. Thank you. Yabba Dabba Doo!

Thank you Brenna Daugherty Gerhardt, AKA my special agent, for kicking me in my butt into Sue's writing class and believing in me over the last few years. Thank you for telling me that I had to write this memoir and to be honest you're a force to be reckoned with so I did what you told me to do. You my friend have opened some really cool doors for me. Thank you.

Thank you Gary Adkisson for taking the time and reading my rough draft and providing beneficial feedback. I appreciate the editing that you suggested and the kindness that you have shown me. I will be forever grateful for all your support and your willingness to continue to help me with some marketing strategies. Thank you.

Thank you for always believing in me, my beautiful wife. You have been on this journey of sobriety and many firsts. You have loved me unconditionally and made so many things in our life lovely. You have pushed me to believe in myself and you have honored our family with your unconditional love. I love watching you with our kiddos and your unwavering ethical beliefs to uphold the law. Thank you for taking care of our life on all of the Sunday afternoons I was gone writing. Together we are strong and I am blessed that I get to spend the rest of my life with you. I am grateful that you get to be the happy ending in my story. Thank you.

I need to thank Ms. DeForest, an amazing human being who believed in my big heart when almost everyone was against me. You looked me in my eyes when everyone else ran away. You told me that you believed in me when I didn't believe in myself. The impact that you have had on my life in some of my darkest times allowed me to continue to fight. I love seeing you in random places and it fills my heart with happiness seeing how excited you get to see me. Thank you for helping me with my college algebra when I thought that it was going to kill me. You made a difference in my life and I am grateful that I was blessed to have you as my high school teacher and to call you my friend today.

I would like to thank all the people who have believed in me over my lifetime. A special thank you to my mom and my brothers for watching me walk through my darkest times and still showing me love. If you are a person who planted a seed of hope in my life when I had no hope, I would like to tell you that your seed grew, even if you couldn't see it grow. My heart felt your kindness, even if I wasn't able to tell you at the time. And today I am strong because of your love! Thank you.